Literary Theory Today

Literary Theory Today

Edited by PETER COLLIER
and HELGA GEYER-RYAN

Polity Press

First published 1990 by Polity Press
in association with Blackwell Publishers

First published in paperback 1992

Editorial office:
Polity Press, 65 Bridge Street,
Cambridge CB2 1UR, UK

Marketing and production:
Blackwell Publishers
108 Cowley Road, Oxford OX4 1JF, UK

ISBN 0 7456 0477 3
ISBN 0 7456 0972 4 (pbk)

British Library Cataloguing in Publication Data
A CIP catalogue record for this book is available from
the British Library.

Typeset in 10/12 pt Baskerville by Photo·graphics,
Honiton, Devon
Printed in Great Britain by T. J. Press (Padstow) Ltd.

Contents

Notes on Contributors

HOMI K. BHABHA   Lecturer at the School of African and Asian Studies, University of Sussex. Author of *Nation and Narration* (London: Routledge and Kegan Paul, forthcoming).

PETER BÜRGER   Professor of French and Comparative Literature at the University of Bremen. Author of *Theory of the Avant-garde* (Manchester: Manchester University Press and Minneapolis: University of Minnesota Press, 1984) and *The Decline of Modernism* (Cambridge: Polity Press, forthcoming).

PETER COLLIER   Lecturer in French at the University of Cambridge and Fellow of Sidney Sussex College. Author of *Proust and Venice* (Cambridge: Cambridge University Press, 1989). Co-editor of *Visions and Blueprints. Avant-garde Culture and Radical Politics in Early Twentieth-century Europe* (Manchester: Manchester University Press, 1988) and *Modernism and the European Unconscious* (Cambridge: Polity Press, 1990).

HELGA GEYER-RYAN   Associate Professor of Comparative Literature at the University of Amsterdam. Author of *Der andere Roman. Versuch über die verdrängte Ästhetik des Populären* (Amsterdam and New York: Heinrichshofen, 1983) and *Fables of Desire* (Cambridge: Polity Press, forthcoming).

STEPHEN GREENBLATT   Professor of English, University of California, Berkeley. Author of *Renaissance Self-fashioning. From More to Shakespeare* (Chicago: Chicago University Press, 1980), and *Shakespearian Negotiations. The Circulation of Social Energy in Renaissance England* (Oxford: Oxford University Press, 1988). Editor of *Allegory and Representation* (Baltimore: Johns Hopkins University Press, 1981).

HANS ROBERT JAUSS   Professor of Literary Criticism and Romance Philology, University of Konstanz. Author of *Toward an Aesthetic of Reception*

(Brighton: Harvester and Minneapolis: University of Minnesota Press, 1982), and *Aesthetic Experience and Literary Hermeneutics* (Manchester: Manchester University Press and Minneapolis: University of Minnesota Press, 1982).

ANN JEFFERSON   Lecturer in French at the University of Oxford and Fellow of New College. Author of *The Nouveau Roman and the Poetics of Fiction* (Cambridge: Cambridge University Press, 1980), and *Reading Realism in Stendhal* (Cambridge: Cambridge University Press, 1988). Co-editor of *Modern Literary Theory. A Comparative Introduction* (London: Batsford, 2nd edition, 1986).

BARBARA JOHNSON   Professor of French and Comparative Literature, Harvard University. Author of *Défigurations du langage poétique. La seconde révolution baudelairienne* (Paris: Flammarion, 1979), *The Critical Difference. Essays in the Contemporary Rhetoric of Reading* (Baltimore and London: Johns Hopkins University Press, 1980), and *A World of Difference* (Baltimore and London: Johns Hopkins University Press, 2nd edition, 1989).

SARAH KOFMAN   Philosopher, University of Paris I (Sorbonne). Author of *Nietzsche et la métaphore* (Paris: Galilée, 1983), *The Enigma of Woman. Woman in Freud's Writings* (Ithaca: Cornell University Press, 1985), *Nietzsche et la scène philosophique* (Paris: Galilée, 1986), *The Childhood of Art* (New York: Columbia University Press, 1988), and *Freud and Fiction* (Cambridge: Polity Press, 1990).

JULIA KRISTEVA   Professor in the Department of Textual and Documentary Sciences, University of Paris VII. Practising psychoanalyst. Author of *About Chinese Women* (London: Boyars, 1977), *Desire in Language. A Semiotic Approach to Literature and Art* (New York: Columbia University Press and Oxford: Basil Blackwell, 1980), *Powers of Horror* (New York: Columbia University Press, 1982), *Revolution in Poetic Language* (New York: Columbia University Press, 1984), *Tales of Love* (New York: Columbia University Press, 1987), and *The Kristeva Reader*, ed. Toril Moi (Oxford: Basil Blackwell, 1986).

MICHAEL RIFFATERRE   Professor of French, Columbia University. Author of *Essais de stylistique structurale* (Paris: Flammarion, 1971), *Semiotics of Poetry* (Bloomington: Indiana University Press, 1978 and London: Methuen, 1980), and *Text Production* (New York: Columbia University Press, 1983).

GAYATRI CHAKRAVORTY SPIVAK   Professor of English, University of Pittsburgh. Author of *In Other Worlds. Essays in Cultural Politics* (New York and London: Routledge Methuen, 1988). Co-editor of *Selected Subaltern Studies* (New York and Oxford: Oxford University Press, 1988).

ELAINE SHOWALTER   Professor of English, Princeton University. Author of *A Literature of Their Own. British Novelists from Brontë to Lessing* (Princeton: Princeton University Press, 1977 and London: Virago, 1978), *The Female Malady: Women, Madness and English Culture 1830–1980* (London: Virago, 1987). Editor of *The New Feminist Criticism. Essays on Women, Literature and Theory* (New York: Random House, 1985 and London: Virago, 1986).

ROBERT WEIMANN   Member of the Academy of Arts, German Democratic Republic. Author of *Shakespeare and the Popular Tradition in the Theater. Studies in the Social Dimension of Dramatic Form and Function* (Baltimore and London: Johns Hopkins University Press, 1978), and *Structure and Society in Literary History* (Baltimore and London: Johns Hopkins University Press, 2nd edition, 1984).

ALBRECHT WELLMER   Professor of Philosophy, University of Konstanz. Author of *Critical Theory of Society* (New York: Herder and Herder, 1971), *Ethik und Dialog. Elemente des moralischen Urteils bei Kant und in der Diskursethik* (Frankfurt: Suhrkamp Verlag, 1986), and *In Defence of Modernity* (Cambridge: Polity Press and Boston: MIT Press, forthcoming).

Acknowledgements

The editors and publishers would like to thank the following for their kind permission to reproduce copyright material:

The Hogarth Press and W. W. Norton & Company, Inc. for an extract from *The Four Fundamental Concepts of Psycho-Analysis* by Jacques Lacan;

Edward Arnold for an extract from *Passage to India* by E. M. Forster.

Introduction: Beyond
Postmodernism

I

Literary and cultural theory are in ferment today because literature and culture themselves appear threatened in our 'postmodern' age, a post-industrial age of instantaneous electronic communications, where the privileged status of the text and the coherence of cultural activity are increasingly destabilized. Jean-François Lyotard has described this world (too indulgently, perhaps) in *The Postmodern Condition*. But although it could be argued that this 'postmodern' ideology is itself a product of the anarchic liberalism of the new right, disguising prescription as description when it declares modernism to be played out and artistic experimentation and ideological critique outdated, one has to admit that there is little virtue in trying to revive an idealized past. Moreover, the crisis of culture and its theory indicate above all the precarious state of what Habermas has called 'the project of modernity', thus threatening the most vital discourses of legitimation and critique which we have inherited from the European Enlightenment. Even in the recent past, cultural discourse seemed regulated by what Lyotard calls 'grand narratives', which included the reassuringly subversive discourses of twentieth-century modernism – formalism, marxism, psychoanalysis. The arguments of Saussure, Marx and Freud initially inspired the most acute languages of modern literary criticism, seemingly able to make the poem or the novel totally explicable by an all-powerful theory. But our late twentieth-century world has seen these originary, totalizing theories called into question and their unquestioning exponents lose their authority. Perhaps the very sophistication of their later practitioners, cutting the theories loose from their original, specific militancy, has weakened their claim to reveal hidden meaning. Roland Barthes moved from complex systems of coded semiotic meaning to a position of apparently capricious textual enjoyment; Pierre Macherey and Louis Althusser argued that the ideology expressed by a text was a practice largely independent of the socioeconomic infrastructure; Lacan, moving beyond Freud's study of the process whereby the artist unwittingly impressed his own symbolic meaning into the work of art, found that there was no essential self behind the shifting mental hall of mirrors which constituted the 'subject' of thought and discourse.

The claims of criticism based on such universal and holistic premises, then, have come to seem increasingly 'perverse', and have been radically challenged by less totalizing movements like 'deconstruction', 'new historicism', or 'feminism', which are as partisan in their way as the 'grand narratives', but which acknowledge and assume their own partial character. There is none the less much continuity – deconstruction, for instance, derives its model of close reading from formalism, its ideological demystification from marxism, and its hermeneutic reversal from psychoanalysis. So it seems to be possible to acknowledge the strength of Lyotard's postmodern analysis, agreeing that there are no transcendental foundations of knowledge, no privileged viewpoints – and yet not feel bound passively to lament the loss of 'the project of modernity' and the lack of any effective modern critique, or actively to connive at the creation of a world where all cultural activity might be judged equally meaningful or meaningless. Thus the authors of the essays in this volume all acknowledge the crisis in literary and cultural theory, but they all suggest ways of working through and beyond it.

Even a postmodern critic like Lyotard does in fact assume the powers of critical discourse, while refusing to elaborate any 'narrative' of its legitimation. And although the dominant current of poststructuralist criticism today, deconstruction, eschews legitimation, since it pursues a negative hermeneutics, showing in every author studied a self-contradictory discourse, and since it follows no principle other than the quest for 'difference/deferment' (rejecting, as metaphysical illusion, any originary discursive meaning inscribed within writing, or any founding humanist significance), its representatives have none the less in practice directed their theories towards the dissection and subversion of the powerful symbolic institutions which support the status quo. However, what these dismantlers of ideology and symbolic domination still tend to avoid is a theoretical rationale, for fear of complicity with the very metaphysics and essences which they have attacked not only for being false but also for supporting an oppressive social hegemony. In his post-Marxian *Aesthetic Theory* Adorno already tries to banish transcendental aesthetics from his appreciation of the fragmented, negative artifacts of his archetypal modernist artists, Beckett, Kafka and Celan. Beckett's work, for instance, is designated as a tendentiously silent artistic act of resistance to the meliorative project of bourgeois aesthetics. And Derrida, the philosopher who haunts all poststructuralist criticism, has found a blind spot vitiating the conscious project of every philosopher and writer he has discussed, from Plato to Nietzsche and Heidegger, from Rousseau to Freud.

Yet a series of recent articles and books has revealed the cruel paradox which lies at the heart of this deconstructive purism. The pro-Nazi stances of Heidegger and Paul de Man, both writers who had seemed dauntingly, quintessentially independent, have been experienced retrospectively as catastrophic. Whereas the right-wing politics of Yeats, Pound, Eliot and Lewis, not to mention Marinetti, Céline or Gottfried Benn, have long been the subject of critical discrimination between degrees and kinds of commitment in expression and action, Heidegger and de Man were somehow assumed to have deactivated the crude relation of philosophy and literature to personality and society, making their play of argument sublimely inclusive of, yet untouched by, contingency. So that the shock was the greater when, at the height of the sway of American deconstruction (when it appeared to have subsumed the other languages of criticism into its negative hermeneutics), there was a return of the repressed voice of its political and philosophical 'other'. Indeed, in the crisis unleashed by the revelation of Paul de Man's wartime collaboration, the political repressed resurfaced in its most grotesquely 'uncanny' form, as fascism. For the languages of modern criticism, even in their poststructuralist forms, supposed at least a negative principle behind their critical practice: rejecting the dangerously simplistic languages of fascism – racism and imperialism, patriarchy and coercive identity, strictly monological or binary thinking, utilitarian rationality. Yet one advantage of the crisis is that now, the history of modern literary theory has to be scrutinized and its unresolved questions used to rethink the future.

For these reasons Barbara Johnson's critical review of Paul de Man and the politics of deconstruction, which urges a reinterpretation of the political mistakes and misconstruals of the founder of American deconstruction, opens this book's reassessment of modern literary theory. It exemplifies a crucial conjuncture in the postwar history of literary theory. Johnson rejects the charge that deconstruction must lead to a total uncertainty of language and ideology, and shows how an analysis of de Man's wartime collaborationist writings, and of their suppression, just like Schiller's denial of violence in Kant's aesthetics, can teach us the need to admit the political parameter into literary theory.

The separation of the literary text from society and with it the repression of the problems of interpretation and literary value are discussed by Peter Bürger in a critique of Pierre Bourdieu, whose authoritative *Distinction* shows up the social strategies and identifications disguised behind positions of aesthetic taste and judgement. Bürger admits that all criteria of evaluation are historically limited, although he is suspicious of Adorno's tendency to interpret the innovations of the artistic avant-garde as manifestations of an objective development of the artistic material. For Bürger it is vital to assert the continuing possibility of differentiating aesthetic values against what he sees as a pessimistic reduction by Bourdieu of cultural consumption to social determinism, where literature and culture are considered primarily as an apparatus for the distribution of cultural 'capital' and social distinction.

The philosophical implications of both Barbara Johnson's revision of deconstruction, and Bürger's challenge to Adorno's *Aesthetic Theory*, are explored in Albrecht Wellmer's analysis of Adorno's *Negative Dialectics* as a concept of reason conscious of the seductive alliance between the power of critique and the temptation of metaphysics. Despite Adorno's attempt to replace Kant's faculty of reason, judged metaphysical, with concrete artistic practice, Wellmer argues that the theories of Derrida show that Adorno himself was tempted to invest aesthetics with metaphysical presence.

In fact, the essays by Johnson, Bürger and Wellmer, which constitute Part I of this book, form the cornerstones of our field of investigation: the repositioning of critical practice after the misadventures of theory, once its lingering metaphysical assumptions (as to truth, value, use) and its discursive integrity (seeking a pure position from which to approach other positions) had been called into question. Their essays tackle the extremes of political collusion, the collapse of aesthetic values, and philosophical nihilism, which seem to threaten the deconstructive position. All three argue that critique is still possible despite the crisis but that it can only advance by taking its very difficulties as the starting point of its analyses.

II

The paramount importance of history in shaping, determining and legitimizing our perception and interpretation of works of art, and creating an archeology of texts from the past, is the theme of the second part of our book. Both Hans Robert Jauss and Stephen Greenblatt are concerned with the dialectical process which establishes relations of continuity and/or difference between past and present. Jauss's 'reception theory' takes as its starting point the context within which commentators on the Bible established different interpretative strategies, according to whether they saw themselves retrieving original meaning, recording accreted significance, or reinterpreting in the light of new situations. Jauss moves in the last analysis to emphasize the historical continuity of the activity of interpretation, despite the shifts of content and context emphasized by reception theory, where the parameters of meaning are displaced by the creative input of the reader.

Greenblatt, like Jauss, insists on 'the historicity of texts' and the 'textuality of history', and he too rejects universal criteria of value and meaning. Yet he goes further than Jauss in foregrounding discontinuities in the encounter between past and present. His 'new historicism' questions the acts of cultural interpretation and selection which assign value to some artifacts rather than to others. He considers the fate of the divergent objects which are invested with value by museums, and which are caught in the dialectic of the respectful 'resonance' which the work's rooting in a cultural context tends to inspire, and the shock of 'wonder' which original (and hence alien) creativity may provoke. Greenblatt gives preference to the specificity of the historical moment and its alienating, disruptive effect on the normalizing assumption of continuity, accepting the fact that the historical perspective of his *own* theory is thereby called into question. And, in formulating the

challenge that his 'new historicism' offers to teleological aesthetics, Greenblatt traces the contingent historical accidents of his personal trajectory and
research.

But the problems of founding such an interpretative strategy may well
seem to threaten to render all cultural production entirely arbitrary. And
it is against the danger of turning the precariousness of representation itself
into an ontological absolute that Robert Weimann, adapting the Marxian
concept of appropriation, shows how different literary forms represent different stages of the crisis of representation. He rejects the two extreme poles
of the relation of language to reality, the structuralist position that sign-
systems are autonomous, and the vulgar Marxist view that they directly
reflect reality. In constructing a history and sociology of modern forms of
self-reflexive literary representation, he shows how certain key works by
Flaubert, James and Hemingway signal self-consciously and self-critically
the reference of their own texts to the world they attempt to appropriate.

III

The violence and constraints affecting the relation of the historical to the
textual had traditionally been ignored by advocates of a strictly structuralist
semiotics, from the Russian Formalists in the 1920s, who defined literature
by its 'literariness', excluding all other criteria, to the French critics of the
1960s, whose semiotics were inspired less by linguistic theory itself than by
its conjunction with the structural anthropology of Claude Lévi-Strauss.
But since then there has been a revolution within linguistics itself. The
whole development of pragmatics has challenged not only the self-contained
systems of structuralism, but also, it would seem, the generally self-consum-
ing theories of the lack of overarching meaning which Derrida's philosophy
has inspired.

Thus the third part of our book opens with chapters by Michael Riffaterre
and Ann Jefferson, who acknowledge the need to redefine the aims of a
poststructuralist formalism. Their 'targets' are the 'undecidability' which for
Jacques Derrida, and critics like Geoffrey Hartmann, removes key literary
texts from monologic significance, and the 'literariness' which for Roman
Jakobson cuts off the text from the world. Michael Riffaterre shows how an
ambiguous poetic discourse can yield effective meanings without the principle of 'undecidability' paralysing hermeneutic activity; using texts by Blake
and Wordsworth which are notoriously difficult to interpret, he shows how
the reader calls on a wider cultural judgement to override the primary
'undecidability' of the text as provisionally segmented, and thus deploys a
heightened hermeneutic awareness, leading to a reprocessing of the work in
terms of a revised principle of segmentation. This second stage of interpretation then frees the meaning which was blocked within the text, but also
opens it up to wider areas of public interpretation, through intertextual
activity. Ann Jefferson re-evaluates the two key figures of the tradition of

Russian Formalism and suggests that Roman Jakobson's quest for stylistic universals has oversimplified the operation of language by ignoring its socio-political dimension, which is better formulated by the aesthetic theory of Mikhail Bakhtin, whose notion of fiction as a polyphonic and carnivalesque activity is grounded in a theory of socio-linguistic agonistics.

As critics working from a linguistic basis have needed to refocus structuralism and contextualize its interpretative activities, so psychoanalytic critics have seen the power and principles of their founding exegetical system simultaneously exploited and challenged. Sarah Kofman, who has published elsewhere her theoretical studies of Freud's aesthetics, here conducts a detailed reading of one of Freud's own exemplary readings, that of *The Merchant of Venice*, in order to deconstruct an over-simplified psychoanalytic symbolism. It transpires that, even though Freud avoided being entirely constrained by the transformational structures suggested by his own model of the dream work, he still did not bring out the social dimension of meaning which Shakespeare's language and structure convey in the case of his female and his Jewish subjects, whose discourse is laden with subversive symbolic connotations and values which challenge simplistic readings.

The critique of a given and stable psychoanalytic symbolism continues in the next chapter, where all of Julia Kristeva's experiences as a pioneer of semiotics, a supporter of feminism, and a practising psychoanalyst feed in to her theoretical and discursive strategies. She demonstrates how Lacan's notion of 'identification' illuminates both a case history and a reading of Joyce. But Kristeva's essay moves beyond a position of simple Freudian or feminist ideology, for, if a notion of identity is necessary to render the psyche operational, the semiotic pleasure of readerly projection implies a concomitant strategy of reversal of identification. She finds the figure of the wandering Ulysses as significant a psychological position as that of Freud's classic Oedipus complex; her model highlights the powerful circulation of desire not only in the modernist text, but also in the controversial transferential postures she explores in her therapeutic work.

IV

The need to revise modes of analysing the expression and representation of women is implicit in Kristeva's essay, as it is in Kofman's. But the relation of the underlying ideology to the mode of reading practised, and the social position it implies, is explicitly brought into focus by Elaine Showalter's survey of the developments and prospects of feminist criticism. She shows how interpretations of the feminine are inescapably related to questions of race and class, how psychoanalytic or other theories must be contextualized in relation to their different frames of institutionalized literary and cultural activity. Showalter refuses the comforts of an essential feminine nature. But she also rejects naive double-binds like those allegedly opposing 'equality' to 'difference', or 'Anglo-Saxon pragmatists' (compiling a female literary history) to 'French theoreticians', (conceptualizing a quintessentially female language). As she unfolds the different diachronic stages and synchronic strategies of a feminist literary enterprise she comes to the conclusion that the most urgent issue of today's theoretical debate, beyond the relationship between the concepts of difference and identity in the discourse of gender, is the power of a radically new discourse, questioning all given institutions, to displace not only literary canons and gender stereotypes, but all the parameters of critical discourse in other fields.

The consequent project, to re-situate oneself as critical subject while maintaining a position of effective agency and rejecting the temptations of (patriarchal) essentialism or (institutionalized) pragmatism, has implications beyond feminism and opens a debate on the place of the critical subject in terms of race and class, as well as in terms of the role of the teacher and critic, and the importance of non-literary cultural activity. And as Showalter unwrites patriarchal discourse, so Homi Bhabha and Gayatri Spivak challenge the identities imposed by Western discourse in general on the third world, thus calling into question the limited horizons within which many critics tend to operate. Homi Bhabha points out the ambiguity of the most critically aware literary visions of Empire, those of Forster and Conrad, even or particularly when they claim to speak on behalf of the non-European, and he reads their limitations in the light of the contradictory ideology of non-literary administrative documents, whose repressed sub-text he elucidates using the models of Derrida's 'in-between' and Freud's uncanny. Gayatri Spivak argues that the role of the teacher should be scrutinized, in order to focus on, for example, women's expression in a Bengali film, rather than on a traditional (white, patriarchal) literary text. She engages Foucault as well as Marx in her self-critical exposure of the difficulties of the commentator wishing to assume her marginal position without rendering it unproblematically dominant. Both Bhabha and Spivak, then, elaborate the difficulties of articulating a notion of cultural identity. They reject that identity whenever it is defined merely as the 'other' (the negative image) of a position of coercive power, and their models take on a resonance which disturbs our own readings and positions, whatever our progressive intentions.

Indeed, it is precisely this spirit of critical and self-critical enquiry which has inspired this volume of original essays, precluding any monolithic conclusion as to the current state of literary and cultural theory and its future prospects. None the less the very variety and energy of the authors' different responses is already a kind of answer. We find that the sophisticated voices of the new feminist consciousness and the post-colonial third-world intelligentsia are not to be contained by traditional ideologies, even those speaking in their favour. They will use the terminology of Marx and Freud, but they will constantly question the ideological schemata which these systems also presuppose. However, they do not contradict the new political conscience of deconstruction or the heightened social awareness of post-Freudian psychoanalysis. And formalism is able to criticize its linguistic foundations, while still providing a model of critical reading, compatible, moreover, with the aims of critical hermeneutics and reception theory. Marxism and the Frankfurt School have distanced themselves from any simple theory of the relation between culture and society, but the models of appropriation and negative dialectics which they inspired still furnish important theoretical instruments. New developments in historical and social theory reopen the whole question of cultural and aesthetic value, ebulliently in the new historicism, more problematically, perhaps, in the case of modernist fiction and ethnic cinema. The destabilization of the critical metalanguages of modernism has, clearly, not been fatal.

In her opening chapter, Barbara Johnson quotes Paul de Man on the uncertain relations of language and art to the world:

> *it is not a priori certain* that language functions according to principles which are those or which are *like* those, of the phenomenal world. It is by no means an established fact that aesthetic values are *in*compatible. What is established is that their compatibility, or lack of it, has to remain an open question.

The contributors to this book show how important, and exhilarating, it is for them to call into question the bases of their own interpretative activity. Certainly, no one critical language can now claim hegemony. Metaphysics and politics will not disappear. The lesson for the critic is to remain vigilant, and *foreground* their interference with interpretation, instead of wishing it away. Formalism must compose with reader-response strategies, psychoanalysis must open up its symbolic systems to feminist models. Marxism must come to terms with a dissolution of nineteenth-century genres as well as class-models. Each position is insecure: the place of the sacred Jewish texts in Greenblatt's museum is no less fragile than the authority of Spivak's Bengali film critic. Bürger cannot prevent life overrunning art in Beuys' piles of felt and traces of fat, nor can Kristeva isolate the polymorphous liberation of the Joycean text from the surrogate maternal identity which she offers to disturbed female desire. But their openness is not to be confused with total relativity. The circulation of textual, social and mental energies driving contemporary criticism to transgress boundaries is objectively unsettling; it is still emotionally and intellectually allied to the vast enterprise of demystification and liberation that mark our modern age.

It has been suggested by Gianni Vattimo, in a synthesis of earlier reactions by Benjamin, Adorno, and Heidegger, that we are now faced with 'the death or decline of art', where avant-garde critics as well as avant-garde artists are forced to enact the options of 'utopia' (a naive belief in the suffusion of the whole of life with aesthetic power), 'silence' (using a vestigial, self-destructive art negatively, to resist any social recuperation of culture), or 'kitsch' (a manipulative mass culture). We believe that the present volume shows that avant-garde criticism is able to resist these extremities, and that, without succumbing to an unjustified 'pathos of the future', it shows its ability to maintain a vigorous critical and self-critical project, precisely by taking these apparent limitations as its thematic challenge.

Peter Collier and Helga Geyer-Ryan
Cambridge 1990

Part I

Part I

BARBARA JOHNSON

The Surprise of Otherness: A Note on the Wartime Writings of Paul de Man

If I perceive my ignorance as a gap in knowledge instead of an imperative that changes the very nature of what I think I know, then I do not truly experience my ignorance. The surprise of otherness is that moment when a new form of ignorance is suddenly activated as an imperative.
Barbara Johnson, 'Nothing Fails Like Success' in *A World of Difference*

As the dedications in two of my books will attest, Paul de Man was extremely important to me both intellectually and personally. He was both an unforgettably challenging and generous teacher and a reliable and interesting friend. When Jonathan Culler first informed me of the existence of over 150 articles written by de Man during 1940 to 1942 for a Belgian newspaper, the regular editorial staff of which had been replaced by collaborators, and the editorial line of which was distinctly anti-Semitic and pro-Nazi, my first impulse was a desire to rename my dogs (Nietzschie and Wagner). That is, my reaction was symptomatic of a logic of purification, expulsion, the vomiting of the name. It was as though the milk of de Man's writing, which I had already drunk, had turned to poison. Yet the logic of contamination and purification is the very logic of Nazism. Surely this 'good breast/bad breast' split was too simplistic a way of dealing with what amounted to an urgent imperative to historicize? De Man's later writings had to be re-read in the light of their own history.

If the quantity and intensity of the articles already published on the subject of de Man's wartime writings are any indication, there is clearly something at stake in this bibliographical discovery. Beyond the fact that Nazism is always news and that people love a fall, what is it that transforms this archival revelation into an *event*? I will begin a rather roundabout approach to these questions by quoting from one of de Man's last discussions of the nature of historical occurrences:

When I speak of irreversibility and insist on irreversibility, it is because in all
those texts and those juxtapositions of texts, we have been aware of something
which one could call a progression though it shouldn't be, a movement from
cognition, from acts of knowledge, from states of cognition, to something
which is no longer a cognition but which is to some extent an occurrence,
which has the materiality of something that actually happens, that actually
occurs. And there, the sort of material occurrence . . . that . . . leaves a trace
on the world, that does something to the world as such, that notion of
occurrence is not opposed in any sense to the notion of writing.[1]

It is a fitting illustration of Paul de Man's theory of history as the disruption
of a cognitive progression by the intrusion of something like writing that
his wartime writings should have been unearthed not by a critic but by an
admirer, Ortwin de Graef, a Belgian graduate student. Although de Man
had in fact referred to his *Le Soir* articles in the course of his later life (in
particular, in a letter to the Chairman of Harvard's Society of Fellows),
they had remained, like the purloined letter, exposed but invisible, open
but unread, until the relentless progress of archival devotion delivered them
from sufferance. However those articles might have contributed at the time
of their first publication to the shape of events in occupied Belgium, they
have now entered history a second time with the full disruptive force of an
event. It is an event that is structured *like* what de Man describes in the
above quotation as an 'occurrence' – an irreversible disruption of
cognition – but it is a disruption that is happening *to* his own acts of
cognition. It is as though de Man had tried to theorize the disruption of
his own acts of theorizing, had tried to include the theory's own outside
within it. But that theory's outside was precisely, we now know, always
already within. And he could not, of course, control the very loss of control
he outlined as inevitable and defined as irony. 'Irony comes into being
precisely when self-consciousness loses its control over itself', he told Robert
Moynihan. 'For me, at least, the way I think of it now, irony is not a figure
of self-consciousness. It's a break, an interruption, a disruption. It is a
moment of loss of control, and not just for the author but for the reader as
well.'[2] The arrival of this purloined letter, then, is an event not only for de
Man but for his readers, however uncannily his theory might have predicted
its inevitability. His death makes it necessary to face the letter without him,
but in any case he could not have served as guide to its interpretation. All
the wisdom he had on the subject, he had already delivered. Indeed, this
is one of the things that has become newly readable in his late work. As
Christopher Norris, Cynthia Chase, and doubtless many others are in the
process of arguing, the critic to whom de Man now appears to have been
most polemically and mercilessly opposed was his own former self. But who
was that masked de Man?

National Literatures, Genre Theory, and Racial Hygiene

Thus, in the framework of three lectures, Professor Domini has given us a complete overview of Italian poetry, which seems to be realizing most felicitously the hope expressed by Mussolini when he declared that 'It is especially at the present time that poetry is necessary to the life of a people.'

Paul de Man, *Le Soir*

Paul de Man was born in Antwerp on 6 December 1919, to a rather well-to-do family that was both patriotically Flemish and cultivatedly cosmopolitan.[3] One of his strongest early influences seems to have been his uncle, Hendrik de Man, a prominent socialist theorist, president of the Belgian Labour Party, and a minister in several governments. Hendrik de Man was the only important member of the Belgian government who agreed with the timing and mode of King Leopold's decision to capitulate to the Germans in May 1940. In a Manifesto to the members of the Belgian Labour Party, published in July 1940, Hendrik wrote:

> Be among the first rank of those who struggle against poverty and demoralization, for the resumption and work and the return to normal life.
> But do not believe that it is necessary to resist the occupying power; accept the fact of his victory and try rather to draw lessons therefrom so as to make of this the starting point for new social progress.
> The war has led to the debacle of the parliamentary regime and of the capitalist plutocracy in the so-called democracies.
> For the working classes and for socialism, this collapse of a decrepit world is, far from a disaster, a deliverance.[4]

As Minister of Finance in the prewar years, Hendrik de Man had been appalled by the power wielded by high finance in the Belgian political process. He was indeed so disgusted by the sleaze factor that he was ready to abandon the democratic process altogether. His mistake in 1940 was to see capitalism as a worse evil than Nazism. Hendrik's enthusiasm for the new 'revolution', however, did not last. In his struggle on behalf of the working classes, he fell increasingly out of favour with the German authorities until he left Belgium in late 1941 for an Alpine retreat in France. The book he published in 1942 was immediately seized by the Nazis. In 1944 he took refuge in Switzerland, where he learned of his conviction for treason, *in absentia*, by a Belgian military court. He died in a car accident in 1953.

The impact of Hendrik's intellectually and politically picaresque career on Paul – both the Paul of 1940 to 1942 and the Paul of 1953 to 1983 – is incalculable. It is tempting to see the young Paul as beguiled into pro-fascist sympathies by his uncle's utopian hopes just as it is tempting to see the older Paul's warnings against the 'unwarranted hopeful solutions'[5] of idealistic political activists as stemming from his uncle's catastrophic misjudgement. But these suppositions are at once impossible to verify and fundamentally inadequate in the sense that they reduce a complex political and ideological over-determination to a personal and psychological 'case'. Paul de Man's early writings are part of a much larger intellectual and literary configuration, most of whose sinister consequences would have been hard to predict. Let us look briefly now at those writings.

Between December 1940, and November 1942, Paul de Man wrote 169 book and music reviews for the francophone Brussels' newspaper *Le Soir*, and contributed another ten articles to a Flemish newspaper, *Het Vlaamsche Land*. Most of the essays have little apparent relation to politics beyond a vague assent to the new order. Their aim is rather to develop and practice a kind of literary criticism that is best summed up in a review of René Lalou's *Histoire de la Littérature Française contemporaine*. After criticizing Lalou for spending too much time on the specificity of individual authors, de Man writes:

> By thus excessively multiplying his differentiations (*différencier à outrance*), he ends up giving the impression of a jungle of trees and creeping vines. And he will have missed the principal goal of any critical exposé: to give an image of the spirit, a synthesis of the thought, of a century.
>
> For what matters most is not the subtle differences of expression between two authors but their common submission to implacable rules. It is manifest that each period forges, sometimes unconsciously, its own esthetic law. There may perhaps exist some eternal and immutable Beauty but it is nonetheless true that that Beauty is illuminated, in each era, from a different angle. A conscious critic must determine what that angle is and deduce his criteria from it.[6]

De Man's general concern in these reviews is with the orderly development of different literary genres and national traditions. This makes for rather repetitive reading. Indeed, while slogging my way through the pile of eye-straining xeroxes of the young de Man's chronicles, I began to wonder why *Le Soir* itself didn't send out the hook for him. What good is a book review that tells you only about the place a novel holds in the evolution of the genre and never gives you a clue about the plot? Did de Man seriously think his readers were going to run out and buy the latest novel because it had timidly begun the necessary synthesis of French rationalism and German mysticism?

More to the point for our purposes, is the question of the politics of this kind of literary history. The following quotation from one of the articles in *Het Vlaamsche Land* begins to show the sinister side of the notion of 'proper traditions':

> When we investigate the post-war literary production in Germany, we are immediately struck by the contrast between two groups, which moreover were also materially separated by the events of 1933. The first of these groups celebrates an art with a strongly cerebral disposition, founded upon some abstract principle and very remote from all naturalness. The in themselves very remarkable theses of expressionism were used in this group as tricks, as

skillful artifices calculated for easy effects. The very legitimate basic rule of artistic transformation, inspired by the personal vision of the creator, served here as a pretext for a forced, caricatured representation of reality. Thus [the artists of this group] came into an open conflict with the proper traditions of German art which had always and before everything else clung to a deep spiritual sincerity. Small wonder, then, that it was mainly non-Germans, and in specific, Jews, that went in this direction.[7]

In the notorious essay entitled 'Jews in Contemporary Literature' (the only other one of the 179 articles that mentions Jews), de Man pushes these ideas to their appalling conclusion:

The fact that they [Western intellectuals] have been able to preserve themselves from Jewish influence in as representative a cultural domain as literature is proof of their vitality. One would not be able to hold out much hope for the future of our civilization if it had let itself be invaded, without resistance, by a foreign force. In keeping, despite Semitic interference in all aspects of European life, an intact originality and character, it [our civilization] has shown that its profound nature was healthy. In addition, one can thus see that a solution to the Jewish problem that would aim towards the creation of a Jewish colony far from Europe would not entail, for the literary life of the West, any deplorable consequences.[8]

How can one avoid feeling rage and disgust at a person who could write such a thing? How can I not understand and share the impulse to throw this man away? The fact that 'Jews in Contemporary Literature' was written for a special issue of *Le Soir* on anti-Semitism does not excuse it. The fact that it is the only example of such a sentiment expressed in the 179 articles does not erase it. The fact that de Man seems not to have been anti-Semitic in his personal life between 1940 and 1942 (and certainly showed no trace of it in later years) only points up a too-limited notion of what anti-Semitism is. And the fact that, as Derrida puts it, 'de Man wants especially to propose a thesis on literature that visibly interests him more here than either anti-Semitism or the Jews'[9] is also no comfort. If there hadn't been people who, without any particular personal anti-Semitism, found the idea of deportation *reasonable*, there could have been no holocaust. In his eagerness to preserve differences *between* European national traditions (including Flemish) and to allow for productive cross-fertilization and exchange among them, de Man judges as extraneous and distracting any 'foreign' differences *within*, which might blur the picture of the organic development of forms. Never has the repression of 'differences within' had such horrible consequences. But is genre theory therefore fascist? Is comparative literature *völkisch*?[10] Things can hardly be so simple.

The Question of Deconstruction

The de-construction of a text does not proceeed by random doubt or arbitrary subversion, but by the careful teasing out of warring forces of signification within the text itself.

Barbara Johnson, *'The Critical Difference'*

Whatever Paul de Man is doing in these early essays, it is certainly no deconstruction. Indeed, deconstruction is precisely the dismantling of these notions of evolutionary continuity, totalization, organicism, and 'proper' traditions. No one could be more different from *Le Soir*'s suave synthesizer than the de Man who wrote:

> *Allegories of Reading* started out as a historical study and ended up as a theory of reading. I began to read Rousseau seriously in preparation for a historical reflection on Romanticism and found myself unable to progress beyond local difficulties of interpretation.[11]

Indeed, the later de Man's work exhibits all the negative characteristics cited by the young Paul: cerebrality, abstraction, a tendency to *'différencier à outrance. . .'.* But if de Man was not doing deconstruction between 1940 and 1942, why have the deconstructors become so defensive?

One answer, of course, is that some critics of deconstruction have taken this occasion to conflate the early and late work of de Man and to proclaim, as reported in *Newsweek*, that 'the movement is finished. As one Ivy League professor gleefully exclaims, "deconstruction turned out to be the thousand-year Reich that lasted 12 years" ' (15 February 1988). This 'gleeful' joy in annihilation clearly draws on the energies of the evil which opponents think they are combatting. The recent spate of publicity has produced somewhat contradictory capsule descriptions of deconstruction ('a crucial tenet of deconstruction is that the relation between words and what they mean is sometimes arbitrary and always indeterminate', *Newsweek*; 'Deconstruction views language as a slippery and inherently false medium that always reflects the biases of its users', *The New York Times*, 1 December 1987, p. 81). It is no wonder that deconstructors should want to set the record straight. But what seems to be clearer than ever in the extreme violence and 'glee' of the recent attacks on deconstruction is the extent to which any questioning of the reliability of language, any suggestion that meaning cannot be taken for granted, violates a powerful taboo in our culture. To say that deconstruction is *'hostile* to the very principles of Western thought' (*Newsweek*) is like saying that quantum mechanics is hostile to the notion of substances. No one could have been a more enthusiastic upholder of the integrity of Western thought than the Paul de Man of 1940–2. It is not a question of hostility but of analysis.

The journalists and polemicists are not wrong in locating the specificity of de Man's theory in his focus on language. Their mistake, however, lies in reassigning the certainties they say he takes away. If language is no longer guaranteed to be reliable or truthful, then it must 'always' be unreliable, false, or biased. If not necessary, then arbitrary; if not meaningful, then indeterminate; if not true, then false. But de Man's analyses did not perform such certainty-reassignments. Rather, they question the very structure and functioning of such either/or logic. To question certainty is not the same as to affirm uncertainty:

> In a genuine semiology as well as in other linguistically oriented theories, the referential function of language is not being denied – far from it; what is in question is its authority as a model for natural or phenomenal cognition. Literature is fiction not because it somehow refuses to acknowledge 'reality', but because *it is not a priori certain* that language functions according to principles which are those, or which are *like* those, of the phenomenal world.[12]

> It is by no means an established fact that aesthetic values and linguistic values are *in*compatible. What is established is that their compatibility, or lack of it, has to remain an open question.[13]

What complicates the picture even further is the fact that, while we might be able to tell the difference between linguistic and purely phenomenal or aesthetic structures ('no one in his right mind will try to grow grapes by the luminosity of the word "day" '), the distinction is not at all clear in the case of ideology or politics, because 'what we call ideology is precisely the confusion of linguistic with natural reality, of reference with phenomenalism'. From this de Man goes on to assert:

> It follows that, more than any other mode of inquiry, including economics, the linguistics of literariness ['literature as the place where this negative knowledge about the reliability of linguistic utterance is made available'] is a powerful and indispensable tool in the unmasking of ideological aberrations, as well as a determining factor in accounting for their occurrence.[14]

In the years just prior to his death, de Man seems indeed to have been moving toward establishing a more explicit link between his own theoretical stance and a critique of the ideological foundations of Nazism. Christopher Norris has pointed to that link by entitling his study of de Man *Deconstruction and the Critique of Aesthetic Ideology*. As Walter Benjamin was one of the first to point out, fascism can be understood as an *aestheticization* of politics. In several late essays, de Man locates a crucial articulation in the construction of a protofascist 'aesthetic ideology' in Schiller's misreading of Kant's *Critique of Judgement*. Schiller's misreading of the aesthetic in Kant involves a denial of (its own) violence. Schiller's vision of 'the ideal of a beautiful society' as 'a well executed English dance' has exerted a seductive appeal upon subsequent political visions. In an essay entitled 'Aesthetic Formalization',[15] de Man juxtaposes to this notion from Schiller a short text by Kleist, *Über das Marionettentheater*, in which the grace of such a dance is shown to be produced by substituting the mechanical (a puppet or a prosthesis) for the human body. Schiller's 'aesthetic state' is thus an ideal that can only be produced by mutilation and mechanization. The dance-like harmony of a state can only arise through the repression of differences within. In one of the last lectures de Man delivered before his death, he makes the political ramifications of this aesthetic state even clearer:

> As such, the aesthetic belongs to the masses . . . and it justifies the state, as in the following quotation, which is not by Schiller:
>
>> 'Art is an expression of feelings. The artist is distinguished from the non-artist by the fact that he has the power to give expression to what he feels. In some form or another: the one in images, a second in clay, a third in words, a fourth in marble – or even in historical forms. The statesman is an artist too. The leader and the led ("Führer und Masse") presents no more of a problem than, say, painter and colour. Politics are the plastic art of the state, just as painting is the plastic art of colour. This is why politics without the people, or even against the people, is sheer nonsense. To shape a People out of the masses, and a State out of the People, this has always been the deepest intention of politics in the true sense.' [*Michael. Ein deutsches Schicksal in Tagebuchblättern* (1929).]
>
> It is not entirely irrelevant, not entirely indifferent, that the author of this passage is from a novel of Joseph Goebbels. Mary Wilkinson, who quotes the passage, is certainly right in pointing out that it is a grievous misreading of Schiller's aesthetic state. But the principle of this misreading does not essentially differ from the misreading which Schiller inflicted on his own predecessor, namely Kant.[16]

De Man's insistence on violence – disfiguration, death, mutilation – is not a personal predilection for horror, but rather a deep suspicion of false images of harmony and enlightenment. Hidden within the aesthetic appeals of the political images by which he himself was once seduced were forms of violence unprecedented in human history. It seems undeniable that if 'the linguistics of literariness is a powerful and indispensable tool in the unmasking of ideological aberrations, as well as a determining factor in accounting for their occurrence', the ideological aberrations he is unmasking were once his own.

It could be objected that his relation to such 'aberrations' remains purely cognitive, that 'accounting for' occurrences may not be the only possible response to history, and that the ideology de Man 'unmasks' remains, in fact, masked. The political implications of his *cognition* remain at odds with the political implications of his *performance*. His refusal to tell his own story, which can be see both as self-protection and as self-renunication, was also a silencing of the question of the origins or consequences of his acts of cognition *in the world*. His unmasking of aberrant ideologies maintains a metaphorical, rather than a metonymical, relation to history. Yet those acts of cognition, however insufficient they may seem now, are not to be discarded because of this refusal to go further. In the absence of any guarantee as to Paul de Man's moral character or political vision, his writings remain indispensable in their insistence that the too-easy leap from linguistic to aesthetic, ethical, or political structures has been made before, with catastrophic results.

If it were easy to remain grounded in the morally good, the history of the twentieth century would look quite different. While deconstruction cannot be reduced to an outcome of one individual's biography, it may well be that it has arisen as an attempt to come to terms with the holocaust as a radical disruption produced as a logical extension of Western thinking. If idealism can turn out to be terroristic, if the defence of Western civilization can become the annihilation of otherness, and if the desire for a beautiful and orderly society should require the tidying action of cattle cars and gas chambers, it is not enough to decide that we now recognize evil in order to locate ourselves comfortably in the good. In Nazi Germany, the seduction of an image of the good was precisely the road to evil.

It is thus not out of 'hostility' to the moral values of Western civilization that deconstruction has arisen, but out of a desire to understand how those values are potentially already different from *themselves*. By rereading the texts of writers and philosophers that have made a difference to Western history, it might be possible to become aware of the repressions, the elisions, the contradictions and the linguistic slippages that have functioned unnoticed and that undercut the certainties those texts have been read as upholding. If certainty had never produced anything but just and life-affirming results, there would be no need to analyse it. It is because of the self-contradictions and ambiguities already present within the text and the history of even the clearest and most admirable statements that careful reading is essential. Such a reading does not aim to eliminate or dismiss texts or values, but rather to see them in a more complex, more *constructed*, less idealized light. And this applies as much to the work and life of Paul de Man as it does to any of the texts he deconstructed.

Notes

1 Paul de Man, 'Kant and Schiller', in *Aesthetic Ideology*, edited by Andrzej Warminski (forthcoming, University of Minnesota Press).

2 Robert Moynihan, *A Recent Imagining: Interviews with Harold Bloom, Geoffrey Hartman, J. Hillis Miller, and Paul de Man* (Hamdon, Conn.: Archon Books, 1986), p. 137.

3 Factual support for this section comes from the following sources: Ortwin de Graef, 'Paul de Man's Proleptic "Nachlass"', forthcoming; Peter Dodge, *A Documentary Study of Hendrik de Man, Socialist Critic of Marxism* (Princeton: Princeton University Press, 1979); and Henri de Man, *Cavalier Seul* (Geneva: Les Editions du Cheval Ailé, 1948).

4 Dodge, *Documentary Study*, p. 326.

5 Paul de Man, 'Image and Emblem in Yeats', in *The Rhetoric of Romanticism* (New York: Columbia University Press, 1984), p. 238.

6 *Le Soir*, 8 April 1941, p. 6 (translation mine).

7 Paul de Man, 'A View on Contemporary German Fiction', *Het Vlaamsche Land*, 20 August 1942, p. 2 (trans. from Flemish by Ortwin de Graef).

8 *Le Soir*, 4 March 1941, p. 10 (translation mine).

9 Jacques Derrida, 'Like the Sound of the Sea Deep within a Shell: Paul de Man's War', *Critical Inquiry* 14 (Spring 1988), p. 626.

10 *Völkisch* thinking, on which Adolf Hitler based many of his ideas, is described by the scholar of Nazism, George L. Mosse, in his book *The Crisis of German Ideology: Intellectual Origins of the Third Reich* (New York: Schocken Books, 1964), as the conflation of soil, blood (race) and culture: 'According to many Völkisch theorists, the nature of the soul of a Volk is determined by the native landscape. Thus the Jews, being a desert people, are viewed as shallow, arid, "dry" people, devoid of profundity and totally lacking in creativity. Because of the barrenness of the desert landscape, the Jews are a spiritually barren people. They thus contrast markedly with the Germans, who, living in the dark, mist-shrouded forests, are deep, mysterious, profound. Because they are so constantly shrouded in darkness, they strive toward the sun, and are truly *Lichtmenschen* (pp. 4–5). A desert is only a desert, but darkness is also light. One glimpses here the dangers not only of an ahistorical essentialism but also of allowing a contradiction to appear logical and natural.

11 Paul de Man, *Allegories of Reading* (New Haven: Yale University Press, 1979), p. ix.

12 Paul de Man, 'The Resistance to Theory', in *The Resistance to Theory* (Minneapolis: The University of Minnesota Press, 1986), p. 11 (emphasis mine).

13 Paul de Man, 'The Return to Philology', in *The Resistance to Theory*, p. 25 (emphasis mine).

14 De Man, 'Resistance to Theory', p. 11.

15 Paul de Man, 'Aesthetic Formalization: Kleist's *Über das Marionnettentheater*', in *The Rhetoric of Romanticism* (New York: Columbia University Press, 1984).

16 De Man, 'Kant and Schiller'.

PETER BÜRGER

The Problem of Aesthetic Value

Translated by Shaun Whiteside

Culture as status-symbol: Bourdieu's sociology of culture

In the face of a large number of conflicting artistic programmes and doctrines of aesthetic evaluation[1] Bourdieu takes a radical position: the external
perspective. He does not inquire which aesthetic is the right one, but
whether it is possible empirically to prove that particular aesthetic attitudes
coincide with particular class positions. He does not identify these solely
with reference to their position within the process of production (economic
capital), but also to social origin (social capital) and the level of scholastic
training attained (cultural capital). In his wide-ranging study, *Distinction*,
based on the results of previous surveys, he comes to the conclusion that
people from the ruling (dominant) classes, the petty bourgeoisie and the
ruled (dominated) classes have clearly outlined aesthetic attitudes which,
together with the totality of their modes of conduct, form a unified life-
style, which he traces back to a class-specific *habitus*, a 'practice-unifying
and practice-generating principle'.[2] According to his thesis, the use of
symbolic objects (particularly including their position within hierarchies of
value) serves a strategy of opposition between the higher and the lower
classes: 'the manner of using symbolic goods . . . constitutes one of the key
markers of "class" and is also the ideal weapon in strategies of distinction'
(p. 66).

   That Bourdieu is concerned with more than substantiating a sociological
hypothesis concerning the interrelation of aesthetic attitudes, life-styles and
class positions is made clear from the subtitle of his study: *Social Critique of
the Judgement of Taste* (in the French edition, *Critique sociale du jugement*). In
appropriating the title of Kant's *Critique of Judgement*, he is formulating the
claim to have pronounced the truth about aesthetic discourses, something
that those discourses themselves are incapable of grasping. In fact he has
already stressed in his introductory chapter that any attempt to define the
essence of the aesthetic is doomed to failure because it excludes the collective
and individual genesis of this historical phenomenon (p. 28). And he adds
a 'postscript' to the book, in which he characterizes the Kantian deduction

of the pure judgement of taste as a dual act of distinction from both the 'refined enjoyment' of the courtier and the 'animal enjoyment' of the people (p. 493).

It is not my intention to seek to oppose Bourdieu's enlightening insights with a trans-temporal essentialist definition of aesthetics. But I should certainly like to oppose Bourdieu's claim to have resolved the problem of evaluation. According to Bourdieu's thesis, the aesthetic evaluations that fall within the sphere of legitimate culture and are supported by philosophical theories do not find their basis in their object itself (that is, in the identifiable quality of the works), but emerge solely from the form of existence of the ruling classes and their need for distinction from the lower classes. For in fact Bourdieu certainly wavers between two versions of his thesis, which cannot be seamlessly united with one another. First of all he attributes to the members of the ruling classes an intention of distinction ('self-distinguishing intention', p. 61; 'strategies of distinction', p. 66). He later stresses that he does not wish to suggest that the modes of conduct under discussion are the result of rational calculation ('it is in no way suggested that the corresponding behaviour is guided by rational calculation of maximum profit', p. 86). The contradiction reveals a problem that arises from the basis of Bourdieu's methods. The external perspective of the observer which he has chosen allows him to reveal connections between aesthetic attitudes and social indices such as class origin, educational training and social position; but it does not allow him to pronounce on the intentions and motivations of those who participate in cultural events, except as clearly characterized interpretative hypotheses.

But Bourdieu goes beyond the boundaries of empirical social research and formulates a general judgement about the value of legitimate culture. This is a fetish, he says, generated only by the investment made by those who participate in culture (p. 230). The differentiation of high and low, authentic and trivial culture, has no objective basis in the objects and their uses, but is solely the result of a struggle for status, the rules of which are laid down by the dominating classes. While he believes that the dominated classes, although excluded from the enjoyment of aesthetic values, have, to all intents and purposes, never questioned them, Bourdieu takes on precisely this task, advocating a 'vulgar critique' of the value of legitimate culture. 'It is barbarism to ask what culture is for; to allow the hypothesis that culture might de devoid of intrinsic interest, and that interest in culture is not a natural property . . . but a simple social artifact, a particular form of fetishism' (p. 250).

Let us not be immediately provoked by the radicalism of this thesis, but instead let us recognize, for the moment, how fertile it is. Bordieu traces all claims to an innate aesthetic competence back to the results of family and educational socialization. He also plausibly argues that cultural value (like the value of culture) is primarily the product of those who participate in cultural life. We can accept both of these propositions; similarly the fact that in aesthetic value judgements the structural distinction from the valueless always carries a social connotation (here I have considerably toned down Bourdieu's own formulation). But the conclusion that Bourdieu draws from his results and interpretations, namely that the evaluation of the works of legitimate culture is not based in the object itself but is, rather, mere fetishism, does not seem to me to be compelling. He takes a position familiar to us from early Enlightenment critiques of religion, which saw myths as insubstantial because the evidence that they provide cannot be empirically proven.

The fact that a practice relies on the convictions of its agents and would break down without them does not express anything about the values towards which that practice is oriented. The fact that even the economic system itself is based on values of trust (*valeurs fiduciaires*) was something that even Valéry recognized; nevertheless, a multinational concern is a real power. The banking institution too, as is well known, depends on the fact that customers trust the idea that their invested money will retain its value within certain margins; this idea is not a mere fiction. Something similar might be true of culture. It too is dependent on the psychical energies with which producers and recipients attribute value to cultural objects; but that does not make them into mere fetishes. Of course, this only demonstrates the possibility of undertaking aesthetic evaluations, but says nothing about criteria of evaluation and the principle behind them.

Approaches to the Problem of Evaluation

Anyone who goes to modern museums will, on some occasion, have come across that stack of neatly layered felt rectangles crowned by a copper plate in the same shape. Or he or she will at least have seen pictures of the fat smeared in the corner of a museum by the same artist. The question of whether these are art works, and, if so, whether there are any standards for the evaluation of such objects, is not one that occurs only to members of the lower classes, who, because of their origins and their lack of educational training, have been unable to attain any aesthetic competence, but certainly also affects museum visitors who have been socialized in a bourgeois way, who are thoroughly familiar with modern art from Cézanne to Informel. It would not be difficult to propose far more extreme examples than these works by Beuys, with regard to the problematic of aesthetic evaluation today. We should for the moment be equally suspicious of the expert stance of the person who already dismisses as philistinism the very question of whether or not these are art works, and the indignation of those who claim they could produce such objects themselves. Instead of doing this, let us consider the matter.

Before discussing criteria of aesthetic evaluation, its validity and its foundation, we should be clear about the particular status of (aesthetic) value judgements. While epistemological judgements about objects from the outside world are, to a large degree, independent of the judging subject, the same is not true of value judgements. They do not express anything about the object, but rather about the relation of the subject to the object. The judging subject itself is one of the two poles which this judgement places in relation to one another. Of course we cannot think of the value judgement as an isolated confrontation of the judging subject with the object (the work); for the subject brings to his or her judgement everything that he or she has acquired through family and educational socialization and the experiences structured around it. Immediacy of judgement is an illusion which we must recognize as such, and which Bourdieu also rightly criticizes.

If we inquire further into the basis of the validity of (aesthetic) value judgements, we find that it can only, at best, be found in the sediments, however fragmentary, of previous experience of art works. Whether these have solidified into linguistically formulated norms or are cultivated as pre-linguistic sensibility, an institutionalized practice of the consideration of art works is the basis of evaluation. Bourdieu, who concludes from this that aesthetic values are not based on anything substantial, thus reveals that he too is still attached to the chimera of trans-historical values which he sees as metaphysically assured.

In so far as the subject, as a historical subject, is constitutive of the aesthetic judgement, the criteria of evaluation are also historical. Does this mean that they are arbitrary, like changing fashions? (Bourdieu suggests as much, p. 232 n.) An example: 20 years ago, nineteenth-century historicist architecture was considered monstrous by the aesthetically competent viewer. In the meantime the façades of those buildings have been repainted in lighter colours, their ornaments delicately emphasized, and the same viewer must admit that he or she finds pleasure in looking at the buildings. A second example: a large number of the works of Informel in the 1950s and 1960s, which were generally appreciated at the time, now look curiously pallid to today's viewer: an unremarkable decorative school of painting that is not without charm, but this charm is quickly exhausted. Must we conclude from this that aesthetic judgement is arbitrary? I do not find this conclusion compelling. In the 1950s and 1960s the impact of modernism had, at least in Germany, a profound historical necessity, following on as it did from the suppression of artistic Modernism during the Nazi era. It is possible that the distancing from Stalinist architecture and Socialist Realism provided artistic Modernism with political connotations of which the supporters of Modernism might not at the time have been necessarily aware at all.

More distanced in time from the Nazi era, and in a climate in which East–West tensions were relaxing, those powers which made non-figurative painting and functionalist architecture seem like the only legitimate forms of expression for the age went into decline. As far as architecture is concerned, the new reverence for historicism reveals the critique of a certain modern style of building, which Mitscherlich criticized some time ago in his studies on the desolation of cities.[3] At the time, this critique was widely acknowledged; but it did not produce any change in aesthetic attitudes. Only the intensification of ecological awareness and the doubts it cast on industrial society, which relies on the principle of the constant expansion of production, also had their effects on the appreciation of aesthetic modernism (in so far as it was bound up with modern society). Consequently, the changes in aesthetic attitudes which we have experienced in our most recent past are revealed to be not arbitrary but, rather, conditioned by sociohistorical and everyday experiences.

Let us try to schematize the various positions which one can take with regard to the question of aesthetic evaluation:

(1) Traditional doctrines of evaluation take as their starting point the idea that there are aesthetic values which have trans-historical validity. The great art work is accorded a self-evidence of which contemporaries are not necessarily aware but which becomes plain in the course of history. The systematic aesthetician sees changes in evaluation, from which the historian deduces the historicity of standards, as an approach towards or deviation from a correct understanding of artistic value. The weaknesses of this position are well known: the hypostatization of the great work of art into the sole, unquestionable source of aesthetic value, an ahistorical concept of art and blindness to the fact that in Modernism, normative discourses on art form an independent sphere which shapes the production and reception of art to the same extent and does not coincide with the works themselves.

(2) In contrast to traditional doctrines of value, the 'material aesthetic', represented particularly by Adorno, reflects its own historicity and admits that even the most important work depends on the work of its predecessors, which is stored in its material. As is well known, Adorno saw the development of music from Beethoven via Wagner to Schönberg as a consistent development of a musical material with an inherent logic; that is, a direction laid down within the material itself. The superiority of the 'material aesthetic' over traditional doctrines of value is beyond doubt: it enables us to formulate value judgements without forcing us to deny the historicity of the criteria of value, and has at its disposal, in the concept of historically advanced material, a historico-philosophically assured, quasi-objective standard. Of course we cannot ignore the fact that Adorno pays a high price for the consistency with which he links the construction of history to evaluation. His polemic on Stravinsky in the *Philosophy of the New Music* is not simply the expression of the idiosyncrasy of the pupil of Berg, but has a thoroughly systematic place within his aesthetic. As he sees only the twelve-tone technique as an advanced state of musical material, he is unable to appreciate either the avant-garde early Stravinsky of the *Histoire du Soldat* or the Neo-Classical composer. The decisionism at work in determining what material can be seen as advanced and which material may be defined as advanced is impossible to overlook – quite apart from the difficulties which we would encounter if we attempted to consider the twentieth-century narrators whom Adorno also canonized (Proust, Kafka, Joyce and Beckett) as exponents of a single material tradition. Finally it must be stressed that

even in the 'material aesthetic' the autonomy of normative discourses about art has not yet been acknowledged. Certainly, in his interpretation of the Sirens episode in the *Odyssey*, Adorno touched upon the dark origins of the autonomy of art; but he did not, as far as I can see, return to it. The fact that Odysseus' comrades have to row with plugged ears, while he, bound and therefore held back by force from practice, listens to the song of the Sirens, is seen by the authors of the *Dialectic of Enlightenment* as an allegory for the idea that blunting of the sensibility of the working masses is a precondition for the pure artistic enjoyment of the privileged classes.

(3) In Bourdieu's sociology of culture, on the other hand, and in the sociology of institutions, normative discourses about art or literature are seen as an autonomous sphere, and the functional definitions of literature and the criteria of evaluation are understood as an object of social conflict.[4] Apart from this important common feature a crucial difference should nevertheless be stressed; while Bourdieu concentrates primarily on the effect of distinction from the lower classes, the sociology of institutions is concerned first with the concrete discussion of evaluative criteria and the definition of functions of literature, secondly with the complex relations of conditions which produce changes in the normative frame of the production and reception of literature, and finally with the various experiences of meaning produced by high and low literature.

I should like to explain this briefly with an example. The critique of mass literature, which in Bourdieu's perspective appears as a strategy of the ruling classes, or of an intellectual stratum within them, in the struggle for cultural power, becomes a more complex and contradictory phenomenon when subjected to an institutional–historical analysis.[5] We must first be aware that the dichotomy of literature is not a trans-temporal phenomenon, but the result of a historical process. As long as the *doctrine classique* held sway in France, the problem of evaluative appreciation, for example, was not resolved by means of a clean separation between high and low literature (the little books of the *'Bibliothèque bleue'*, which were consumed by the masses, were hardly even seen by the educated classes of the seventeenth and eighteenth centuries), but by means of the hierarchy of genres. Certainly, long before 1800 there was something like 'light fiction'; but it was only the crisis of the Enlightenment concept of literature (in the last third of the eighteenth century), paradoxically a result of its success, that made it a problem. If the thinkers of the Enlightenment on the one hand saw the literary market as the primary condition for reaching the greatest possible number of readers, on the other hand they could not avoid being aware that this market was developing a dynamic of its own which in no way corresponded to their idealized concept of a public effecting is own Enlightenment. 'Books have now become a commodity like sugar, coffee and snuff, ' said Wieland's 'Teutscher Merkur' in 1780.[6] That means: the authors were out for profit, not (as the Enlightenment concept of literature expects) the truth, and the readers demanded an agreeable entertainment, addressed primarily to the emotions, rather than participation in the process of self-enlightenment.

The Enlightenment thinkers themselves were helpless in the face of this crisis in the Enlightenment concept of literature produced by the expansion of the literary market; they were unable to develop a concept that could claim to resolve the crisis of which they were fully and acutely aware. But the proponents of the theory of aesthetic autonomy had such a concept at their disposal. Where the Enlightenment thinkers still took as their starting point the unity of author and readers within a *République des lettres*, the proponents of autonomy distinguished between 'the elite of a nation and that nation's mass' (Schiller in his polemic on G.A. Bürger)[7] and concluded, from the market-dependence of literature, that its higher functions could be saved only at the cost of a separation from the practice of life and hence by being made elitist. Faced with the progressive erosion of the validity of religious values and a development that increasingly submitted the bourgeois subject too to the demands of daily work, enabling him to learn only partial skills, literature was to become the site of the interpretation of the world as meaningful and of holistic experience. This sublime function could, of course, be fulfilled only by a literature that had turned away from the desire of readers for entertainment as much as from their need for practical (*lebenspraktisch*) (moral) orientation in everyday life. The institutionalization of the aesthetics of autonomy therefore necessarily resulted in the struggle against the Enlightenment's instrumental concept of literature, which was now exposed to the accusation of triviality. It had the further consequence that certain needs such as the moral orientation of readers in high literature lost their right to existence.

It is therefore absolutely understandable that some Enlightenment thinkers saw the literary debate led by the Weimar Classicists as the strategy of an ambitious clique of intellectuals, violating the rules of literary urbanity and endeavouring to enforce their own position as the only legitimate one. Such an interpretation, which proceeds along entirely the same lines as Bourdieu's argument, grasps only one side of the complex process of dichotomization. The proponents of the programme of artistic autonomy were not only enforcing their power interests, but formulating an internally coherent answer to the crisis in the Enlightenment concept of literature brought about by the expansion of the literary market. Over and above this, they were reacting to certain normative problems resulting from the social process of modernization (the problem of alienation and a loss of meaning). The fact that the solution they had sought would in turn be the source of new problems is something that we cannot pursue beyond what we have indicated already. We might only recall the concept of 'affirmative culture' introduced by Herbert Marcuse. But it must be clear by now that an analysis aimed solely at the problem of 'class distinction' must miss the theoretical content of the discussions around the definition of the function of literature and the criteria of literary evaluation. This does not cast doubt on the value of the works of Bourdieu and his school, but reveals them to be one-sided in the strict sense of the word.

The approaches outlined diverge not least in the position that they accord to the institutions of art. The proponents of traditional doctrines of evaluation remain trapped in the perspective of the participant. That works of art represent ideal values is, for them, as certain as the trans-historical validity of aesthetic norms. Even Adorno still lives entirely within the art world, whose norms he is of course able to recognize as being historically variable. In contrast, Bourdieu adopts an external perspective on the institution of art; he observes its participants as an ethnologist would observe the rites of a native tribe. The approach of the sociology of institutions finally claims to unite these two perspectives and to examine the idea of the historicity of art not only at the level of the material but also at that of the institution, that is, of the normative framing conditions of the production and reception of art. Since the attack of the historical avant-garde movements on the institution of art revealed it to be an institution,[8] the carpet has been rudely pulled out from beneath the substantialism of traditional doctrines of evaluation. Adorno made a great theoretical effort when he sought compellingly to establish unambiguous evaluative decisions, at least within a particular era; but since his death the theorem of the most progressive material has become recognizable as the programme of the producer. The coexistence of different stages of material can nowadays only be rejected on an arbitrary basis, without compelling grounds. That is certainly true of classical modernism: in fact it would be extremely difficult to locate the canonized narrators of the twentieth century (Proust, Joyce, Kafka, Musil and Beckett) within a single material tradition. Even more clearly, painting from the early years of our century presents us with a variety of material traditions, each of them with its own unmistakeable characteristics. While Adorno still started out from the idea that the aesthetic norms valid in a given period are based on the correspondence between artistic material and the state of development of society as a whole, this theorem was weakened by the surrealist painters' falling back on the material of nineteenth-century salon painting, if not before. And while Adorno was able once more to equate a particular modernism with contemporary art as such because he lived within it and only within it, this attitude is no longer possible today, now that the historical avant-garde movements have violently torn the auratic veil from autonomous art. (Adorno therefore resisted, consistently from his point of view, the avant-garde's rhetoric of destruction.) Certainly, the aura is reproduced in every act of authentic reception; but the restored aura is no longer the original one. We know, or at least we can know, that we ourselves produce the magic that enchants us. It has been true, since the historical avant-garde movements, that anything that we declare to be an art work is an art work. Since then, as Hegel anticipated, art is existing as 'post-art'.

If art has passed through the stage of self-criticism in this way, producers and recipients can no longer unproblematically adopt the attitude of the participant, for whom value adheres to objects as magical power does to fetishes. Instead they are encouraged to see through the experiences produced by their contact with the objects as a practice based only on itself and not on a metaphysical, ontological or anthropological principle. This means that if they seek to make the historical condition of the institution of art their own, they are forced to take both the internal perspective of the participant and the external perspective of the critical observer. In other words: though the historical avant-garde movements were, in their attack on the institution of art, unable to bring art back into the practice of life (*Lebenspraxis*), they still effectively shattered the attitude of native immediacy (which does not mean that this attitude is not still adopted, now as before). It has been replaced by an 'as-if' attitude that sees through the illusoriness of the aesthetic experience and nevertheless continues to take it seriously.

A discussion of the problem of aesthetic evaluation which places itself in a hermeneutic relationship to its object must take as its starting point the historical state of the development of the institution. What applies to producers and recipients of art affects to an even greater extent the theorist concerned with the understanding of the problematic of value. The theorist too must unite the perspective of the participant with the perspective of the observer in order to show that the experience that can be had from the works is limitless. While the reflecting recipient seeks nothing more than a well-founded value-decision, the theorist must thematize the question of the legitimation of value-decisions and their limits. The theorist will be aware that his or her own words are bound up with the historical state of development of their object, that is, of the institution of art. The theorist's effort, too, can only be a systematization of that which can be experienced in the present day. If it seeks to be more, it ignores its own historicity, becoming naively ontological or pseudo-objective.

In Modernity, aesthetic experience is always embedded in descriptive and normative discourses; but these have no foundation other than the experience that structures them. In other words: there is no bottom line from which we can answer questions of aesthetic evaluation, even if only for our own age. This does not mean that value decisions are only subjective preferences or group-specific strategies of distinction; they can definitively be traced back to principles, but these too are subject to discussion.

Anyone who abandons Adorno's theorem concerning historically advanced material (and we are obliged to do so by our awareness of the arbitrariness at its basis) is confronted by a large number of rival material traditions. Expressionist, Cubist, Constructivist, Surrealist and Neo-Realist painting accumulate in the first third of our century but do not allow us to discern a material of the age. And yet the coexistence of the various stages of material is not arbitrary; rather, there are entirely recognizable principles concerning the relation of the material to reality. (In what follows I shall restrict myself to a schematic outline that serves only the purpose of illustration.) Behind the painting of the Expressionists there is a vision that defines art as an expression of the subject. Against a world that constantly demands a higher level of conformity from the individual, the Expressionists set a programme of the liberation of the subject. A quite different principle is at work in the Constructivism of the Dutch group, De Stijl, that of rationality. Here the modern world, governed by technology and science, does not appear as a constraint but as the promise of an historical progress unique in the history of humanity. The subjective character of the means of expression sought by the Expressionists is rejected by Mondrian and his comrades-in-arms, in favour of a material the simplicity and clarity of which is aimed at universality. Yet another principle underlies surrealist painting: that of radical protest against bourgeois society, a protest that includes the very art in which the Expressionists still put their trust.

Let us end this outline here. It will have become plain at least that the various stages of material each have a different relation to reality. The principles inherent within them can neither be deduced from one another nor traced back to a higher principle. Attitudes to reality are expressed in them which are made effective in the material. It is not a single material that reflects the totality of the age; rather, in the different material traditions different relations to contemporary reality are articulated. If, today, we can see paintings by Schmidt-Rottluff, Mondriaan and Magritte placed next to one another without privileging one material tradition over the others, this is because they present an attitude to bourgeois society the legitimacy of which (or at least the historical legitimacy of which) is comprehensible to us. The longing for the period style that would be inevitably and universally compelling is in the final analysis diametrically opposed to a society that continually undermines its inherent tendencies towards unification by means of newly-created differentiations. That Modernism finally contains no material that could be described as having been definitively rejected has been clearly shown by the Surrealists in falling back on nineteenth-century salon painting. The only decisive thing is whether the material can be used to articulate a relation to reality.

Does our argument, which sought to prove the aesthetic legitimacy of various material traditions, not refer the value decision to the discussion of the individual work, where, with a lack of general criteria, the problem must be even more insoluble than it is on the level of the material? In a certain sense this is true. The concept of form on which Modernist art is based refers to the work in its particularity; it resists all attempts to encapsulate it in generally applicable rules. There is also the problem that the concepts exchanged as tokens of communication in evaluative discourses have a semantic content that is, in both historical and group-specific terms, very diverse. If, for example, a word such as harmony (*Stimmigkeit*) in the context of a classicist vision of art, connotes something like harmonic formation, then the advocates of radical Modernism can link it to a fragmentary character of the work beyond all boundaries of accepted anti-aesthetics (the harmonic work would then also be '*schrottig*', 'scrappy'). Nevertheless, aesthetic evaluations are not merely arbitrary and subjective decrees, for the simple reason that the individual work, in the strict sense, does not exist. All works exist in a context, even if it is only that of the other works by the same artist, and are embedded in descriptive and evaluative discourses. Comparison and criticism (which already defines the process of production) ensure the possibility of evaluation without requiring precisely defined criteria. This is the problem with aesthetic evaluation for a rationalist position that insists on a prior definition of criteria. But just as we can communicate in colloquial speech without defining the meaning of the words beforehand, individuals and groups communicate about the aesthetic value of artistic works without having solid criteria at their disposal.

Has this not involuntarily brought us close to Bourdieu's position, in which he contends that no criteria for evalution are present in the object itself? In at least two respects that is not so: in the first place we have reached the conclusion that there are no solid (or even trans-historically valid) criteria of value, but that the institutional discourse that continually confronts works with one another – although without any conceptual focus – permits rational value decisions. On the other hand we have attempted to show that a practice that is based solely on itself can also belong to the order of authentic experiences. But Bourdieu doubts that. The very radicalism of his critique, which unmasks the ruling ideology of art as fetishism, misses its target, because it does not, in turn, dialectically question its own result again – from the perspective of the participant. Thus he paradoxically maintains a substantialist concept of art, which he has rightly criticized among the proponents of traditional doctrines of evaluation. Instead, we have attempted to show the lack of metaphysical guarantees in the sphere of art (and, linked with this, the historicity of the processes of evaluation) not as a fundamental lack in the institution of art, but as an indication that the only truly liberated art is the one revealed as a ritual practice.

But how, we might ask, does this relate to Beuys's pile of felt and fat-smeared corner? Are they works of art, and if so, are they major works? Unfortunately this question cannot be answered with a conclusive yes or no. The importance of the artist Joseph Beuys does not consist, or at least not primarily, in the works shown by the museums, but in the consistent elaboration of the position of an avant-garde concept of art after the collapse of the historical avant-garde movements. The latter, as is well known, had wanted to bring art back into the practice of life; but their works ended up in the museum. Beuys adopts a position on this situation. He sees neither the possibility of returning to the production of works within the autonomous institution of art, nor that of directly taking up the avant-garde attack on the institution. He finds a way out of this dilemma by occupying the impossible space between art and life. Continually overstepping the boundary that separates art and life, he remains still an artist. Beuys seeks to rescue the social–critical function of art, which can no longer be fulfilled either by the autonomous work or the avant-garde act of protest as such, by crossing frontiers and thus declaring the experiential material of his life to be both the material of art and a supra-artistic effective substance (felt and fat were the materials to which he attributed his rescue from freezing to death after crashing his plane in Russia). Only someone who can connect

the sensory impression of the stack of felt with the allegorical meaning that
Beuys gives to it (that of producing life-energy), and can account for the
incongruity of the two, will grasp something of the content of this work,
which is always, at the same time, a non-work.

Notes

1 Cf. the critical account by J. Schulte-Sasse, *Literarische Wertung* (Stuttgart:
   Sammlung Metzler, 1976).
2 Pierre Bourdieu, *Distinction, A Social Critique of the Judgement of Taste*, trans.
   Richard Nice (Routledge and Kegan Paul, 1984), p. 101. The page numbers
   given refer to this edition.
3 A. Mitscherlich, *Die Unwirtlichkeit unserer Städte. Anstiftung zum Unfrieden*, ed.
   Suhrkamp (Frankfurt, 1965).
4 I developed the terms 'the institution of art' and 'institution of literature' to
   designate the normative framing conditions of artistic and literary production in
   an essay which has now been translated into English: *The Institution of 'Art' as a
   Category in the Sociology of Literature*, in *Cultural Critique* (Department of English,
   University of Minnesota, Minneapolis), 2 (Winter 1985–6), pp. 5–34. On
   criticism, cf. P. -U. Hohendahl, *Beyond Reception Aesthetics*, in *New German Critique*,
   28 (Winter 1983), pp. 108–43; 135ff. A comprehensive account of the institution
   of literature in Germany is provided by P. -U. Hohendahl's *Literarische Kultur im
   Zeitalter des Liberalismus 1830–1870* (Munich: Beck, 1985). Cf. also the volume
   Zum Funktionswandel der Literatur, edited by P. Bürger (*Hefte für kritische Literaturwissenschaft*, 4; ed. Suhrkamp (Frankfurt, 1983), as well as the studies mentioned
   below.
5 The following remarks are based on the works of Christa Bürger and Onno Frels
   in Christa Bürger and others, *Aufklärung und literarische Öffentlichkeit* (*Hefte für
   kritische Literaturwissenschaft*, 2; ed. Suhrkamp (Frankfurt, 1980)); and *Zur Dichotomisierung von hoher und niederer Literatur* (*Hefte für kritische Literaturwissenschaft*, 3; ed.
   Suhrkamp (Frankfurt, 1982)).
6 Quoted from O. Frels, 'Die Entstehung einer bürgerlichen Unterhaltungskultur',
   in *Aufklärung und literarische Öffentlichkeit*.
7 Quoted from Christa Bürger, "Einleitung" in *Zur Dichotomisierung von hoher und
   niederer Literatur*.
8 Here and below, cf. my *Theory of the Avant-Garde* (Minneapolis: University of
   Minnesota Press, 1984).

ALBRECHT WELLMER

Metaphysics at the Moment of its Fall

Translated by Shaun Whiteside

In his 'Meditations on Metaphysics', the last chapter of the *Negative Dialectics*, Adorno sought to unfold the concept of a thought beyond metaphysics. This concept remains aporetic in his work. That which can truly be called 'thought' must, for Adorno, participate in the transcending impulse of metaphysics; but this impulse resists the form of conceptual thought. As almost always in Adorno, the aporia results from twofold argument: on the one hand he shows that the 'fall' of metaphysical ideas is irreversible; on the other he argues that the truth of metaphysics can only be grasped at the moment of its fall. The moment of this fall is, in a broader sense, the final stage of the European Enlightenment since Kant, and in a narrower sense it is the crime of Auschwitz as the moment of the accomplishment and self-destruction of that Enlightenment.

The 'Meditations on Metaphysics' is a long analysis of Kant's critical rescuing of metaphysics. Adorno uses it to demonstrate why the fall of metaphysics is irreversible, and at the same time he affirms and appropriates Kant's gesture of critical rescue. I should like first of all to clarify the destructive aspect of his argument. Adorno's critique is aimed against Kant's drawing of boundaries between the spheres of the empirical and the intelligible, the pre-condition of Kant's critical rescue of metaphysics. And indeed Adorno indicates an antimony in the concept of the intelligible which, unlike Kantian antinomies, is not only unavoidable but also insoluble; an antinomy, then, which as well as questioning the knowability of the intelligible world also questions its *thinkability*. The substance of the antinomy is that transcendental ideas cannot attain objective reality, and that if they are to be the expression of intelligent thought, they *must* attain reality. That transcendental ideas cannot attain objective reality, that there is no possible experience that corresponds to them, has been repeatedly shown by Kant himself. Adorno shows, on the other hand, that they would be empty as mere thoughts if they were not thought from the point of view of possible experience, that is, as an objective reality that is at least *possible*.

The ambiguity of the Kantian concept of ideas may be grasped in the transition from the *Critique of Pure Reason* to the *Critique of Practical Reason*.

In the light of practical reason, in fact, the ideas of God, freedom and immortality no longer appear simply as regulative ideas but rather become *constitutive* ideas, 'because they are reasons for the possibility of *realizing* the *necessary object* of pure practical reason (the supreme good)'. So that the 'supreme good' may be conceived of as a *possible reality*, God, freedom and immortality must be conceived of as real – even if unknowable. But as names of the real, these ideas are only thinkable because in terms of their meaning they are always – in a way which Kant did not perceive – related to possible experiences, or to the conditions of possible experience. In fact, they assume, in their different ways, the concept of an individuated spiritual being, or rather that of a world of individuated spiritual beings; in the concept of a spiritual being, however, in the only way in which we can conceive of it, its physicality, and therefore space and time and possible experience are always implied from the beginning. This naturalness, this physicality of individuated spiritual beings, is tacitly assumed and at the same time denied *as* a necessary assumption in the central concepts in terms of which Kant conceives of the realm of the intelligible. The ambiguity of transcendental ideas – between a 'regulative' and a 'constitutive' meaning, between transcendence and immanence – is explained by the fact that the concept of the intelligible means not only a Beyond of *knowable* nature, but at the same time a Beyond of *evil* nature (and of a meaningless history). As a Beyond of evil nature, the realm of the intelligible represents an infinite task facing finite rational beings – the realization of the supreme good, the overcoming of the 'natural' character of the will – as well as the possibility of a solution for this task, for which historical experience alone provides no clues. As the task is imperative, the ideas of God, freedom and immortality must have reality; for only if they have reality can the task itself be both meaningful and the index of the meaning of the natural and historical world. This circle of postulates no longer expresses a critical–epistemological, but rather a practical–teleological connection of the intelligible with the empirical world. The intelligible refers to the fundament and the goal of this teleology. Ony if the fundament – God, freedom, immortality – is real can the goal refer to a possibility. In Kant, this goal is designated by a series of borderline concepts such as those of a 'perfectly good' or 'holy' will, a kingdom of ends, of the supreme good, the realm of God, etc., in which the empirical world can be said to transcend itself towards the intelligible.

All of these borderline concepts are paradoxical in that they can only designate their practically unattainable borderline values for sentient rational beings by eliminating the condition of 'naturalness' from the borderline status itself. The concept of a 'pure rational being' is also involved in this paradox: it designates a *telos* of finite rational beings, whose irrationality it negates; it thus describes an ideal of rationality. But the formulation of the ideal also negates all those conditions according to which finite rational beings must be *individuated*, that is, real rational beings: naturalness, physicality, sensuousness, will. The ambiguity of the concepts in terms of which Kant conceives of the realm of the intelligible is thus repeated on various levels: they transcend the boundaries of possible experience and yet *mean* possible experience. This is even true of the idea of the immortality of the soul. Adorno scoffs at the 'spiritualism' of a metaphysics – even that of Kant's – which can only rescue the doctrine of immortality at the cost of total spiritualization, for the soul alone:

> But what hope still clings to, as in Mignon's song,[1] is the transfigured body. Metaphysics will hear nothing of that. It will not lower itself to material things ... Yet the idealist construction, which proposes the elimination of earthly remains, becomes void once it entirely removes that 'selfhood' which served as a model for the concept of the spirit ... Christian dogmatics, in which souls were imagined as awakening simultaneously with the resurrection of the flesh, was metaphysically more consistent, more enlightened, if you like – than speculative metaphysics, just as hope means a physical resurrection and feels cheated of the best part by being spiritualized.[2]

Kant's attempt at a critical rescue of the truth of metaphysics, and with it the truth of theology, is doomed to fail from Adorno's point of view, because the drawing of the boundary between that which is knowable and that which is merely thinkable and logically necessary but not knowable, and indeed the concept of the intelligible itself, must remain aporetic. Kant's philosophy proves helpless in the face of the maelstrom of the progressive Enlightenment into which metaphysical ideas are drawn.

Thus the accusations which Kant applied to the earlier form of metaphysics also apply to his own: its ideas are 'mirages of thought'; they represent not only unknowable things, but also unthinkable things; they are the imaginary of thought, a dream of reason. To this extent Adorno is in agreement even with the positivist Enlightenment. Nevertheless the historical moment in which metaphysics as a theory is irreversibly revealed to be wrong by the Enlightenment, is for Adorno also the moment when it becomes possible to rescue its truth; the truth of metaphysics may only be understood at the moment of its fall. Only at a moment when all the objectivist and apologist claims of metaphysics, which assumed the inheritance of theology as an ideology, collapse, does it become clear what irreversibly separates it from the false Enlightenment, and how – even where it conformed to this Enlightenment in the form of systematic thought (*Systemdenken*) in philosophy – it had always been opposed to it. But now, only at the moment of its disintegration – the historical moment of fully developed modernity – does the truth-content of metaphysics become apparent; or rather at the same moment it also becomes clear why the need for metaphysics is imperative to a consciousness that does not wish to eliminate itself *as* consciousness. This paradoxical intensification of the problem contains a concentration of motifs through which Adorno's meditations on metaphysics come ambiguously close both to the critique of religion of the young Marx, the poststructuralist critique of metaphysics and the critique of relativism by transcendental pragmatism. In what follows I should like to pursue these affinities a little further.

Adorno sees the truth content of metaphysics in its impulse to transcend everything merely existent towards an absolute. This transcending impulse is nothing but the 'transcending moment' in all thought, without which, for Adorno, the idea of truth – which he, in an apparently un-Kantian manner, describes as 'supreme' among metaphysical ideas[3] – would be reduced to nothing. I say *apparently* un-Kantian in order to show that Kant's attempt to deal with the concept of truth below the level of ideas of reason, so to speak, is always immanently questionable. Adorno is referring to this possibility when, from Kant's doctrine of Ideas, he derives the thesis that 'theory without metaphysics is impossible'.[4] If Adorno's thesis on the metaphysical character of the concept of truth is correct, it becomes clear that his defence of the concept of truth – and it is this that concerns him – must assume the characteristics of aporia. Or rather: it becomes the unfolding of an aporia; and while Adorno is unfolding this aporia, he is also seeking to read the aporetic aspects of Kantian metaphysics as the mark of an insight through which Kant proves finally superior to those who have left him behind either through idealism or positivism.

For Adorno, the possibility of truth coincides with that of an objective meaning. Hence, with the idea of truth, duration is postulated in a dual sense: first of all the duration of the truth itself. 'For a characteristic of truth is that – together with its nucleus of time – it will last. Without duration there would be no truth, and its final trace would be swallowed up by death, the absolute.[5] And on the other hand it is also the duration of those living subjects *for* whom truth exists. For 'the thought that death should be the ultimate thing is unthinkable'.[6] 'If death were that absolute which philosophy vainly sought to conjure up in a positive way, then everything is nothing; also, everything that we think is thought into the void; none of it is truly thinkable.[7] The thought that in the idea of truth death is negated not only metaphorically – as the death of the true – but also literally, stresses a theological motif both with and against Kant. What is Kantian is the primacy that Adorno assumes of practical over theoretical reason, and the connection with the Kantian doctrine of Postulates which Adorno, in a characteristic modification, relates not to the reform of the culprits but to the suffering of the victims: 'That no reform within the world was enough to do justice to the dead; that none touched the wrong of death was what leads Kantian reason to hope against reason. The secret of his philosophy is the unthinkability of despair.'[8] On the other hand, what is un-Kantian, and is in fact posited in opposition to Kant, is when Adorno emphasizes a materialist motif within the theological motif, aimed at the *secularization* of the transcending impulse. The course of history forces metaphysics into the materialism in opposition to which it was initially conceived;[9] it forces it to descend on to the 'stage of suffering', the 'somatic layer of life distant from meaning',[10] since in the camps 'every consolatory aspect of the spirit was burned away, leaving man utterly comfortless'.[11] The transcending impulse does not mean a Beyond of the historical world but rather a different state of the world itself. The vanishing-point of demythologization – first that of theology, then of metaphysics – is a constellation of immanence and transcendence that is just as necessary to be thought as it is unthinkable to be conceived of.

> The thing that would not be affected by demythologization would not be an argument . . . but the experience that thought which is not beheaded will flow into transcendence, through to the idea of a vision of a world in which not only would existent suffering be abolished, but the suffering that is irrevocably past would be revoked.[12]

This is Adorno's version of Marx's critique of religion, to which it is also related in that the disenchantment of the world, the collapse of all religious and metaphysical guarantees of meaning accompanying the process of capitalist modernization becomes evident as the precondition of a secularization of metaphysics. In the light of this more reflective repetition of Marx's critique of religion, Kant's aporias appear as signs of an insight which, contrary to Kant's opinion, can only be formulated aporetically. The ambiguities of Kant's doctrine of Ideas, which I indicated at the start, are, for Adorno, correct in that the Absolute cannot be conceived of either as being – which would be metaphysics as ideology – or as non-being – which would be positivism as a prohibition on thinking. In ever-new modifications, Adorno repeats this thought in the closing section of the *Negative Dialectics*. Thus he says about Kant: 'Forced by the convergence of all thoughts in an Absolute, he went further than the absolute boundary between the Absolute and the Existent; though he was no less forced to draw that line. He maintained his hold on metaphysical ideas, and yet forbade jumping from thoughts of the Absolute which might one day be realized, like eternal peace, to the idea that the Absolute therefore exists.'[13] Or, more concisely: 'The concept of the intelligible realm would be the concept of something which does not exist, and which, however, does not only not exist';[14] and 'the concept of the intelligible is neither a concept of something real nor of something imaginary. Rather it is aporetic.'[15]

However, Adorno finally goes beyond the aporia. For a brief moment he throws all dialectical caution to the winds and unguardedly yields to speculation. And he does employ a Hegelian objection to Kant, in order to demonstrate, in a quite un-Hegelian way, the thinkability of a concept of transcendence materialistically modified, a hope of reconciliation materialistically modified. Adorno criticizes Kant's doctrine of the 'indestructible block', his teaching of immutably given forms of thought and knowledge from which human consciousness, condemned, so to speak, to eternal imprisonment within them,[16] is not in principle able to escape. Hegel's critique of the Kantian dualism of form and content has pointed out the dogmatic aspect of this Kantian conception. From this Adorno concludes:

> But the forms are not the Ultimate described by Kant. By virtue of the reciprocity between them and existing content, they too evolve. Yet this is irreconcilable with the conception of the indestructible block. Once the forms

become elements of a dynamic – as would be truly in keeping with the view
of the subject as original apperception – their positive appearance cannot be
stipulated for all future cognition any more than any one of the contents
without which they do not exist, and with which they change.[17]

It is as if, for Adorno, this thought opened a narrow crack in the door,
through which a feeble glimmer of salvation fell upon the benighted world,
enough to question Kant's claim to metaphysical agnosticism as the final
word. 'We cannot know it' is replaced by 'we do not know it *yet*'. 'The naive
consciousness towards which probably even Goethe was inclined – that we
do not know yet, but that some day, perhaps, the mystery will be solved after
all – comes closer to metaphysical truth than Kant's *ignoramus*.'[18] Admittedly
Adorno is careful, at this point too, not to yield to a 'passage to affirmation',
[19] but the status of his observation remains unambiguous: he uses the
historical character of forms of recognition as an argument for the idea that
a hope of salvation materialistically understood need fear nothing from the
claims of enlightened reason.

However, Adorno's reversion to a Hegelian argument against Kant reveals
the point where he does not critically surpass but rather precritically under-
cuts Kant. Admittedly reference to the possibility of a future alteration in
our forms of thought and apperception can lend plausibility to the idea that
the aporetic relationship of necessity and yet impossibility in metaphysics,
as it presents itself to Adorno, is not the ultimate for philosophy, and does
not need to be its final word: the aporia could vanish, for example, if
philosophy went beyond the concepts, problems or premises which appeared
necessarily to produce the aporia, or if it reformulated the questions which
apparently permitted only aporetic answers. But only at the cost of philosophical naiveté could one conclude from the historical character of our
forms of thought and apperception that the Absolute as reconciliation – or
that absolute reconciliation – could become a historical reality. In fact, we
can know *already* that we cannot anticipate as real that which we cannot
even consistently *think* as real; hence the resolution of the aporia, the
disentanglement of the riddle could not mean what Adorno attempts to
conceive of as an Absolute that does not yet exist: the fulfilment of a
messianic hope through the transfiguration of historical reality. If the hope
of salvation were to be fulfilled in history, it would not be the hope of
salvation that was fulfilled (but rather that of a fulfilled life). On the other
hand, if what was fulfilled were really the hope of salvation, this would still
not designate a new condition of *history*.

It becomes apparent here that Adorno's attempt to outdo Marx's critique
of religion through a materialistic appropriation of theology remains trapped
in an insoluble conflict between materialistic and metaphysical (i.e.
theological) motifs. In the medium of the concept this conflict could only
be resolved by regressing to a precritical metaphysics. But all of Adorno's
thought is thought against the possibility of such a regression. This is why
he could finally only transfer the unthinkable thought of reconciliation to

aesthetic experience. But as this cannot on its own lend credence to anything that does not withstand philosophical critique, Adorno could not on the other hand relinquish the attempt philosophically to decipher the aesthetically coded thoughts of reconciliation. The *Negative Dialectics* and *Aesthetic Theory* refer aporetically to one another; in this aporetic referential connection, however, there actually circulates a piece of unreconstructed metaphysics – which is not redeemed by critical argument – that Adorno could neither abandon nor openly admit.

If, as Adorno claims, the concept of truth is 'supreme' among metaphysical concepts, then the idea of reconciliation also renders the concept of truth untenable, and turns 'truth' into a dream, as it were, which reason dreams about itself. This is how it had been seen by Nietzsche, with whom Adorno is secretly negotiating in the 'Meditations on Metaphysics'. Adorno's defence of the concept of truth means, in Nietzschean terms, an attempt to invert the positive and negative; one has only to think of Nietzsche's celebrated formulation 'that even we seekers after knowledge today, we godless anti-metaphysicians still take our fire, too, from the flame lit by a faith that is thousands of years old, that Christian faith which was also the faith of Plato, that God is the truth, that truth is divine'.[20] Neither Nietzsche nor Adorno is concerned with the usual propositional or factual truth; according to Adorno, this should rather be called simply 'correctness', while Nietzsche quite similarly attributes it to the 'conceptual dice-game', within which 'truth' means 'using every die in its designated fashion, counting its dots precisely, forming the correct categories and never contravening the order of class and rank'.[21] But why, one would like to ask, from the point of view of the modern philosophy of language, should such a concept of truth be inadequate? I should like to return to this question later, but here I would like to attempt to supply a provisional answer: 'truth', as an inherent property in the 'conceptual dice-game', is pluralistic; so many truths like language games, paradigms, concept systems of interpretations of the world. If this were all, if every truth were 'relative' to a language system of reference, which as such could not even be judged in terms of 'truth' and 'untruth', then only *truths* could exist, but not *the* truth. But however easily such a conclusion may fall from the lips of a modern relativist, it must appear nonsensical if we consider its consequences. It states that truth is a matter of perspective, and that every perspective is, in terms of truth, as good as any other. But then, 'in truth', truth does not matter; truth, and reason along with it, is radically devalued. The idea of truth would be something like a transcendental illusion, namely 'the kind of *error* without which a particular kind of living being could not live'.[22] All thought, even all of Nietzsche's thought, inevitably presupposes this idea, as it is impossible to think *within* a linguistic system of reference and also, in the same act of thinking, to make the thought relative *to* that linguistic system of reference. However, in the end thought itself would, in the name of truth, have to question the idea of truth. Such a critique of truth in the name of truth could not be formulated without pragmatic self-contradiction; but this alone would still not be an argument against it, in so far as the critique had really identified an untenable presupposition in the idea of truth. But if the critique were correct, then we could no longer dismiss as nonsensical the suspicion that the will to truth masked a will to power. Nietzsche had sufficient courage, imagination and consistency not to underrate the problems that resulted from his critique of metaphysics; this above all differentiates him from most modern relativists.

I have shown why Adorno's attempt to use the idea of 'reconciliation' to rescue a 'strong' concept of truth from both Nietzsche and positivism was doomed to failure. The really interesting question, however, is why Adorno saw himself forced into the impossible attempt to yoke together a Marxist and a theological motif in order to rescue truth. I believe that the answer to this question is that Adorno, in his critique of "identity-thinking" (*Identitätsdenken*) had rendered himself so dependent on certain premises contained in Nietzsche's critique of concepts that he could only fend off its consequences by force. Adorno's postulated solidarity with metaphysics in the moment of its fall[23] basically means fidelity to the idea of truth. But is it really the case that we cannot escape metaphysics as long as we cling to truth? And what exactly would it mean if we answered 'yes' to this question? *Two* questions which Adorno's answers do not deal with satisfactorily. In order to clarify these questions somewhat further, I should therefore like to undertake a brief examination of the continuation and reformulation of Adorno's (and Nietzsche's) problematic in the more recent discussion of the philosophy of language, particularly in Apel, Habermas and Derrida. Naturally the following references can only be rough stylizations. But I hope at least to render more precise the issues contained in the two questions posed above.

Apel, Habermas and Derrida agree in their criticism of the philosophy of consciousness, in relation to which they stress the linguistic nature of reason and also the linguistic constitution of consciousness. They also agree that a 'strong' concept of truth is present in the basic structures of reason seen from a linguistic point of view. But while Apel and Habermas seek to explain this concept of truth in a new way and thus release it from its imprisonment within the metaphysical tradition, Derrida sees the concept of truth as one of those fundamental concepts which are basically infected with metaphysics – others would be, say, 'meaning' and 'understanding' –– which, because they are built into the grammar of our languages, are inevitable but no less illusory for that. What interests me here above all is that aspect of Derrida's philosophy that is concerned with the theory of meaning, which is central to our problem and which he elaborated early in his career, in his analysis of Husserl's phenomenology and the structuralist theory of language. In terms of the theory of meaning, there are some notable similarities between Derrida's critique of Husserl's theory of signs in *Speech and Phenomena* and Wittgenstein's critique of the theory of signs of the *Tractatus* in the *Philosophical Investigations*. In a certain sense even their conclusions are comparable: both Wittgenstein and Derrida criticize the idea that linguistic signs are, so to speak, invested with meaning by consciousness and thus become the bearers of *intentions* of meaning, and both instead 'locate' linguistic meanings (1) horizontally, in the context of references of a totality of linguistic signs, and (2) vertically, in an iteration of the *use* of signs which is inconclusive in principle. However, in contrast to Wittgenstein, who resolved the paradoxes of the intentionalist theory of meaning by explaining the concept of the understanding of meaning in terms of a practical knowledge of rules, Derrida retains the intentionalist standard of the 'presence' of meanings for consciousness. By using this standard, he reaches the conclusion that the meaning of linguistic expressions can never be present to consciousness, but that it is rather 'something' infinitely deferred in the chain of iteration, something withdrawing from context to context, something constitutively different from itself, in short that it 'is' not that 'something' which it must always be assumed to be in the differentiation between sign and meaning, between signifier and signified; that, therefore, in terms of this assumption, it *is not*. In this way the concepts of meaning, of sense, of understanding, of interpretation, communication, sign, etc., the whole semantic and hermeneutic vocabulary – which Derrida correctly takes to be deeply rooted in the reflexive structure of our linguistic practice – is revealed as a site of 'transcendental illusion', in which Derrida sees the true, hard kernel of metaphysics. Why of metaphysics? Derrida's answer amounts, to some extent, to a reversal of Wittgenstein's reflection on 'meaning', 'sense' and 'understanding'. What Derrida states is that within the concepts of meaning, of sense, of the decoding of a sense, of understanding, etc., are implied the ideas of a consciousness that is transparent to itself, of a sense that is completely present, an end to the work of decoding, of truth as the revelation of being. In the apparently innocent concept of the sign – which here represents a whole range of concepts – language itself sees itself, as it were, *sub specie aeternitatis*, dreaming of a truth which 'escapes play and the order of the sign', that is, of a return from the 'exile' of language.[24] The difference between (tangible) sign and (intangible) meaning contains the opposition between the sensible and the intelligible world;[25] if we posit a meaning that is present to consciousness and a subject that is both 'present' (*gegenwärtig*) and transparent to itself in its intentions, we thereby posit being as 'presence'. But in this process, thought is posited as metaphysical, focused on the ideas of truth, of the foundational, of meaning, in which language transcends itself towards an invariant being. 'It could be shown,' says Derrida, 'that all the names related to fundamentals, to principles, or to the centre have always designated an invariable presence – *eidos, arché, telos, energeia, ousia* (essence, existence, substance, subject), *aletheia*, transcendality, consciousness, God, man and so forth.'[26] But for Derrida this also means that in the grammar of our language, and in particular the language of philosophy, 'the metaphysical unity of man and God, the relation of man to God, the project of becoming God as the project constituting human-reality'[27] is always already assumed. But this assumption, this 'onto-theology' rooted in language, is nothing but the transcendental illusion that is produced by those concepts in which language thinks itself.

It is plain that a destruction – or 'deconstruction' – of metaphysics under these conditions is only possible if thinking succeeds in overcoming metaphysics – and that means the language of philosophy, the language of thought – by turning its own momentum against itself. This is the purpose of Derrida's effort 'to use the concept to rise above the concept' – to couch Derrida's anti-philosophy in Adorno's terms. In Derrida, unlike Adorno, this effort is not carried out in the name of solidarity with a metaphysics in the process of falling, but rather, aware of a primarily inevitable complicity with metaphysics, it aims at its fall. One might also speak of a reversal of positive and negative here; a reversal that is actually a *re*-reversal, in the sense of a return to Nietzsche. And there are good reasons for this re-reversal of signs, at least when seen from within, for Adorno's philosophy could easily be characterized as the expression – albeit interrupted – of a metaphysical longing for 'presence'. But is it then correct to say that 'meaning', 'the fundamental' and 'truth' are metaphysical concepts? I should like, following a suggestion by C. Menke-Eggers,[28] to differentiate, in my discussion of this question, between an aspect of Derrida's basic theses that is, in a narrow sense, related to the theory of meaning and one that is related to the theory of argumentation (or truth). The aspect relating to the theory of meaning is comparatively easily dealt with. Here, in fact, Wittgenstein's treatment of the problem simply appears more consistent and convincing. Wittgenstein also criticizes the fundamental ideas of an intentionalist semantics as well as the hypostatization of meanings into intelligible objects. But at the same time he resolves the transcendental illusion in the concepts of meaning and understanding by reconstructing their *non-metaphysical use* in language. In particular, Wittgenstein refers to the moment of *practical* knowledge, of 'knowing one's way around' in the understanding of a language, without which linguistic communication in a common language, and one which is assumed to be common, would be unthinkable. In Wittgenstein, radical scepticism, which leads to the subversion of concepts such as 'meaning', 'thought' and 'understanding', is only ever a transitory point on the way towards the resolution of false mentalist ideas which have accreted to the philosophical use of those concepts. Yet Derrida must state that the false mentalist standard is built into the very concepts in question; only thus can one justify the thesis of their metaphysical character and hence a hermeneutic anarchism which *radically* questions the possibility of understanding and self-understanding.

Certainly Derrida himself has one reservation: he repeatedly refers to the possibility – and the necessity – of liberating the central concepts at issue here, and also that of 'intention' or 'subject', from the metaphysical frame of reference in which he sees them as being trapped, in order, as it were, to sublate them into a postmetaphysical grammar of language. But since Wittgenstein has already successfully philosophically destroyed the idealism of the concept of meaning, and thus shown how we can avoid the paradoxes which Derrida says are inevitable for the moment, I can see no reason why we should spend any more time on these paradoxes.

Things become more complicated when we consider the aspect of Derrida's critique of metaphysics that relates to the theory of truth. It could indeed be argued that Derrida's critique of the implied idealism of the concept of meaning only becomes virulent in relation to the problem of truth. I should like to elucidate the problem at issue here by using the example of Apel's and Habermas' consensus theory of truth. Once more I am obliged to resort to stylizations; stylizations that apply more thoroughly to Apel's stronger version of consensus theory than to Habermas' cautiously fallibilist version.

The consensus theory of truth can be understood as an attempt to resolve Adorno's intention – the rescue of an emphatic concept of truth encompassing theoretical and practical reason – without falling back on metaphysical figures of thought. An attempt such as this – in the form in which the problem is first encountered – can only be successful if it succeeds in freeing the concept of truth from the immanence of particular language games. As long as we consider language games from within, a connection between the claims of truth and possible reasons, and hence also between 'truth' and a possible 'rational consensus' based on the meaning of linguistic expressions, always seems to be at least partially assured. A concept of truth that encompasses language games would, on the other hand, require that even linguistic systems of reference themselves, *within* each of which a connection is defined between the truth claims and possible reasons, can once more be criticized and revised with good reasons: that they too can be held to be, if not actually 'true' or 'false', still to a greater or lesser degree 'appropriate' from the point of view of truth. This presupposes that the concept of rationality or of a rational justification too can be understood as encompassing all particular languages. The consensus theory of truth accordingly attempts to conceptualize an 'absolute', that is, a non-relativist concept of truth in terms of a non-relativist concept of rationality. According to this, a consensus would be rational in a non-relative sense if it came about under the conditions of an ideal structure of communication; and 'truth' would be the content of such a consensus. Habermas has characterized the ideal conditions under which a consensus could be called 'rational' with reference to the formal structures of an 'ideal speech situation'. Apel took up this characterization of an ideal structure of communication and brought it into his concept of an 'ideal communication community'. It is this concept that interests me here; I believe, in fact, that it is here that the consensus theory of truth has found its most consistent expression.

Originally, Apel had introduced a concept taken from C.S. Peirce, that of an *unlimited* communication community as the 'supreme point' of a transcendental philosophy reformulated in language pragmatic terms, that is, as 'an intersubjective analogue to Kant's "transcendental unity of consciousness" '.[29] In transcendental philosophy transformed via language prag-

matics, the concept of truth assumes, as it were, the leading role. Apel
declares truth to be the 'ultimate opinion' of an unlimited communication
community. But for Peirce, the 'ultimate opinion' could only be the 'true'
opinion because its rational genesis had been guaranteed by the logic of the
process of investigation. A generalization of Peirce's approach towards
practical truth and interpretative truth, as Apel saw it, could therefore only
succeed if the rationality of the 'ultimate opinion' were guaranteed in some
other way. This is why the ideal – in the sense of being
unlimited – communication community must also be seen as ideal in the
sense of an ideal *structure* of communication. It is therefore the consequence
of Apel's aproach that definitions enter into the concept of truth which in
Kant appear only in practical philosophy. The 'regulative principle' of the
realization of an ideal communication community necessarily also takes on
the traits of a constitutive principle: for every claim to validity and for
every argument the possibility of the realization of an ideal communication
community must be assumed. At the same time, however, the explication
of 'truth' as being the 'ultimate opinion' of an ideal communication community is revealed precisely as the solution of the problem that I formulated
above; for in this explanation the *appropriateness* of the linguistic system of
reference is guaranteed by the *ideal* nature of the communication structure,
while at the same time stability, that is, the definitiveness of the consensus,
results from the two definitions taken together.

But if the idea of an 'ultimate' language must be thought together with
that of an ideal communication structure in the concept of the ideal communication community, it follows that this concept not only describes ideal
conditions for communication but also a situation of ideal *communicated-ness*.
What is *meant* as a situation of ideal communication is revealed as a situation
beyond the necessity of linguistic communication. In the borderline value
of the ideal communication community the constitutive plurality of sign-
users is eliminated in favour of the singularity of a (collective) transcendental
subject that communicates with itself without friction, which as something
that has evolved, exists, so to speak, *in truth*. The ultimate, ideal language
would be a language beyond language, a language 'beyond play and the
order of the sign'. Within transcendental philosophy the problem of Kant's
borderline concepts of practical reason is reproduced once more in terms of
language pragmatics: in the borderline value of its realization the ideal
communication community would mean the negation of a linguistically
embodied reason; the *telos* of linguistic communication would imply the end
of communication.[30]

Consequently, within the concept of truth, metaphysics appears to triumph even in the moment of its fall; Nietzsche and Derrida would be right,
and so, in a different sense, would Adorno. This conclusion would certainly
only be justified if it were to become clear that *every* explication of the
concept of truth encountered problems analogous to those encountered by
consensus theory. None the less I do not believe that this is the case. Rather
I believe that the contrast between relativism and foundationalism (with

reference to the problem of truth and justification), or between hermeneutic anarchism and metaphysical objectivism (with reference to the problem of the understanding of meaning) only makes sense in terms of the premises of an 'onto-theological' tradition of thought, in which even empiricism is still trapped. But here is not the place to substantiate the grounds of this thesis.[31] Instead of elaborating a ground, however, I should like to supply some pointers – albeit merely negative ones – and return once more to Derrida in this context. The consensus theory of truth seemed to affirm Derrida's suspicion that 'truth' and 'justification' – and hence also 'reason' – are metaphysical concepts. But what has actually become apparent is that there is a philosophical understanding of these concepts – we might call it 'metaphysical' – which is *connected* to a concept of meaning and significance in Derrida's sense that is at once idealist and objectivist. I believe that this connection could, without great difficulty, be shown, through a whole series of basic concepts and problem formulations which have repeatedly played a crucial role in the discussion of the problem of truth and rationality. One of these basic concepts is that of a linguistic system of reference that is self-contained in terms of meaning and possible argumentation – a paradigm, a language game, a 'jargon' in Rorty's sense – at the *limit* of which the truth-criteria and rules of argrumentation which *internally* constitute it become unusable, with the result that 'truth' and 'rationality' are each defined only *within* a linguistic system of reference. If we accept such a problem formulation, we can either draw relativist conclusions – like Kuhn, or Rorty who, neither accidentally nor quite correctly, refers to Derrida – or we must seek a 'ground' – or a point of reference – beyond the particularity of language games, from which the particular truths and rationalities can be understood as manifestations of – or as deviations from – *one* truth and *one* reason. The latter would be the 'foundationalist' solution, of which Apel provides a particularly impressive example. Yet I hold the premises on which the alternative positions agree to be false. That the idea of a self-contained language game is a myth is something that Derrida could also teach us. And while I hold the assumption that metaphysics survives in such myths to be plausible, I see no reason for accepting them philosophically. I do not want to deny that such myths might be deeply rooted in contemporary scientific culture; that would of course be a reason to take their persistence empirically into account. What I dispute is that we cannot think *against* them without at the same time being entrapped by them – unless we were to abandon the medium of discursive language and thus cease to think. Philosophical thought today is knotted up precisely in alternatives like the last – alternatives which should be left behind. Going beyond them would mean freeing not only the concept of meaning but also the concepts of truth, of discursive justification, of rationality from the embrace of metaphysics, which leaves us only with the choice between foundationalism and relativism, between rationalism and irrationalism, between ultimate foundations and the end of argumentation. As could be easily demonstrated, this is precisely the point towards which impulses central to Adorno's and Habermas' philosophy are directed. To defend them would mean defending an idea of the end of metaphysics which does not mean a leaving-behind of reason and modernity, but rather their critical self-affirmation. Perhaps this is what one might call solidarity with metaphysics at the moment of its fall.

Notes

1 'Mignon' is a character in Goethe's *Wilhelm Meister* novels [Editor's note].
2 Theodor W. Adorno, *Negative Dialektik, Gesammelte Schriften*, vol. 6 (Frankfurt, 1973), p. 393.
3 Ibid., p. 394.
4 Ibid., p. 377.
5 Ibid., p. 364.
6 Ibid.
7 Ibid.
8 Ibid., p. 378.
9 Ibid., p. 358.
10 Ibid.
11 Ibid.
12 Ibid., p. 395.
13 Ibid., p. 378.
14 Ibid., p. 385.
15 Ibid., p. 384.
16 Ibid., p. 378.
17 Ibid., pp. 378–9.
18 Ibid., p. 379.
19 Ibid., p. 378.
20 F. Nietzsche, *The Gay Science*, trans. Walter Kaufmann (New York: Vintage Books, 1974), p. 283.
21 F. Nietzsche, 'Über Wahrheit und Lüge im außermoralischen Sinn', in *Werke*, vol. 3 (Darmstadt, 1960), p. 315.
22 F. Nietzsche, *Werke*, vol. 3, p. 844.
23 Adorno, *Negative Dialektik*, p. 400.
24 J. Derrida, 'Structure, Sign and Play in the Discourse of the Human Sciences, in *Writing and Difference*, trans. Alan Bass (London: Routledge and Kegan Paul, 1978), p. 292.
25 Ibid., p. 281.
26 Ibid., pp. 279–80.
27 J. Derrida, *Margins of Philosophy*, trans. Alan Bass (Brighton: Harvester Press, 1982).
28 C. Menke-Eggers, *Nach der Hermeneutik. Zur Negativität ästhetischer Erfahrung*, Dissertation (Konstanz, 1987), pp. 220ff.
29 K. O. Apel, 'Von Kant zu Peirce: Die semiotische Transformation der Transzendentalen Logik', in *Transformation der Philosophie*, vol. 2, (Frankfurt, 1973), p. 164. (A modified translation of this work is published as *Towards a Transformation of Philosophy*, trans. Glyn Adey and David Frisby (London: Routledge and Kegan Paul, 1980). Also cf. 'Szientismus oder transzendentale Hermeneutik?' (Scientism or transcendental hermeneutics?) in the same volume.

30 I have developed this critique further in *Ethik und Dialog. Elemente des moralischen Urteils bei Kant und in der Diskursethik* (Frankfurt, 1986), Part VIII, pp. 81ff.
31 But see also A. Wellmer, 'Intersubjectivity and Reason', in L. Hertzberg and J. Pietarinen (ed.), *Perspectives on Human Conduct* (forthcoming).

Part II

HANS ROBERT JAUSS

The Theory of Reception: A Retrospective of its Unrecognized Prehistory

Translated by John Whitlam

I

The aesthetics of reception is one of those theories which has established itself so successfully with a new approach that, looking back, it is difficult to understand why the problems surrounding it were ever really regarded as problems. After 1950, 'reception' appeared for the first time as a methodological concept in jurisprudence, theology and philosophy. In those fields it signalled a reorientation of historical research, freed from the dogmatic premises of positivism and traditionalism and on the way to developing a new theory of history following analogous hermeneutic principles. Since 1967 there has been a comparable reorientation in traditional philologies arising from the new concept of an aesthetics of reception (Rezeptions- und Wirkungsästhetik). It required the history of literature and the arts to be seen henceforth as a process of aesthetic communication in which the three logically distinguishable entities – author, work and recipient (reader, listener or observer, critic or audience) – participate in equal measure. This involved reinstating the recipient in his own right as receiver and mediator, in short: as the bearer of all aesthetic culture – a right which had been denied as long as the history of the arts had been dominated by the traditional aesthetics of the work of art and its function of representation. Reception theory posed once more the problems of defining the work by its effect, of the dialectic of effect and reception, of canon formation and restructuring and of dialogic understanding through the distance of time (mediation between different horizons). In short, it renewed the question of what aesthetic experience could mean when viewed as a productive, receptive and communicative activity. It is quite justified to speak of a paradigmatic shift in literary theory when we consider the worldwide repercussions of reception theory conceived by the Constance School,[1] for this new theoretical approach opened up a field of research that had lain fallow for a long time. After all, an attempt to represent the problems of reception through its history requires a process of reconstruction and confirms the hermeneutic principle that the prehistory of a significant shift of events can only be fully recognized by looking at its post-history.

II

In the European tradition, prehistories are only truly considered worthy if they can trace their origins to Homer or the Bible. Disregarding for a moment the late appearance of the concept of *receptio* and looking to the hermeneutic problem which arose much earlier, the theory of reception could invoke both these sources. For the problem of reception was first posed in the interpretation of Homer and then again in the exegesis of the Bible, when temporal distance from the original text was so great that Homer's poetry and the revelations contained in the Holy Scriptures had ceased to be immediately understandable; indeed, when for the time being their canonic meaning had become obscure, if not displeasing or offensive. What is to be done when an authority, distant in time and preserved only in writing, has forfeited the immediacy of living speech or address which it had in the oral culture whence it originated when, more particularly, its doctrine or message is no longer in tune with the world view, the attitudes and morals of a later time?

An authority which has grown out of date in this way may simply fall victim to criticism and be replaced by new authorities. But if not, there are two ways in which it might be salvaged, as tested in the case of Homer in the Hellenistic philology of the Alexandrian and Pergamine schools. These are grammatical interpretation and allegorical exegesis. The foreign-sounding wording of the old text can be explained in contemporary language and thereby be retrieved from obscurity. However, through a new interpretation it is also possible for this wording to be given a double meaning by distinguishing between *sensus litteralis* and *sensus allegoricus*, if the first, literal meaning is transposed into a second, allegorical one and the old sense of the text is thus adapted towards a new understanding.

These two procedures reciprocally imply the oldest form of reception theory. They serve to salvage a diminished authority, and are, by their very nature, conservative and modern at the same time. For both procedures, both grammatical and allegorical exegesis, have the same goal of hermeneutic application: to forge a link between the past and present, between the canonic sense of the text and the sense 'for us'. Reception in this form goes by the motto 'From the Old, create the New'. But such an approach is still far distant from modern, historical thought. Grammatical interpretation seeks to save the literal meaning, but not yet in a 'historical' way, still less for its own sake. Instead, it seeks to reconstruct the past meaning in order to translate it into a form understandable in the present. Allegorical exegesis, on the other hand, attempts not simply to set aside the literal sense of the text, but to interpret the text for the recipient's changed situation in such a way that the new spiritual meaning is still justified as an adaptation of the old, literal meaning. The two procedures can be regarded, in the end, as the two sides of a single, continuous process of reception, as the work of historical understanding, applied to the canonic text: they forge the same link between the sense established by the text and the understanding established by us with the only difference being that the one aims at a more reconstructive hermeneutics, the other at a more applied hermeneutics. Both the grammatical and allegorical approach set out to salvage the authority of the canonic text in an act of reception which is protected from subjective arbitrariness by the objective 'spirit' of the text concealed in its literal wording. In such a way, both the grammatical translation and the new (even manifoldly complex) interpretation become legitimated. This is particularly true for the doctrine of fourfold meaning in writing which was developed later. The famous formula distinguishes between four forms of reception, namely literal (historical), allegorical, tropological (moral) and anagogical (eschatological) meanings: *littera gesta docet, quid credes allegoria, moralis quid agas, quo tendas anagogica.* Even when the spiritual meaning is divided among different recipients and different domains of application – to the Church and its dogmatic teaching, to the conduct of the individual believers as well as to the metaphysical and eschatological mysteries[2] – any difference of interpretation is still referred back to the objective meaning of the text, as the condition of all further understanding. In the older theory of text interpretation, reception is first seen as a passive act of receiving, while understanding is seen as a process of recognizing, or remembering, something already known. It is only when the refinement and variety of possible interpretations are no longer founded on the objective content of the literal meaning but rather on the subjective conditions of understanding, or, more precisely, on the results of a variety of approaches, that there is a shift to modern hermeneutics. Once this has happened, the sense of the text is no longer regarded as an authoritatively given but rather as an open structure demanding productive understanding. Only then is the horizon of understanding opened up to the possibility of seeing the text in a later context in unendingly different ways or, more precisely, in ways that answer questions that could not be asked in the primary context. It is not until the transitional period between the Middle Ages and the modern age that this move from passive to active reception, from merely receiving to producing, is seen in the history of the concept itself. I shall now turn to this history, first concerning myself with theology, with jurisprudence and with the history of philosophy before I turn to the history of the fine arts and of literature.

III

The word *receptio* appears for the first time in Middle Latin in the context of scholastic theology: *Quidquid recipitur ad modum recipientis recipitur* (Whatever is received can only be received in the manner of the recipient). This is probably the earliest expression of the reception concept and the starting-point from which we can trace the entire progress of theology from the dogmatic interpretation of the scriptures to an historical–critical hermeneutics.[3] The scholastic principle was inferred by Thomas Aquinas from the *Liber de causis*.[4] It mediates between the Bible's claim to speak *secundum dicentem deum* (in God's words) and the claims of finite, imperfect man, who is unable to grasp the truth of what is revealed in a complete or immediate way. This is the principle that any truth is received only according to the measure of the receiver, a principle circumscribed and defined by the recognition of God through the *analogia attributionis*, the neo-Platonic doctrine which posits an incomplete similarity between effects and their causes. Yet the same Thomas Aquinas was prepared to admit that theoretical sciences could gradually move from the incomplete to the complete, so that even those coming later were still able to recognize some truth in the mistakes of their predecessors.[5] The text of the Bible in particular was to reveal its plain truth only in a successive way, from one gloss to the next one, until the process of reception was completed by the last reader. This person could finally see the truth of the text in its complete richness, as inspired and foreseen by the wisdom of God, from the beginning. Evidence of this can be found in the *topos* probably first formulated by Gregor the Great (*Moralia in Job*, XX, I, 1) *Scriptura sacra . . . aliquo modo cum legentibus crescit* (The Holy Scripture grows with all those who read it). Also in the twelfth century there is first evidence that it was possible to interpret and legitimate secular poetry in the same way as the Holy Scriptures. Marie de France may well have adapted a famous statement by Priscian in saying 'The ancients were already conscious of the fact that those coming after them would be wiser because their successors would be able to gloss the wording of the text and thereby enrich its meanings'.[6] In the Talmudic tradition, the *Scientia Cabalae* is explicitly equated with tradition in the sense of reception: 'Cabala among the Hebrewes signifying no other than the Latin *receptio*: A learning by the ancients held in high estimation and reverence and not without great reason . . .'.[7] Directed against rabbinical legalism, the revisionist cabbala set out to reinterpret the revealed Scriptures for Jews in their present situation of exile and persecution. In the cabbalistic tradition there is also an exegetic word game which promises the greatest reward for all the hard work on fourfold meaning in Scripture. It connects with a famous story in the Talmud which tells of four great teachers who managed to 'reach Paradise' with their esoteric studies. Moses de Leon who wrote his lost work *Pardes* before 1290, explained the title which literally means 'paradise', as being an abbreviation for the four levels of meaning in the Torah: 'each consonant in the word PaRDeS points to one of these levels: P stands for *Peschat*, the literal sense of the word; R for *Remes*, the allegorical sense; D for *Deresha*, the Talmudic and Agadic interpretation; S for *Sod*, the mystical sense.'[8] Much later, at the peak of the bourgeois culture of reading, it was possible for the solitary reader to think that nothing brought him closer to paradise lost than lying on the sofa reading a novel. But this profane 'paradise of words' – a theme which can be traced from Thomas Gray[9] via Marcel Proust to Roland Barthes' *Le plaisir du texte* – has never regained the richness of its religious origins.

The scholastic concept of reception, which Ockham turned against Thomas Aquinas,[10] can also be found in Luther's work directed against Zwingli and Oecolampadius, both of whom sought to differentiate between word and spirit: '*et ita mentiuntur et definiunt verbum non secundum dicentem Deum, sed secundum recipientem hominem*' (and thus they lie by not defining the word according to what God said but according to the man receiving it).[11] This highlighted once more the problem of the anthropomorphic speech of God, which Spinoza, in the name of true recogition from the natural light of reason, was the first to devalue as mere accommodation (*accomodatio* rather than *receptio*) of revelation to historical man.[12] In response to this, Protestant hermeneutics will gradually upgrade accommodation as it attempts to acknowledge revelation expressed *secundum modum recipientis hominis* as a truth in its historical development.[13] Catholic hermeneutics acknowledged reception as an ecclesiological reality only very recently, adopting' the concept from legal history. It was applied to a limited extent in the process of reaching consensus on the pronouncements of an infallible church and later in the slow processes of imposing the dogmatic resolutions of the Church councils.[14] It is obvious that the principle of infallibility always makes it difficult fully to accommodate hermeneutic principles of interpretation.

IV

In legal history, the concept of reception was already in use in the thirteenth century in the process of adopting Roman law in Central Europe. Yet it was only explained in a methodical way much later, as a result of the debate on the ideological question of whether, in adopting Roman law, the Germans had merely taken over foreign concepts and sacrificed their own. Even as late as 1952, Franz Wieacker speaks out against the misunderstanding surrounding the word *Rezeption*, 'as if it were at all possible for living people to adopt a foreign system of law without making it entirely their own and thereby transforming it'.[15] According to Wieacker, in cases where the recipient is not the subject but only the object of the activity defined by reception, we cannot talk about reception in the true sense of the word. In this very sense, reception is raised to the level of a basic concept in historical continuity which takes place during cultural exchange in the interactive processes of encounter and appropriation, response and impetus to bring forth one's own creation, either as a continuation or as a revision of authoritative tradition. On this basis, the reception of an earlier or foreign culture (Greek through Roman, classical through medieval) could be described in comparable phases: the adoption of civilization (luxury goods, writing, measures, coinage, elementary schools), religion (denomination, ritual, sacred art) and law clearly precedes the appropriation of spiritual goods (philosophy, sciences, arts). The adoption of literature, on the other hand, often has three phases: dependency (translations), independency (classicism) and emancipation (modernity).[16]

After 1950, a further concept of reception took its place as part of legal hermeneutics: concretization (as opposed to subsumption), seen as a progressive (also legally creative) interpretation of legal norms, which may be required in judging a particular case.[17] A judge who has to pass judgement on a dispute is often unable to make a decision based on the scheme of case and rule, that is, by subsuming the issue under the appropriate norm. There are often legal problems to be solved for which the law originally had no answer, where there is a gap in legislation or where various regulations, sometimes even contradictory ones, have to be taken into consideration. To solve such cases, the law itself must be reinterpreted; that is, in considering the case, we must concretize a meaning of the legal norm which was not yet acknowledged or foreseen when the law was first formulated. Thus the judgement itself can become an act which creates a legal precedent if the particular case does not fall under the given general norm, but instead demands a further concretization of what it prescribes in a new or different way, so that one decides through the judgement what should be considered law now and in the future.[18]

There is a certain analogy between particular case and norm in the application of law and individual work and aesthetic norm in literary hermeneutics: if a literary work is to be defined in its capacity as an event, as an innovation on the horizon of tradition, an aesthetic judgement of it necessitates grasping the particularity and norm-setting achievement of the work in relation to the aesthetic norms pertaining up until that time. The canonic rules of genre and models of style are always varied and modified by a new work and are therefore concretized in an equally new or different way.[19] For this reason, it is not by chance that, subsequent to Roman Ingarden, both the Prague literary theorists and the Constance School, though in ignorance of legal hermeneutics, made concretization a key concept in literary semiotics and the aesthetics of reception. By concretization the Prague structuralists since 1969 (Felix Vodička, following Jan Mukařovský) understand the representation of the work in the consciousness of those for whom the artifact becomes an aesthetic object; it is only the reception of the work which, in progressive interpretations, brings its structure within the infinite range of concretizations and forms of reception to historical life. Meanwhile, in a critical continuation of Roman Ingarden's phenomenological aesthetics, the Constance School has since 1967 been investigating and systematically describing the constitution and development of meaning which takes place in the appropriation of the aesthetic object and in the history of its reception. The aim of this School is to describe the nature of aesthetic activity, firstly in the realm of the *implicit* reader, and secondly in the realm of the *historical* reader, which involves a continuous change of horizon in and through understanding and interpretation. (This brief formula is intended to indicate to what extent Wolfgang Iser's theoretical approach and my own complement one another.)[20]

V

The interest shown by philosophers in the history of their authorities' reception arose at a later date. Aristotle, who wrote a first doxographic account, was interested only in the doctrines of his predecessors and not in the acceptance and influence which they had had. And even Hegel, who in the history of philosophy, sought to reveal within it the logic behind its succession of systems, declared in a sweeping statement at the beginning of his lectures: 'I shall not dwell on the dissemination of a doctrine, its fate and those who merely passed it on.'[21] It was Hans Blumenberg who brought the concept of reception into the history of philosophy and science in 1958.[22] His interpretation of the supplanting of ancient philosophy by the Christian theology of late antiquity deconstructs the substantialist view of tradition together with the mythicized concept of event. The shift from old to new is not recognizable just by looking at historical junctures, but only by looking at the dividing line of 'epoch thresholds' which come about almost imperceptibly *in re* and only become discernible *post rem*. We must look at the reallocation of functions in the organization of the former world model against which the new doctrine must impose itself with its own answers to old questions. An event like the 'Copernican Revolution' only became 'epoch-making' when considered in the light of the historical work of its preparation and reception; a myth gains its historical power from the beginning through the interpreting activity of reception which denies the primacy of its origin and constantly enriches the meaning of the myth by telling it in new ways.[23] In his analyses of historical zones of transition, decline and reformation of meaning Blumenberg discovered a historical dynamics at the base of the history of science, an approach which is not discussed in Thomas S. Kuhn's later theory of paradigmatic change, which has subsequently become so successful.[24] Hans-Georg Gadamer, meanwhile, based his philosophical hermeneutics on the analysis of the authority of tradition and on what he called the consciousness of the history of influence or effect (*wirkungsgeschichtliches Bewusstsein*).[25] Literary hermeneutics extended his principle of the history of effect by which the work cannot be understood without regard for its effect, to the correlative principle of the history of reception, which does not have as its starting-point the presumed objective truth of the work but rather the comprehending consciousness seen as the subject of aesthetic experience. Such an approach requires differentiating

the horizons in an active sense (instead of the fusion of horizons in a passive
sense). Today, the interaction of effect and reception is commonly defined
in such a way that *effect* is the name given to the element of concretization
determined by the text, while *reception* is the element determined by the
person to whom the text is addressed. Thus the implication of the text and
the explication of the addressee, the implicit and the historical reader, are
dependent on one another, and the text itself is thus able to limit the
arbitrariness of interpretation, guaranteeing the continuity of its experience
beyond the present act of reception.

VI

In the history of the arts there was little investigation into reception. The
canon of works and authors was extended to their posthumous fame, passing
over in silence their impact on recipients, the very bearers of tradition. The
topic of reception was of interest first and foremost in rhetoric, for a while
in the anti-art polemics of the Church fathers, later in moralistics, in the
doctrine of affects and the norms of taste, and finally in the sociology of
art, but not in classical aesthetics. Classical aesthetics saw any inquiry into
the effects of art as outside the purview of art.[26] The great exception to this
in the philosophical tradition is Aristotle's poetics in antiquity and Kant's
Critique of Judgement in the modern age. Yet neither Aristotle's doctrine of
catharsis nor Kant's important turn towards an aesthetics of reflective
judgement set up a theory of reception as the experience of the receiving
subject which could form the basis of a tradition. There are only sporadic
traces of its 'prehistory' – the first of these, as we would expect, in Montaigne.[27]

VII

'Un suffisant lecteur descouvre souvent ès escrits des perfections autres que
celles que l'autheur y a mises et apperceues, et y preste des sens et des
visages plus riches' (An intelligent reader often discovers in texts perfections
other than those which the author put in or noticed, and thus the reader
endows the old text with richer meanings and aspects).[28] With this step
from the passive act of receiving to an active, meaning-extending and
therefore itself productive reception, Montaigne simultaneously created the
essay genre and marked it as a literary form of productive reading which
conveyed text and self-experience. The testimony of Montaigne from his
tower room that he arranged for solitary reading presupposes the invention
of printing, the setting up of a private library, and thus the liberation of
the secular reader from institutional reading. Before this time, in the age of
rare manuscripts, all reading was controlled by the Church, the University,
and the judiciary, and was limited to compulsory interpretation of canonic

texts.[29] In a review of his *Principle Features of the Present Age* (1804–5), Fichte traced the dawn of the modern age to the changes brought about by printing and the Reformation. He emphasizes the high value placed on the written word in Protestantism: 'it became the almost indispensable means of achieving salvation, and without being able to read, one could no longer justifiably be a Christian'. In Fichte's view, it was not only the written word, but also one's own understanding of it, following the maxim that 'one should not be convinced by anything except what one understands', a thesis which contributed to the belief in the dignity and merit of the person, the most important result of the Enlightenment.

Yet as early as 1804, Fichte had recognized the fatal consequences of printing with regard to the never-ending flood of documents it produced, and envisaged the end of all writing and reading 'which by its highest effect cancels its effect'. Since no one had the time to read everything any more, 'in this system books would merely be printed so that they could be reviewed' by scholars, and the receiving party, the readers, would always be trying to get hold of the newest things without remembering the old, so that reading would become a permanent narcotic. 'Anyone who has tasted only once the sweetness of this state wants to enjoy it for ever more and may do nothing else in life; he now reads without drawing on any literary knowledge or progression with the age, merely so that he reads and spends his life reading and represents the pure reader.' Yet the extent to which today's reader risks drowning in the sea of material produced at book fairs, which nobody could ever hope to wade through, may have exceeded Fichte's ironic prediction.[30]

VIII

With the Enlightenment turning towards the aesthetics of effect in the eighteenth century, there is more evidence of a new interest in the receiving subject's experience of art and the active imagination of the beholder and reader. The first piece of evidence is the belated reception of the pseudo-Longinean text *On the Sublime*. There we can read that the truly great work which goes beyond impeccable mediocrity and even the appearance of perfect beauty, 'sets the spiritual powers of the beholder in motion since it contains more than has been stated'. From this one may conclude that 'the receiver is completing a process that had begun with the producer'. Furthermore (in chapter 7, 2): 'for by its very nature, our soul is lifted up by the truly sublime, and in the process of taking this happy impetus, it is filled with joy and pride, *as if it itself has produced what it has heard.*'[31] There is an echo of this sentiment in the view of art after 1750: 'To the "fiction that the beholder does not exist", this time responds with a second, equally productive fiction, the "fiction that the picture does not exist".' What is meant here is a restructuring of the beholder's attitude, a phenomenon for which the Pygmalion myth, popular at the time, is symptomatic.[32] As the artist Pygmalion attempts to bring the dead marble of the work to life, so too now the enthusiastic beholder wishes to transcend the boundary between art and nature, to forget its artistic character, in order to grasp a piece of true nature in the picture – like Diderot, who transported himself directly into Vernet's landscapes as a beholder. If now the beholding of art could become a medium of self-experience for the receiving subject, this shift in aesthetic experience could occur because of the awakening self-awareness of the bourgeois individual. Work and observer enter henceforth into a reciprocal relationship, which Hegel expressed in appropriate terms: the work takes on its substantial truth only for and through the beholding subject because 'beholder and work can each attain awareness of themselves only through the other'.[33]

The rise of the bourgeois reader who, as a 'common reader' – not as the trend-setting person of professional criticism – affirms the public claim to self determination, is testified by Samuel Johnson's concession: 'By the common sense of readers uncorrupted with literary prejudices, after all the refinements of subtility and the dogmatism of learning, must be finally decided all claim to poetic honours.'[34] The beginnings of a readers' aesthetics are found in theories of the nature of the human mind in the Age of Sensibility. Lessing demands a self-judging reader; Schlegel even a reader who is also creative: 'The synthetic writer constructs and creates for himself a reader as a reader should be; he imagines his reader not as passive and dead, but as alive and interactive. The writer allows what he has invented to grow in stages before the reader's eyes or entices him to invent himself. He does not set out to have a particular effect on the reader, but rather he enters with the reader into the sacred relationship of deepest sym-philosophy and sym-poetry.'[35] However, the emancipation of the bourgeois reader reaches its peak and a temporary end in the autonomous art of German idealism, in a sphere of contemplation which once again excluded the question of effect and the part played by reception. The autonomous work of art is allowed to have only 'inner expediency' and may not serve any external purpose. According to Adam Müller, with every observer which this type of work of art draws into the 'workshop of genuine art' it extends its own sphere to a free world behind historical reality: 'thus any poetry, any picture, and after that any cycle of poetry and pictures form a little aesthetic state around them from their readers and beholders. The beholders are as it were the free subjects of the work and its master; with each newcomer, the dominion or the importance of this small sovereign increases.'[36]

IX

While the aesthetics of autonomous art in this way severed the connection between the work and its effect on the public, Hegel maintained the idea of a 'progressive development [of art] to existence for others'. 'However much it may seem to form a cohesive and rounded world, the work of art nevertheless does not exist as a real, individualized object for itself, but for us, for a public which looks at the works of art and appreciates it.'[37] The aesthetic historiography of the nineteenth century followed Hegel's insight into the historical progression of the arts, at the same time adopting those elements of hermeneutic insights which had begun to emerge in the theory of history since Chladenius. His insight into the hermeneutic function of the 'point of view' was the beginning of a theory of historical perspective which saw in the point of view of eye witnesses or historians not only their necessarily limited horizons, but at the same time a chance to put the increasing wealth of facts into perspective; in other words, to represent them in an abridged and rejuvenated form by means of fiction and thereby to renew their meaning for the present time. In the words of Reinhard Kosel-leck: 'The doctrine of historical perspective legitimates the historical change in cognition by ascribing a cognitive function to the passage of time. Historical truths, when seen from a temporal perspective, become superior truths.'[38] Yet the historical theory of an ever-changing point of view also required and allowed history to be constantly rewritten. Goethe provides the clearest evidence of this. For history, he admitted the principle of the unity of work (or event) and effect which he denied to autonomous poetry, when he stated that history had to be rewritten from time to time 'because a person living in advancing time is placed in standpoints from which the past can be viewed and judged in a new way'.[39] The idea of a progressive reception of past art is found again in Heine's *Travel Pictures*: 'Every age, when it gets new ideas, gets new eyes and sees a lot of new things in the old works.'[40] The same idea is taken up by Karl Marx in the concept of *appropriation*, which can be applied equally to nature and history. This is also evident from an observation which he first explains with reference to Roman law and later with reference to the three unities of classical drama, the putative misunderstanding of Greek drama. When considering historical processes dialectically, later modifications are not at all to be seen as incorrect interpretations, but rather as interpretations appropriate to the new time or its artistic needs: 'Otherwise it could be said that every achievement of an older period which is *appropriated* by a later one, is a misunderstanding of the old.'[41]

In contrast to this hermeneutic position, the later view of literature taken by the materialists as well as by their opponents in the history of ideas is characterized by reciprocal one-sidedness after the decline of aesthetic historiography. Franz Mehring's *The Legend of Lessing* (1892) separated the 'true', materialistically reconstructed Lessing from the history of his recep-tion in order to show this reception to be nothing more than a 'legend' of bourgeois interpretation. Mehring's paradigm lives on in Marxist theory in as much as it reduces the history of reception to the critique of ideology and claims that its way of analysing works of art is the only true way.[42] Conversely, according to Julian Hirsch's *The Genesis of Glory* (1914), in the tradition of Nietzsche, it was precisely the appearance, that is, the changing image of a work in the eyes of contemporary and subsequent generations, which was the real essence of the work and the object of a kind of 'phenogra-phics' with which he sought to replace positivist biographics. Afterwards, in *Nietzsche. Essay on Mythology*, Ernst Bertram surpassed all historicism and perspectivism with a radical concept of reception. In his view, a legend originates first of all in the act of always reading in a different way, for us as 'witnesses of a past which never *appears* in the same way.' Yet the act of reception is here not merely an arbitrary act of positing on the part of the interpreter, but it is bound to the historical moment in the awareness that this image of the work 'only "appears" in this way today, for us, momentarily'.[43]

X

Compared with the high-flown German history of ideas, the evidence from outside Germany seems more modest. For the aesthetics of Saint-Simon, the only thing of interest in art was its didactic and rhetorical function.[44] The renewal and systematization of the historical method by the positivists followed the rigorous standard of the natural sciences, but it was by no means limited to research into those data-rich sources and influences, that could be corroborated in fact.[45] The educational authorities, Gustave Lanson in France and Wilhelm Scherer in Germany, subordinated actual literary history to a canonization of literary evolution, a concept which was also intended to subsume the correlation of writer and public, literary work and social reality. Yet Lanson's demand, 'Le livre, donc, est un phenomène social qui évolue', was to remain unfulfilled as long as the biographical individual had to act as an intermediary and assume sole responsibility for the diversity of cultural, social and class factors. Likewise, in Scherer's *Poetics* (published posthumously in 1888), there is a chapter entitled 'Writer and Public' which seeks to combine economics, the aesthetics of effect and rhetoric with astonishingly modern-sounding observations on the 'exchange value of poetry and literary intercourse' and the 'aesthetic threshold' of the public's receptiveness ('It is only possible to appreciate what one could also, if need be, have oneself produced'). Yet Scherer's poetics with its postulate: 'The variety of the public must necessarily have an effect on the production' had no consequences for the official canon of literary theory for at least 50 more years.

At the beginning of the twentieth century a critique based on the psychology of reception (J. M. Guyan, E. Hennequin) constituted a revolt against the positivist history of literature, and particularly against the paradigm of the unity of life and work. Later, Charles Péguy, A. Thibaudet and others, inspired by Bergson's philosophy of life, postulated even a 'lecture créatrice', which sought to consider the work no longer as the end point of biographical and social determinants but as the starting-point for creative reception. But these still impressionistic approaches are eclipsed by the poetic theory of Paul Valéry, who recognized the indispensable gulf between the aesthetics of production and the aesthetics of reception. With his provocative dictum 'mes vers ont le sens qu'on leur prête' he promoted the merely contemplative reader of the past to the level of co-creator of the *open work* in modern literature. According to Valéry, it was Edgar Allan Poe who first shed light on the relationship between work and reader and made it one of the fundamentals of poetry. But he also demanded an 'histoire vraie de la lecture. Une histoire réelle complète de la littérature – histoire des livres les plus vraiment lus – et leur influence.'[46] This postulate was taken up first by the sociology of literature: by L. L. Schücking (1931) with an inquiry into the functions and types of readers in the formation of literary taste; by A. N. Veselovsky (1939) with the postulate of exposing converging tendencies in the thinking and the image worlds of the receiving side; by R. Escarpit (1961) with research into the reading habits of social groups, involving distribution and consumption, whose new tastes can be a 'creative betrayal', committed against the intention of great literature; and lastly, by G. Grimm (1977), who had already appropriated the aesthetics of reception and effect, albeit critically, with the intention of analyzing empirically the activity of subjects in the history of reception.[47]

I do not want to report specifically on the methodological debate in literary theory over the past two decades.[48] It could be portrayed as a resumption of the 'Querelle des Anciens et des Modernes', in which henceforth author and reader have adopted the earlier opposing positions. With respect to the still unwritten 'literary history of the reader'[49] there has been a rejection principally of those paradigms which – being mistrustful of the reader's aesthetic experience – had denied the dialectic unity of text and reception, and thus the communicative or even society-forming function of literature. We see this opposition, in the first place, in the idealism of an aesthetics of the self-sufficient work (which, in the case of the purist New Critics[50], required the one, ideal reader); secondly, in the substantialism of self-perpetuating tradition (above all the 'afterlife of antiquity' in the wake of Ernst Robert Curtius); thirdly, in structuralism, with the proclaimed 'death of the subject' and the enthroning of self-sufficient écriture; and finally, in the neo-materialism of the critics of ideology who one-sidedly and dogmatically proclaimed the precedence of production and reflection in the history of the Arts.

If today poststructuralist literary theory dates the beginning of this debate back to the denial of logocentrism, or more exactly, to Derrida's *De la grammatologie* (1967), we should remember that, at the same time, the ontological precedence of the work as the place where given truth manifests itself was being disputed not only in Germany but also in Italy. While in the wake of Derrida the theory of textuality, defined as 'the play of differences', remained one-sidedly orientated towards the productive side of aesthetic activity, there was an initial effort of semiotic criticism to rediscover and evaluate the process of communication within the domain of aesthetic experience. Taking serial music as his starting-point, it was primarily

Umberto Eco who, in *Opera aperta* (1962), drafted the first theory of an open, constantly progressing constitution of meaning, a theory by which the work of art, seen as an open structure, requires the active co-production of the recipient and brings about a historical variety of concretizations without in the process ceasing to be *one* work.

I must mention two other important figures who paved the way for the historical–hermeneutical paradigm of reception theory. In his *Essay on Eduard Fuchs* (1937) Walter Benjamin demanded that historians break the continuum of history in order to 'set in motion the experience with history, which for every present time is an original one'. Benjamin's theory of the 'Now of discernibility' was achieved through the 'Now of readability'. He expects the competent reader to abandon 'the calm, contemplative attitude towards the object in order to become aware of the critical constellation in which precisely this fragment of the past is found with relation to precisely this present time'.[51] For Jean-Paul Sartre, the chance of hope lay not in salvaging what is past but in the productive reception of whatever the present offers, that is, of a possible sense of our world revealed by literature in the reciprocal act of writing and reading: 'Ecrire, c'est donc à la fois dévoiler le monde et le proposer comme une tâche à la générosité du lecteur'.[52] Thus in *Qu'est-ce que la littérature?* (1948), literature is justified as being the communicative act in which the human drive towards freedom is able to prove itself by appropriating and changing the world.

XI

Even in the history of science new paradigms do not immediately fall from heaven: the new which has yet to establish itself must set itself apart from the old and legitimate itself before tradition so that the very attitude to the world can change simultaneously with the new view of the object. This mediation of the work of art is particularly true for paradigm change in aesthetic experience, which – according to Paul Ricoeur – concerns in equal measure the relationship between work (text) and world, the communication between man and man and man's understanding of himself.[53] It is not by chance that the shift towards the aesthetics of reception happened in a time – the 1960s – when there was a noticeable change in the perspectives of literature, the arts and the new media: the gradually apparent, epochal threshold between the great authors of the beginning of the twentieth century, now considered as henceforth remote modern classics, and the heralding of an as yet diffuse 'postmodern period'. One of the fundamental literary figures of this time is Jorge Luis Borges. His work *Ficciones* (1941), and particularly his text *Pierre Ménard – Author of Quixote* (written in 1939), demonstrates in an exemplary way that between reception theory and its concomitants and competitors, like reader research, textual linguistics, semiotics and deconstructionism on the one hand, and the practice of postmodern aesthetics on the other, there are in fact analogies worthy of consideration. For his programmatic text, Borges chose the doubly reflective form of a commentary on a fictitious text made up by himself but supposedly written by Ménard, a second-rate French symbolist. Ménard's ambition was to write a *Don Quixote* appropriate to his own time. Not by transferring the former-time hero to Wall Street (naive actualization) nor by combining knight and squire, as Daudet had done in *Tartarin de Tarascon* (productive reception), but instead through total identification (apparently postulated by Novalis) with his predecessor, in the form of a word-by-word repetition of his spontaneously created work! The paradox of this undertaking is the crux of reception theory: the non-identity of what is repeated in the temporal distance of repetition. The identical text has become incomparably richer and more complex after 300 years. A sentence such as the one from chapter 1, page 9 of *Don Quixote*: 'truth whose mother is history, the rival of time, the conserver of deeds, witness of the past, example and explanation of the present, warning for the future', was in Cervantes' time just another rhetorical listing in praise of history. Yet, for Borges, this statement had taken on the proportions of a stupendous idea by Ménard's time, a contemporary as he was of William James. For history was defined henceforth as an origin, and thus not merely as an investigable aspect of reality! Anyone who sets out to reconstruct a past 'as it really was' and to show it in its 'couleur locale' – like Flaubert in *Salammbô* – is on the wrong track. However, Ménard's experiment did not just reveal new meaning in the supposed identity of old and new, in literal repetition; but, at the same time, it made us aware of the fictitious nature of our existence. What are the conclusions to be drawn for postmodern aesthetics? Fiction and reality no longer constitute an ontological opposition: the real itself turns out to be potentially fictitious or fantastic, the supposedly original turns out to be merely a postscript to a previous text, a kind of palimpsest on which appear the traces of what the '*doctor universalis*' had already thought but which in theory any person could think. Thus the final logical step in Ménard's experiment is that, after he has filled thousands of pages with a reproduction of Quixote, he destroys the manuscript itself: he can only escape the fate of his predecessor – the diffusion of his fame in the inexorable process of possible reception – if his own work does not survive by means of another text, but by discovering a way of suspending history within itself.

XII

Finally, I should briefly point out that Borges with *Pierre Ménard* did more than anticipate the shift from the classical aesthetic production to the modern aesthetic reception. As John Barth shows in *The Literature of Exhaustion* (1967), the first document of the American post-modern era,[54] Borges' *Ficciones* marks the end of the classical modern era of the twentieth century while at the same time showing the way for the departure of new avantgardes. For, firstly, Ménard's discovery of consciously anachronistic reading opens the way for an overdue rehabilitation of the reader, the boom in theories on reading and reading traditions and reader types, the project of a 'literary history of the reader' – all of which leads to the poetic and poetological peak of an already widespread movement represented by Italo Calvino's *Se una notte d'inverno un viaggiatore* (1979). Secondly, Ménard's contemporary *Quixote*, seen as a palimpsest or pre-text of the old one, largely anticipates the theories of intertextuality established in the 1970s. It started from the premise that it is not the singularity of a text which defines its literary character but the potential presence of other texts (its 'transtextuality') – a theory which Gérard Genette systematized in his significantly entitled: *Palimpsestes – La littérature au second degré* (1982). Thirdly, it anticipates the now prevalent deconstructionism. In opposition to the secular logocentrism of Western metaphysics, deconstructionism exhibits the inveterate allegorical difference by which any text can say something other than it intends, so that for example *Allegories of Reading* of Paul de Man is a work that constantly reveals the indispensability of *misreading*. At bottom, deconstructionism, as popular as it is today, has come no further in dissolving all constitution of meaning than Borges has with his paradox of the non-identity of what is repeated and with the self-erasure of aesthetic representation in the experiment carried out by his *Pierre Ménard*. Fourthly, if this experiment ends by refuting all originality in the consciousness of the completed *post-histoire*, then this favourite theme of the post-modern era scarcely produced a more grandiose poetic vision than Borges had done with his library of Babel which, thanks to ingenious combinations of 25 letters, makes it possible to present all extant books and all possible books either in their entirety or to include them in a single book with an infinite number of pages.

Yet indulging in new myths about the final state of our world, the death of the subject and the self-destruction of reason is not the last word in Borges' *Ficciones* or *Labyrinths*, and no longer even an object of fascination for literary post-modernism. In 1979 in *Se una notte d'inverno un viaggiatore*, Borges' most important successor, Italo Calvino, thematized the new change of horizon in a way which no longer sees the dawn of the new looking backwards, in epigonic awareness of the *post*, of 'afterwards', of what has come 'too late'. 'I too would like to erase myself and find for each book another I, another voice, another name, to be reborn; but my aim is to capture in the book the illegible world, the world without centre, without ego, without I.'[55] The much-invoked loss of the 'I', of the Cartesian certainty 'I think therefore I am', turns out an unrecognized reverse. The project of a book consisting of 'what the world has not yet said of itself', reveals the benefit of a delimitation of the subject and of language, a new chance to regain the potentiality of the beginning. That is why *Se una notte d'inverno un viaggiatore* consists of ten beginnings of novels, thereby raising the expectation of the reader for the manifold variety of possible worlds. It is not the loss of the 'I', but the loss of the 'You' which would be the real catastrophe. That is why Calvino allows the 'You' of the reader to become the protagonist of his books, a 'You' which cannot become the 'He' of a fixed character, but instead can be an ever-changing 'I' of a narrator, can be erased and reborn and can be unified lastly, contrasting with the stories which cannot find their end, with the 'You' of a female reader. Yet, as the ideal reader, Ludmilla is the real, sympathetic hero of this novel of the novel. In Calvino's Utopia of the complete police state, even the completely self-regulating system of thought control founders on 'her always curious, always insatiable reading', when the almighty, but sensitive director of the state police archive is forced to admit 'In reading something happens over which I have no power.' He has to allow himself to be taught by Calvino's reader that, although he can hinder reading, he cannot prevent it by the decree that itself forbids reading, there will still be read something of the truth that he would wish never to be read. Calvino's reader is able to evade the power of the censor and at the same time win over Ermes Merana, the *genius malignus* of the falsified world, because she follows a hermeneutic maxim which can be interpreted as Calvino's final word and as the quintessence of all reception theory, that which long went unrecognized and which the Constance School gave a name to, and that which, presumably, is still valid in the postmodern era: 'I expect readers to read in my books something I didn't know, but I can expect it only from those who wish to read something they didn't know.'[56]

Notes

1 Thus far, the writings of the Constance School have been translated into 15 languages. See the works by Iser, Jauss, Stierle, Warning and Weber in the Bibliography following. W. Kroll's *Bibliographie deutscher Arbeiten zur Rezeptions- und Wirkungsästhetik* (in *Wortkunst*, special edn, 1977) lists 437 titles for the ten years following 1967.

2 G. Ebeling, 'Hermeneutik', in *Die Religion in Geschichte und Gegenwart* ed. K. Galling, third edition (Tübingen, 1957), p. 247.

3 Note the absence of an article on *Rezeption* in *Die Religion in Geschichte und Gegenwart*.

4 Book of the Prophets, chap. 10; see similarly Boethius, *The Consolation of Philosophy*, Book 5, 4, 25; Thomas, *Summa theologica*, Book I, 75, 5c *inter alia*; cf. Dante, *Convivio*, Book 3, 7, 3.

5 In *Commentary on the Metaphysics of Aristotle*, trans. J. P. Rowan, 2 vols (Chicago: Henry Regnery Company, 1961), cf. vol. 1, Book 2, Lesson 1; see also J. Spörl, 'Das Alte und das Neue im MA', in *Historisches Jahrbuch* (1930), p. 319.

6 Prologue to the *Lays* of Marie de France; see also H. R. Jauss, *Literaturgeschichte als Provokation* (Frankfurt, 1970), p. 21.

7 Henry Reynolds, *Mythomystes* (1632), referred to by H. Bloom, *Kabbalah and Criticism* (New York, 1975), p. 14.

8 G. Scholem, *On the Kabbala and its Symbolism*, trans. R. Mannheim (London, Routledge and Kegan Paul, 1965).

9 According to Sir Walter Scott, *On Novelists and Fiction*, ed. J. Williams (London, 1968), p. 124.

10 William of Ockham, *Ordinatio* (in the *Sentences*, Book 1), d. 35 q. 1.

11 Martin Luther, Sermon no. 3868.

12 Spinoza, *Opera*, ed. G. Gawlik (1979), Book I, 232.

13 See E. Jüngel, 'Anthropomorphismus als Grundprobleme neuzeitlicher Hermeneutik', in *Verifikationen, Festschrift Ebeling*, ed. E. Jüngel et al. (1982), p. 520.

14 See Y. Congar, 'Die Rezeption als ekklesiologische Realität', in *Concilium 8* (1972), pp. 500–14.

15 Franz Wieacker, *Privatrechtsgeschichte der Neuzeit* (Göttingen, 1952), p. 64.

16 Ibid., p. 19; supplemented by a suggestion by M. Fuhrmann.

17 K. Engisch, *Die Idee der Konkretisation in Recht und Rechtswissenschaft* (1953); J. Esser, *Vorverständnis und Methodenwahl in der Rechtsfindung* (1970), pp. 72ff.

18 See M. Kriele, 'Juristische Hermeneutik am Beispiel der Mephisto-Entscheidung', in *Text und Applikation*, ed. M. Fuhrmann et al. (Munich, 1981), pp. 149ff.

19 See R. Ingarden, *The Literary Work of Art: an Investigation on the Borderlines of Ontology, Logic and the Theory of Literature*, trans. G. G. Grabowicz (Evanston, Ill.: Northwestern University Press, 1973); F. Vodička, *Struktura vývoje* (Prague, 1969), p. 82; H. R. Jauss, *Literaturgeschichte als Provokation* (Frankfurt, 1970), pp. 247ff; W. Iser, *The Act of Reading. A Theory of Aesthetic Response* (London: Routledge and Kegan Paul, 1978).

20 See also H. R. Jauss, *Aesthetische Erfahrung und literarische Hermeneutik* (Frankfurt, 1982), Part III, esp. pp. 657–703.

21 Hegel quoted in W. Büttemeyer, 'Gedanken zur Rezeptionsgeschichte der Philosophie', in *La storia della filosofia come sapere critico, Studi offerti a Mario Dal Pra* (Milan, 1984), pp. 718–34.

22 H. Blumenberg, 'Epochenschwelle und Rezeption', in *Philosophische Rundschau 8* (1958), pp. 94–120; and cf. H. Blumenberg, *Aspekte der Epochenschwelle* (Frankfurt, 1976).

23 H. Blumenberg, *Work on Myth*, trans. R. M. Wallace, (Cambridge, Mass.: MIT Press, 1985).

24 Thomas S. Kuhn, *The Structure of Scientific Revolutions* (Chicago: University of Chicago Press, 1962; 2nd edn, 1970).

25 H. G. Gadamer, *Truth and Method*, trans. W. Gen-Doepel, ed. John Cumming and Gerrett Barden (London: Sheed and Ward, 1979).

26 For example, Goethe, *Nachlese zu Aristoteles Poetik* (1827) and letter to Zelter, 23 March 1827; Friedrich Schlegel, *Horen-Rezension* (1796); and T. W. Adorno, *Aesthetic Theory*, trans. C. Lenhardt, ed. Gretel Adorno and Rolf Tiedemann (London: Routledge and Kegan Paul, 1984).

27 Probably the oldest French example of the use of word *réception* can be found in Corneille's *Epistle to Madame de Combalat*: 'le nom [du Cid] au bout de six cent ans vient encore de triompher en France. Il y a trouvé une réception trop favorable pour se repentir d'être sorti de son pays' (quoted by Y. Chevrel in *Degrez*, 12 (1894), p. 5).

28 Montaigne, *Essais, (1580–85)*, Book I, xxiv.

29 See also Heinz Schlaffer, *Als die Menschheit das Lesen lernte – Über die Sucht, Bücher zu verschlingen*, in *Stuttgarter Zeitung*, 13 November 1985.

30 Fichte, *Fifth and Sixth Lectures* (Hamburg, 1956), esp. p. 106.

31 According to M. Fuhrmann, *Einführung in die antike Dichtungstheorie* (Darmstadt, 1973), esp. p. 142 (chap. 7, paras. 2–3).

32 W. Kemp, *Der Betrachter ist im Bild* (Cologne, 1985), esp. p. 184, with respect to research by Neil Flax and Michael Fried.

33 O. Bätschmann, 'Pygmalion als Betrachter' (in Kemp, *Der Betrachter*, pp. 183–224, esp. p. 193) draws on Hegel, *Lectures on the Philosophy of Religion*, trans. R. F. Brow, ed. Peter C. Hodgson vol. 1, Introduction and Concept of Religion (Berkeley, University of California Press, 1984) p. 236 n.137: 'The form, the subjectivity, which the artist has given his work, is only external, not the absolute form of self-knowing, of self-consciousness. Consummate subjectivity is lacking in the work of art. This self-consciousness belongs to subjective consciousness, the intuiting subject. In contrast, therefore, with the work of art, which inwardly is not something that knows, the moment of self-consciousness is the other, but a moment that is utterly a part of the work – a moment that *knows* what is portrayed and represents it as the substantial truth.'

34 According to Frank Kermode, 'The Common Reader', in *Daedalus*, 112 (1983), pp. 1–11, esp. p. 2.

35 According to G. Grimm, *Rezeptionsgeschichte* (Munich, 1977), p. 69; and *Kritische Fr. Schlegel-Ausgabe*, ed. H. Eichner (Munich/Paderborn/Vienna, 1967), vol. 2, p. 161, n.112.

36 Adam Müller, *Vorlesungen über die deutsche Wissenschaft und Literatur*, quoted in R. Mandelkow 'Rezeptionsgeschichte als Erfahrungsgeschichte', in *Studien zur Goethezeit*, ed. H. -J. Mähl (1981), p. 155.

37 Hegel, *Ästhetik*, ed. F. Bassenge (Berlin/Weimar, 1965), vol. 1, p. 259; vol. 2, p. 11. (Translated as *Aesthetics, Lectures on Fine Art*, by T. M. Knox, 2 vols (Oxford: Clarendon Press, 1975).) See also Kemp, *Der Betrachter*, p. 18.

38 R. Koselleck, *Vergangene Zukunft – Zur Semantik geschichtlicher Zeiten*, (Frankfurt, 1979) p. 291. (Translated as *Futures Past; On the Semantics of Historical Time*, by Keith Tribe (Cambridge, Mass.: MIT Press, 1985).)

39 Goethe, *Werke* (Hamburg edn), vol. 14, p. 195.

40 Heine, *Die Nordsee* (1826), in *Sämtliche Werke* (Munich, 1972), vol. 2, p. 79.

41 Letter from Marx to Lasalle, 22 July 1861, quoted in D. Durizin, *Vergleichende Literaturforschung* (Berlin, 1976), p. 138.

42 According to Mandelkow, 'Rezeptionsgeschichte', pp. 157ff.

43 Ibid., pp. 164ff.

44 Example cited in H. Böhringer, 'Avantgarde – Geschichte einer Metapher', in *Archiv für Begriffsgeschichte*, 27 (1978), p. 100.

45 The following can be found in F. Wolfzettel, *Einführung in die französische Literaturgeschichtsschreibung* (Darmstadt, 1982), pp. 228–36 (on Lansonism), and pp. 237–42 (on Bergsonism). On Scherer, see *Poetik*, ed. G. Reiss (Tübingen, 1977), chap. 2, esp. pp. 84, 127, 132, 125.

46 Valéry, *Oeuvres* (Paris: Editions de la Pléiade, 1957) vol. 1, pp. 1346, 1509; vol. 2, pp. 606, 1197.

47 L. L. Schücking, *The Sociology of Literary Taste*, trans. B. Battershaw (International Library of Sociology and Social Reconstruction) (London: Routledge and Kegan Paul, 1966); A. N. Veselovsky, *Introduction to collected papers* (Leningrad, 1939), p. 16; R. Escarpit, *Das Buch und der Leser* (1961), p. 34 (translated by Ernest Pick as *Sociology of Literature*, New Sociology Library, 4 (London: Frank Cass and Co. Ltd, 1971); G. Grimm, *Rezeptionsgeschichte* (Munich, 1977).

48 For more information on this debate, the reader is referred to the recent American research by R. C. Holub, *Reception Theory* (London, 1984).

49 H. Weinrich, 'Für eine Literaturgeschichte des Lesers', in *Merkur*, 21 (1967),
    pp. 1026–38. Recently Weinrich has diagnosed a return swing in the pendulum
    from reception theory back to a theory of production, which once again prior-
    itizes the author with regard to the reader (*Autor des Lesers*) as the 'first witness
    to the super-individual meaning of a text – the second is the reader himself'.
    Der Autor des Lesers, in the literary supplement of the *Neue Zürcher Zeitung*, 13–14
    October 1984, p. 65.
50 The question of the impact of a work is here rejected as 'affective fallacy' and
    thus I. A. Richards' theory of the aesthetic experience (*Principles of Literary
    Criticism*, 1924), which separated the act of reception from its historical setting,
    conceiving to the act purely psychologically, is laid to rest.
51 W. Benjamin, *Gesammelte Schriften* (Frankfurt, 1977) vol. 2, chap. 2, pp. 467ff.
    (Translated as 'Eduard Fuchs, Collector and Historian', in *One-Way Street
    and Other Writings*, trans. Edmund Jephcott and Kingsley Shorter, with an
    introduction by Susan Sontag (London: New Left Books, 1979), pp. 349–86.
    For a reappropriation of Mandelkow's theory of legends, see Mandelkow,
    Rezeptionsgeschichte.
52 J. P. Sartre, *Qu'est-ce que la littérature?* (Paris, 1962) p. 109. (Translated as *What
    is Literature?* by B. Frechtman (London: Methuen, 1950).)
53 P. Ricoeur, 'The Text as Dynamic Identity', in *The Identity of the Literary Text*,
    ed. M. J. Valdes and O. Miller (Toronto, 1985), p. 184.
54 John Barth in *The Atlantic Monthly* (1967), pp. 29–34.
55 Quoted in the English translation *If on a Winter's Night a Traveller*, by William
    Weaver (London, Secker and Warburg, 1981).)
56 I am very grateful to my friend Alan Paskow of the University of Maryland
    for the many helpful suggestions which he made during my revision of the
    English translation of this chapter.

Suggested Reading

W. Barner, 'Neuphilologische Rezeptionsforschung', in *Poetica* 9 (1977), pp.
499–521.
K. Berger, *Exegese des Neuen Testaments* (Heidelberg, 1977).
H. Blumenberg, *Epochenschwelle und Rezeption*.
P. C. Boris, 'Attualità di un detto antico? "La sacra Scrittura cresce con chi la
legge" ', in *Intersezioni* 6 (1986).
L. Daellenbach, 'Théorie de la réception en Allemagne', in *Poétique* special issue 39
(1979).
C. Dahlhaus, *Grundlagen der Musikgeschichte* (Cologne, 1977), in particular pp. 237–59
(Probleme der Rezeptionsgeschichte).
U. Eco, *Opera aperta* (Milan, 1962).
G. Grimm, *Rezeptionsgeschichte*.
H. U. Gumbrecht, 'Soziologie und Rezeptionästhetik', in *Neue Ansichten einer künftigen
Germanistik*, ed. J. Kolbe (Munich, 1973), pp. 48–74.
P. U. Hohendahl, *Sozialgeschichte und Wirkungsästhetik* (Frankfurt, 1974).
R. C. Holub, *Reception Theory*.
W. Iser, *Die Appellstruktur der Texte* (Konstanz, 1970).
——— *The Act of Reading. A Theory of Aesthetic Response* (London: Routledge and Kegan
Paul, 1978).

—— *The Implied Reader: Patterns of Communication from Bunyan to Beckett* (Baltimore: Johns Hopkins University Press, 1974).

H. R. Jauss, *Literaturgeschichte als Provokation der Literaturwissenschaft* (Konstanz, 1967).

—— *Literaturgeschichte als Provokation* (Frankfurt, 1970).

—— *Ästhetische Erfahrung und literarische Hermeneutik* (Munich, 1977; Frankfurt, 1982).

—— 'Ein Paradigmenwechsel in der Literaturwissenschaft', in *Forschung in der Bundesrepublik Deutschland*, ed. Chr. Schneider (Weinheim, 1983), pp. 121–34.

W. Kemp, *Der Betrachter ist im Bild. Kunstwissenschaft und Rezeptionsästhetik* (Cologne, 1985).

K. Lubbers, 'Aufgaben und Möglichkeiten der Rezeptionsforschung', in *German.-roman. Monatsschrift* 55 (1964), pp. 292–302.

K. R. Mandelkow, *Rezeptionsgeschichte als Erfahrungsgeschichte*.

—— 'Probleme der Wirkungsgeschichte' in *Jb. für internat. Germanistik* 2 (1970), pp. 71–84.

M. Naumann, *Gesellschaft – Literatur – Lesen* (Berlin/Weimar, 1973).

K. Stierle, 'Was heisst Rezeption bei fiktionalen Texten?', in *Poetica* 7 (1975), 345–87.

H. Turk, *Wirkungsästhetik* (Munich, 1976).

R. Warning, *Rezeptionsästhetik – Theorie und Praxis* (Munich, 1975).

H. D. Weber, *Rezeptionsgeschichte oder Wirkungsästhetik* (Stuttgart, 1978).

H. Weinrich, *Der Autor des Lesers*.

STEPHEN GREENBLATT
Resonance and Wonder

The new historicism, like the Holy Roman Empire, constantly belies its own name. The *American Heritage Dictionary* gives three meanings for the term 'historicism':

> 1. The belief that processes are at work in history that man can do little to alter. 2. The theory that the historian must avoid all value judgements in his study of past periods or former cultures. 3. Veneration of the past or of tradition.

Most of the writing labelled 'new historicist', and certainly my own work, has set itself resolutely against each of these positions.

(1) 'The belief that processes are at work in history that man can do little to alter.' This formulation rests upon a simultaneous abstraction and evacuation of human agency. The men and women who find themselves making concrete choices in given circumstances at particular times are transformed into something called 'man'. And this colourless, nameless collective being cannot significantly intervene in the 'processes . . . at work in history', processes that are thus mysteriously alienated from all of those who enact them.

New historicism, by contrast, eschews the use of the term 'man'; interest lies not in the abstract universal but in particular, contingent cases, the selves fashioned and acting according to the generative rules and conflicts of a given culture. And these selves, conditioned by the expectations of their class, gender, religion, race and national identity, are constantly effecting changes in the course of history. Indeed if there is any inevitability in the new historicism's vision of history it is this insistence on agency, for even inaction or extreme marginality is understood to possess meaning and therefore to imply intention. Every form of behaviour, in this view, is a strategy: taking up arms or taking flight are significant social actions, but so is staying put, minding one's business, turning one's face to the wall. Agency is virtually inescapable.

Inescapable but not simple: new historicism, as I understand it, does not posit historical processes as unalterable and inexorable, but it does tend to discover limits or constraints upon individual intervention: actions that appear to be single are disclosed as multiple; the apparently isolated power of the individual genius turns out to be bound up with collective, social energy; a gesture of dissent may be an element in a larger legitimation process, while an attempt to stabilize the order of things may turn out to subvert it. And political valencies may change, sometimes abruptly: there are no guarantees, no absolute, formal assurances that what seems progressive in one set of contingent circumstances will not come to seem reactionary in another.

The new historicism's insistence on the pervasiveness of agency has apparently led some of its critics to find in it a Nietzschean celebration of the ruthless will to power, while its ironic and sceptical reappraisal of the cult of heroic individualism has led others to find in it a pessimistic doctrine of human helplessness. Hence, for example, from a Marxist perspective Walter Cohen criticizes the new historicism as a 'liberal disillusionment' that finds that 'any apparent site of resistance ultimately serves the interests of power', while from a liberal humanist perspective, Edward Pechter proclaims that 'anyone who, like me, is reluctant to accept the will to power as the defining human essence will probably have trouble with the critical procedures of the new historicists and with their interpretative conclusions'.[1] But the very idea of a 'defining human essence' is precisely what critics like me find vacuous and untenable, as I do Pechter's counter-claim that love rather than power makes the world go round. Cohen's critique is more plausible, but it rests upon his assertion that new historicism argues that '*any* apparent site of resistance' is ultimately co-opted. Some are, some aren't.

I argued in *Shakespearean Negotiations* that the sites of resistance in Shakespeare's second tetralogy are co-opted in the plays' ironic, complex but finally celebratory affirmation of charismatic kingship. That is, the formal structure and rhetorical strategy of the plays make it difficult for audiences to withhold their consent from the triumph of Prince Hal. That triumph is shown to rest upon a claustrophobic narrowing of pleasure, a hypocritical manipulation of appearances, and a systematic betrayal of friendship, and yet these manifestations of bad faith only contrive to increase the spectators' knowing pleasure and the ratification of applause. The subversive perceptions do not disappear but, in so far as they remain within the structure of the play, they are contained and indeed serve to heighten a power they would appear to question.

I did not propose that all manifestations of resistance in all literature (or even in all plays by Shakespeare) were co-opted – one can readily think of plays where the forces of ideological containment break down. And yet characterizations of this essay in particular, and new historicism in general, repeatedly refer to a supposed argument that any resistance is impossible.[2] A particularizing argument about the subject position projected by a set of plays is at once simplified and turned into a universal principle from which contingency and hence history itself is erased.

Moreover, even the argument about Shakespeare's second tetralogy is misunderstood if it is thought to foreclose the possibility of dissent or change or the radical alteration of the processes of history. The point is that certain aesthetic and political structures work to contain the subversive perceptions they generate, not that those perceptions simply wither away. On the contrary, they may be pried loose from the order with which they were bound up and may serve to fashion a new and radically different set of structures. How else could change ever come about? No one is forced – except perhaps in school – to take aesthetic or political wholes as sacrosanct. The order of things is never simply a given: it takes labour to produce, sustain, reproduce, and transmit the way things are, and this labour may be withheld or transformed. Structures may be broken in pieces, the pieces altered, inverted, rearranged. Everything can be different than it is; everything could have been different than it was. But it will not do to imagine that this alteration is easy, automatic, without cost or obligation. My objection was to the notion that the rich ironies in the history plays were themselves inherently liberating, that to savour the tetralogy's sceptical cunning was to participate in an act of political resistance. In general I find dubious the assertion that certain rhetorical features in much-loved literary works constitute authentic acts of political subversion; the fact that this assertion is now heard from the left – when in my college days it was more often heard from the right – does not make it in most instances any less fatuous and presumptuous. I wished to show, at least in the case of Shakespeare's histories and in several analogous discourses, how a set of representational and political practices in the late sixteenth century could produce and even batten upon what appeared to be their own subversion.

To show this is the case is not to give up on the possibility of altering historical processes – if this is historicism I want no part of it – but rather to eschew an aestheticized and idealized politics of the liberal imagination.

(2) 'The theory that the historian must avoid all value judgments in his study of past periods or former cultures.' Once again, if this is an essential tenet of historicism, then the new historicism belies its name. My own critical practice was decisively shaped by the America of the 1960s and early 1970s, and especially by the opposition to the Viet Nam War. Writing that was not engaged, that withheld judgements, that failed to connect the present with the past seemed worthless. Such connection could be made either by analogy or causality; that is, a particular set of historical circumstances could be represented in such a way as to bring out homologies with aspects of the present or, alternatively, those circumstances could be analysed as the generative forces that led to the modern condition. In either mode, value judgements were implicated, because a neutral or indifferent relation to the present seemed impossible. Or rather it seemed overwhelmingly clear that neutrality was itself a political position, a decision to support the official policies in both the state and the academy.

To study the culture of sixteenth-century England did not present itself as an escape from the turmoil of the present; it seemed rather an intervention, a mode of relation. The fascination for me of the Renaissance was that it seemed to be powerfully linked to the present both analogically and causally. This two-fold link at once called forth and qualified my value judgements: called them forth because my response to the past was inextricably bound up with my response to the present; qualified them because the analysis of the past revealed the complex, unsettling historical genealogy of the very judgements I was making. To study Renaissance culture, then, was simultaneously to feel more rooted and more estranged in my own values.[3]

Other critics associated with the new historicism – Louis Montrose, Don Wayne and Catherine Gallagher, among others – have written directly and forcefully about their own subject position and have made more explicit than I the nature of this engagement.[4] If I have not done so to the same extent, it is not because I believe that my values are somehow suspended in my study of the past but because I believe they are pervasive: in the textual and visual traces I choose to analyse, in the stories I choose to tell, in the cultural conjunctions I attempt to make, in my syntax, adjectives, pronouns. 'The new historicism', Jean Howard has written in a lively critique, 'needs at every point to be more overtly self-conscious of its methods and its theoretical assumptions, since what one discovers about the historical place and function of literary texts is in large measure a function of the angle from which one looks and the assumptions that enable the investigation.'[5] I am certainly not opposed to methodological self-consciousness, but I am less inclined to see overtness – an explicit articulation of one's values and methods – as inherently necessary or virtuous. Nor, though I believe that one's values are everywhere engaged in one's work, do I think that there need be a perfect integration of those values and the objects one is studying. On the contrary, some of the most interesting and powerful ideas in cultural criticism occur precisely at moments of disjunction, disintegration, unevenness. A criticism that never encounters obstacles, that celebrates predictable heroines and rounds up the usual suspects, that finds confirmation of its values everywhere it turns, is quite simply boring.

If there is then no suspension of value judgements in the new historicism, there is at the same time a complication of those judgements, what I have called a sense of estrangement. This estrangement is bound up with the abandonment of a belief in historical inevitability, for, with this abandonment, the values of the present could no longer seem the necessary outcome of an irreversible teleological progression, whether of enlightenment or decline. An older historicism that proclaimed self-consciously that it had avoided all value judgements in its account of the past – that it had given us historical reality *wie es eigentlich gewesen* – did not thereby avoid all value judgements; it simply provided a misleading account of what it had actually done. In this sense the new historicism, for all its acknowledgement of engagement and partiality, is slightly less likely than the older historicism to impose its values belligerently on the past, for those values seem historically contingent.

(3) 'Veneration of the past or of tradition.' The third definition of historicism obviously sits in a strange relation to the second, but they are not simply alternatives. The apparent eschewing of value judgements was often accompanied by a still more apparent admiration, however cloaked as objective description, of the past. One of the most oppressive qualities of my own literary training was its relentlessly celebratory character: literary criticism was and largely remains a kind of secular theodicy. Every decision made by a great artist could be shown to be a brilliant one; works that had seemed flawed and uneven to an earlier generation of critics bent on displaying discriminations in taste were now revealed to be organic master-pieces. A standard critical assignment in my student years was to show how a text that seemed to break in parts was really a complex whole: thousands of pages were dutifully churned out to prove that the zany subplot of *The Changeling* was cunningly integrated into the tragic main plot, or that every tedious bit of clowning in *Doctor Faustus* was richly significant. Behind these exercises was the assumption that great works of art were triumphs of resolution, that they were, in Bakhtin's term, monological – the mature expression of a single artistic intention. When this formalism was combined, as it often was, with both ego psychology and historicism, it posited aesthetic integration as the reflection of the artist's psychic integration and posited that psychic integration as the triumphant expression of a healthy, integrated community. Accounts of Shakespeare's relation to Elizabethan culture were particularly prone to this air of veneration, since the Romantic cult of poetic genius could be conjoined with the still older political cult that had been created around the figure of the Virgin Queen.

Here again new historicist critics have swerved in a different direction. They have been more interested in unresolved conflict and contradiction than in integration; they are as concerned with the margins as with the centre; and they have turned from a celebration of achieved aesthetic order to an exploration of the ideological and material bases for the production of this order. Traditional formalism and historicism, twin legacies of early nineteenth-century Germany, shared a vision of high culture as a harmoniz-ing domain of reconciliation based upon an aesthetic labour that transcends specific economic or political determinants. What is missing is psychic, social, and material resistance, a stubborn, unassimilable otherness, a sense of distance and difference. New historicism has attempted to restore this distance; hence its characteristic concerns have seemed to some critics off-centre or strange. 'New historicists', writes Walter Cohen, 'are likely to seize upon something out of the way, obscure, even bizarre: dreams, popular or aristocratic festivals, denunciations of witchcraft, sexual treatises, diaries and autobiographies, descriptions of clothing, reports on disease, birth and death records, accounts of insanity.'[6] What is fascinating to me is that concerns like these should have come to seem bizarre, especially to a subtle and intelligent Marxist critic who is committed to the historical understanding of culture. That they have done so indicates how narrow the boundaries of historical understanding had become, how much these boundaries needed to be broken.

For none of the cultural practices on Cohen's list (and one could extend it considerably) is or should be 'out of the way' in a study of Renaissance literature or art; on the contrary, each is directly in the way of coming to terms with the period's methods of regulating the body, its conscious and unconscious psychic strategies, its ways of defining and dealing with marginals and deviants, its mechanisms for the display of power and the expression of discontent, its treatment of women. If such concerns have been rendered 'obscure', it is because of a disabling idea of causality that confines the legitimate field of historical agency within absurdly restrictive boundaries. The world is parcelled out between a predictable group of stereotypical causes and a large, dimly lit mass of raw materials that the artist chooses to fashion.

The new historicist critics are interested in such cultural expressions as witchcraft accusations, medical manuals, or clothing not as raw materials but as 'cooked' – complex symbolic and material articulations of the imaginative and ideological structures of the society that produced them. Consequently, there is a tendency in at least some new historicist writings (certainly in my own) for the focus to be partially displaced from the work of art that is their formal occasion onto the related practices that had been adduced ostensibly in order to illuminate that work. It is difficult to keep those practices in the background if the very concept of historical background has been called into question.

I have tried to deal with the problem of focus by developing a notion of cultural negotiation and exchange, that is, by examining the points at which one cultural practice intersects with another, borrowing its forms and intensities or attempting to ward off unwelcome appropriations. But it would be misleading to imagine that there is a complete homogenization of interest; my own concern remains centrally with imaginative literature, and not only because other cultural structures resonate powerfully within it. If I do not approach works of art in a spirit of veneration, I do approach them in a spirit that is best described as wonder. Wonder has not been alien to literary criticism, but it has been associated (if only implicitly) with formalism rather than historicism. I wish to extend this wonder beyond the formal boundaries of works of art, just as I wish to intensify resonance within those boundaries.

It will be easier to grasp the concepts of resonance and wonder if we think of the way in which our culture presents to itself not the textual traces of its past but the surviving visual traces, for the latter are put on display in galleries and museums specially designed for the purpose. By resonance I mean the power of the object displayed to reach out beyond its formal boundaries to a larger world, to evoke in the viewer the complex, dynamic cultural forces from which it has emerged and for which as metaphor or more simply as synechdoche it may be taken by a viewer to stand. By wonder I mean the power of the object displayed to stop the viewer in his tracks, to convey an arresting sense of uniqueness, to evoke an exalted attention.

The new historicism obviously has distinct affinities with resonance; that is, my concern with literary texts has been to recover as far as possible the historical circumstances of their original production and consumption and to analyse the relationship between these circumstances and our own. I have tried to understand the intersecting circumstances not as a stable, prefabricated background against which the literary texts can be placed, but as a dense network of evolving and often contradictory social forces. The idea is not to find outside the work of art some rock to which literary interpretation can be securely chained but rather to situate the work in relation to other representational practices operative in the culture at a given moment in both its history and our own. In Louis Montrose's convenient formulation, the goal has been to grasp simultaneously the historicity of texts and the textuality of history.

In so far as this approach, developed for literary interpretation, is at all applicable to visual traces, it would call for an attempt to reduce the isolation of individual 'masterpieces', to illuminate the conditions of their making, to disclose the history of their appropriation and the circumstances in which they come to be displayed, to restore the tangibility, the openness, the permeability of boundaries that enabled the objects to come into being in the first place. An actual restoration of tangibility is obviously in most cases impossible, and the frames that enclose pictures are only the ultimate formal confirmation of the closing of the borders that marks the finishing of a work of art. But we need not take that finishing so entirely for granted; museums can and on occasion do make it easier imaginatively to recreate the work in its moment of openness.

That openness is linked to a quality of artifacts that museums obviously dread – their precariousness. But though it is perfectly reasonable for museums to protect their objects – I would not wish it any other way – precariousness is a rich source of resonance. Thomas Greene, who has written a sensitive book on what he calls the 'vulnerable text', suggests that the symbolic wounding to which literature is prone may confer upon it power and fecundity. 'The vulnerability of poetry', Greene argues, 'stems from four basic conditions of language: its historicity, its dialogic function, its referential function, and its dependence on figuration.'[7] Three of these conditions are different for the visual arts, in ways that would seem to reduce vulnerability: painting and sculpture may be detached more readily than language from both referentiality and figuration, and the pressures of contextual dialogue are diminished by the absence of an inherent *logos*, a constitutive word. But the fourth condition – historicity – is in the case of material artifacts vastly increased, indeed virtually literalized. Museums function, partly by design and partly in spite of themselves, as monuments to the fragility of cultures, to the fall of sustaining institutions and noble houses, the collapse of rituals, the evacuation of myths, the destructive effects of warfare, neglect and corrosive doubt.

I am fascinated by the signs of alteration, tampering, even destructiveness which many museums try simply to efface: first and most obviously, the act of displacement that is essential for the collection of virtually all older artifacts and most modern ones – pulled out of chapels, peeled off church walls, removed from decayed houses, seized as spoils of war, stolen, 'purchased' more or less fairly by the economically ascendent from the economically naive, the poor, the hard-pressed heirs of fallen dynasties and impoverished religious orders. Then too there are the marks on the artifacts themselves: the attempt to scratch out or deface the image of the devil in numerous late-medieval and Renaissance paintings, the concealing of the genitals in sculpted and painted figures, the iconoclastic smashing of human or divine representations, the evidence of cutting or reshaping to fit a new frame or purpose, the cracks or scorch marks or broken-off noses that indifferently record the grand disasters of history and the random accidents of trivial incompetence. Even these accidents – the marks of a literal fragility – can have their resonance: the climax of an absurdly hagiographical Proust exhibition several years ago was a display case holding a small, patched, modest vase with a notice, 'This vase broken by Marcel Proust'.

As this comical example suggests, wounded artifacts may be compelling not only as witnesses to the violence of history but as signs of use, marks of the human touch, and hence links with the openness to touch that was the condition of their creation. The most familiar way to recreate the openness of aesthetic artifacts without simply renewing their vulnerability is through a skilful deployment of explanatory texts in the catalogue, on the walls of the exhibit, or on cassettes. The texts so deployed introduce and in effect stand in for the context that has been effaced in the process of moving the object into the museum. But in so far as that context is partially, often primarily, visual as well as verbal, textual contextualism has its limits. Hence the mute eloquence of the display of the palette, brushes and other implements that an artist of a given period would have employed or of objects that are represented in the exhibited paintings or of materials and images that in some way parallel or intersect with the formal works of art.

Among the most resonant moments are those in which the supposedly contextual objects take on a life of their own, make a claim that rivals that of the object that is formally privileged. A table, a chair, a map, often seemingly placed only to provide a decorative setting for a grand work, become oddly expressive, significant not as 'background' but as compelling representational practices in themselves. These practices may in turn impinge upon the grand work, so that we begin to glimpse a kind of circulation: the cultural practice and social energy implicit in map-making drawn into the aesthetic orbit of a painting which has itself enabled us to register some of the representational significance of the map. Or again the threadbare fabric on the old chair or the gouges in the wood of a cabinet

juxtapose the privileged painting or sculpture with marks not only of time
but of use, the imprint of the human body on the artifact, and call attention
to the deliberate removal of certain exalted aesthetic objects from the threat
of that imprint.

For the effect of resonance does not necessarily depend upon a collapse
of the distinction between art and non-art; it can be achieved by awakening
in the viewer a sense of the cultural and historically contingent construction
of art objects, the negotiations, exchanges, swerves, exclusions by which
certain representational practices come to be set apart from other representational practices that they partially resemble. A resonant exhibition often
pulls the viewer away from the celebration of isolated objects and toward
a series of implied, only half-visible relationships and questions. How have
the objects come to be displayed? What is at stake in categorizing them as
of 'museum-quality'? How were they originally used? What cultural and
material conditions made possible their production? What were the feelings
of those who originally held the objects, cherished them, collected them,
possessed them? What is the meaning of my relationship to these same
objects now that they are displayed here, in this museum, on this day?

It is time to give a more sustained example. Perhaps the most purely
resonant museum I have ever seen is the State Jewish Museum in Prague.
This is housed not in a single building but in a cluster of old synagogues
scattered through the city's former Jewish Town. The oldest of
these – known as the Old–New Synagogue – is a twin-nave medieval structure dating to the last third of the thirteenth century; the others are mostly
Renaissance and Baroque. In these synagogues are displayed Judaica from
the Bohemian and Moravian Jewish communities. In one there is a permanent exhibition of synagogue silverworks, in another there are synagogue
textiles, in a third there are Torah scrolls, ritual objects, manuscripts and
prints illustrative of Jewish beliefs, traditions, and customs. One of the
synagogues shows the work of the physician and artist Karel Fleischmann,
principally drawings done in Terezín concentration camp during his months
of imprisonment prior to his deportation to Auschwitz. Next door in the
Ceremonial Hall of the Prague Burial Society there is a wrenching exhibition
of children's drawings from Terezín. Finally, one synagogue, closed at the
time of my visit to Prague, has simply a wall of names – thousands of
them – to commemorate the Jewish victims of Nazi persecution in Czechos-
lovaia.

'The Museum's rich collections of synagogue art and the historical synagogue buildings of Prague's Jewish town', says the catalogue of the State
Jewish Museum, 'form a memorial complex that has not been preserved to
the same extent anywhere else in Europe.' 'A memorial complex' – this
museum is not so much about artifacts as about memory, and the form the
memory takes is a secularized kaddish, a commemorative prayer for the
dead. The atmosphere has a peculiar effect on the act of viewing. It is
mildly interesting to note the differences between the mordant Grosz-like
lithographs of Karel Fleischmann in the pre-war years and the tormented

style, at once detached and anguished, of the drawings in the camps, but aesthetic discriminations feel weird, out-of-place. And it seems wholly absurd, even indecent, to worry about the relative artistic merits of the drawings that survive by children who did not survive.

The discordance between viewing and remembering is greatly reduced with the older, less emotionally charged artifacts, but even here the ritual objects in their glass cases convey an odd and desolate impression. The oddity, I suppose, should be no greater than in seeing a Mayan god or, for that matter, a pyx or a ciborium, but we have become so familiarized to the display of such objects, so accustomed to considering them works of art, that even pious Catholics, as far as I know, do not necessarily feel disconcerted by their transformation from ritual function to aesthetic exhibition. And until very recently the voices of the tribal peoples who might have objected to the display of their religious artifacts have not been heard and certainly not attended to.

The Jewish objects are neither sufficiently distant to be absorbed into the detached ethos of anthropological display nor sufficiently familiar to be framed and encased alongside the altarpieces and reliquaries that fill Western museums. And moving as they are as mnemonic devices, most of the ritual objects in the State Jewish Museum are not, by contrast with Christian liturgical art, particularly remarkable either for their antiquity or their extraordinary beauty. They are the products of a people with a resistance to joining figural representation to religious observance, a strong anti-iconic bias. The objects have, as it were, little will to be observed; many of them are artifacts – ark curtains, Torah crowns, breastplates, pointers, and the like – the purpose of which was to be drawn back or removed in order to make possible the act that mattered: not vision but reading.

But the inhibition of viewing in the Jewish Museum is paradoxically bound up with its resonance. This resonance depends not upon visual stimulation but upon a felt intensity of names, and behind the names, as the very term resonance suggests, of voices: the voices of those who chanted, studied, muttered their prayers, wept, and then were forever silenced. And mingled with these voices are others – of those Jews in 1389 who were murdered in the Old–New Synagogue where they were seeking refuge, of the great sixteenth-century Kabbalist, Jehuda ben Bezalel, known as Rabbi Loew, who is fabled to have created the Golem, of the twentieth-century's ironic Kabbalist, Franz Kafka.

It is Kafka who would be most likely to grasp imaginatively the State Jewish Museum's ultimate source of resonance: the fact that most of the objects are located in the museum – were displaced, preserved and transformed categorically into works of art – because the Nazis stored the articles they confiscated in the Prague synagogues that they chose to preserve for this very purpose. In 1941 the Nazi *Hochschule* in Frankfurt had established an Institute for the Exploration of the Jewish Question which in turn had initiated a massive effort to confiscate Jewish libraries, archives, religious artifacts and personal property. By the middle of 1942, Heydrich, as Hitler's chief officer with the so-called Protectorate of Bohemia and Moravia, had chosen Prague as the site of the Central Bureau for Dealing with the Jewish Question, and an SS officer, Untersturmführer Karl Rahm, had assumed control of the small existing Jewish museum, founded in 1912, which was renamed the Central Jewish Museum. The new charter of the museum announced that 'the numerous, hitherto scattered Jewish possessions of both historical and artistic value, on the territory of the entire Protectorate, must be collected and stored.'[8]

During the following months, tens of thousands of confiscated items arrived from 153 Jewish communities in Bohemia and Moravia, the dates of the shipments closely co-ordinated with the 'donors" deportation to the concentration camps. The experts formerly employed by the original Jewish museum were compelled to catalogue the items, and the Nazis compounded this immense task by ordering the wretched, malnourished curators to prepare a collections guide and organize private exhibitions for SS staff. Between September 1942 and October 1943 four major exhibitions were mounted. Since these required far more space than the existing Jewish Museum's modest location, the great old Prague synagogues – made vacant by the Nazi prohibition of Jewish public worship – were partially refurbished for the occasion. Hence in March 1943, for example, in the seventeenth-century Klaus Synagogue, there was an exhibition of Jewish festival and life-cycle observances; 'when Sturmbannführer Günther first toured the collection on April 6, he demanded various changes, including the translation of all Hebrew texts and the addition of an exhibit on kosher butchering'.[9] Plans were drawn up for other exhibitions, but the curators – who had given themselves with a strange blend of selflessness, irony, helplessness and heroism to the task – were themselves at this point sent to concentration camps and murdered.

After the war, the few survivors of the Czech Jewish community apparently felt they could not sustain the ritual use of the synagogues or maintain the large collections. In 1949 the Jewish Community Council offered as a gift to the Czechoslovak government both the synagogues and their contents. These became the resonant, impure 'memorial complex' they are – a cultural machine that generates an uncontrollable oscillation between homage and desacration, longing and hopelessness, the voices of the dead and silence. For resonance, like nostalgia, is impure, a hybrid forged in the barely acknowledged gaps, the cesurae, between words like State, Jewish and Museum.

I want to avoid the implication that resonance must be necessarily linked to destruction and absence; it can be found as well in unexpected survival. The key is the intimation of a larger community of voices and skills, an imagined ethnographic thickness. Here another example will serve: in the Yucatan there is an extensive, largely unexcavated late-Classic Maya site called Coba, the principal surviving feature of which is a high pyramid known as Nahoch Mul. After a day of tramping around the site, I was relaxing in the pool of the nearby Club Med Archaeological Villa in the company of a genial structural engineer from Little Rock. To make conversation, I asked my pool-mate what he as a structural engineer thought of Nahoch Mul. 'From an engineer's point of view,' he replied, 'a pyramid is not very interesting – it's just an enormous gravity structure. But,' he added, 'did you notice that Coca Cola stand on the way in? That's the most impressive example of contemporary Maya architecture I've ever seen.' I thought it quite possible that my leg was being pulled, but I went back the next day to check – I had, of course, completely blocked out the Coke stand on my first visit. Sure enough, some enterprising Mayan had built a remarkably elegant shelter with a soaring pyramidal roof constructed out of ingeniously intertwining sticks and branches. Places like Coba are thick with what Spenser called the Ruins of Time – with a nostalgia for a lost civilization, in a state of collapse long before Cortés or Montejo cut their paths through the jungle. But, despite frequent colonial attempts to drive them or imagine them out of existence, the Maya have not in fact vanished, and a single entrepreneur's architectural improvization suddenly had more resonance for me than the mounds of the 'lost' city.

My immediate thought was that the whole Coca Cola stand could be shipped to New York and put on display in the Museum of Modern Art. And that impulse moves us away from resonance and toward wonder. For the MOMA is one of the great contemporary places not for the hearing of intertwining voices, not for historical memory, not for ethnographic thickness, but for intense, indeed enchanted looking. Looking may be called enchanted when the act of attention draws a circle around itself from which everything but the object is excluded, when intensity of regard blocks out all circumambient images, stills all murmuring voices. To be sure, the viewer may have purchased a catalogue, read an inscription on the wall, switched on a cassette, but in the moment of wonder all of this apparatus seems mere static.

The so-called boutique lighting that has become popular in recent years – a pool of light that has the surreal effect of seeming to emerge from within the object rather than to focus upon it from without – is an attempt to provoke or to heighten the experience of wonder, as if modern museum designers feared that wonder was increasingly difficult to arouse or perhaps that it risked displacement entirely onto the windows of designer dress shops and antique stores. The association of that lighting – along with transparent plastic rods and other devices to create the magical illusion of luminous, weightless suspension – with commerce would seem to suggest that wonder is bound up with acquisition and possession, yet the whole experience of most art museums is about *not* touching, *not* carrying home, *not* owning the marvellous objects. Modern museums in effect at once evoke the dream of possession and evacuate it.[10]

That evacuation is an historical rather than structural aspect of the museum's regulation of wonder: that is, collections of objects calculated to arouse wonder arose precisely in the spirit of personal acquisition and were only subsequently displaced from it. In the Middle Ages and Renaissance we characteristically hear about wonders in the context of those who possessed them (or gave them away). Hence, for example in his *Life of Saint Louis*, Joinville writes that 'during the king's stay at Saida someone brought him a stone that split into flakes':

> It was the most marvellous stone in the world, for when you lifted one of the flakes you found the form of a sea-fish between the two pieces of stone. This fish was entirely of stone, but there was nothing lacking in its shape, eyes, bones, or colour to make it seem otherwise than if it had been alive. The king gave me one of these stones. I found a tench inside; it was brown in colour, and in every detail exactly as you would expect a tench to be.[11]

The wonder-cabinets of the Renaissance were at least as much about possession as display. The wonder derived not only from what could be seen but from the sense that the shelves and cases were filled with unseen wonders, all the prestigious property of the collector. In this sense, the cult of wonder originated in close conjunction with a certain type of resonance, a resonance bound up with the evocation not of an absent culture but of the great man's superfluity of rare and precious things. Those things were not necessarily admired for their beauty; the marvellous was bound up with the excessive, the surprising, the literally outlandish, the prodigious. They were not necessarily the manifestations of the artistic skill of human makers: technical virtuosity could indeed arouse admiration, but so could nautilus shells, ostrich eggs, uncannily large (or small) bones, stuffed crocodiles, fossils. And, most importantly, they were not necessarily objects set out for careful viewing.

The experience of wonder was not initially regarded as essentially or even primarily *visual*; *reports* of marvels had a force equal to the seeing of them. Seeing was important and desirable, of course, but precisely in order to make reports possible, reports which then circulated as virtual equivalents of the marvels themselves. The great medieval collections of marvels are almost entirely textual: Friar Jordanus' *Marvels of the East*, Marco Polo's *Book of Marvels*, Mandeville's *Travels*. Some of the manuscripts, to be sure, were illuminated, but these illuminations were almost always ancillary to the textual record of wonders, just as emblem books were originally textual and only subsequently illustrated. Even in the sixteenth century, when the power of direct visual experience was increasingly valued, the marvellous was principally theorized as a textual phenomenon, as it had been in antiquity. 'No one can be called a poet', wrote the influential Italian critic Minturno in the 1550s, 'who does not excel in the power of arousing wonder.'[12] For Aristotle wonder was associated with pleasure as the end of poetry, and in the *Poetics* he examined the strategies by which tragedians and epic poets employ the marvellous to arouse wonder. For the Platonists, too, wonder was conceived as an essential element in literary art: in the sixteenth century, the Neo-Platonist Francesco Patrizi defined the poet as principal 'maker of the marvellous', and the marvellous is found, as he put it, when men 'are astounded, ravished in ecstasy'. Patrizi goes so far as to posit marvelling as a special faculty of the mind, a faculty which in effect mediates between the capacity to think and the capacity to feel.[13]

Modern art museums reflect a profound transformation of the experience: the collector – a Getty or a Mellon – may still be celebrated, and market value is even more intensely registered, but the heart of the mystery lies with the uniqueness, authenticity and visual power of the masterpiece, ideally displayed in such a way as to heighten its charisma, to compel and reward the intensity of the viewer's gaze, to manifest artistic genius. Museums display works of art in such a way as to imply that no one, not even the nominal owner or donor, can penetrate the zone of light and actually possess the wonderful object. The object exists not principally to be owned but to be viewed. Even the *fantasy* of possession is no longer central to the museum-gaze, or rather it has been inverted, so that the object in its essence seems not to be a possession but rather to be itself the possessor of what is most valuable and enduring.[14] What the work possesses is the power to arouse wonder, and that power, in the dominant aesthetic ideology of the West, has been infused into it by the creative genius of the artist.

It is beyond the scope of this brief paper to account for the transformation of the experience of wonder from the spectacle of proprietorship to the mystique of the object – an exceedingly complex, overdetermined history centring on institutional and economic shifts – but I think it is important to say that at least in part this transformation was shaped by the collective project of Western artists and reflects their vision. Already in the early sixteenth century, when the marvellous was still principally associated with the prodigious, Dürer begins, in a famous journal entry describing Mexican objects sent to Charles V by Cortés, to reconceive it:

> I saw the things which have been brought to the King from the new golden land: a sun all of gold a whole fathom broad, and a moon all of silver of the same size, also two rooms full of the armour of the people there, and all manner of wondrous weapons of theirs, harness and darts, wonderful shields, strange clothing, bedspreads, and all kinds of wonderful objects of various uses, much more beautiful to behold than prodigies. These things were all so precious that they have been valued at one hundred thousand gold florins. All the days of my life I have seen nothing that has gladdened my heart so much as these things, for I saw amongst them wonderful works of art, and I marvelled at the subtle *ingenia* of men in foreign lands. Indeed, I cannot express all that I thought there.[15]

Dürer's description is full of the conventional marks of his period's sense of wonder: he finds it important that the artifacts have been brought as a kind of tribute to the king, that large quantities of precious metals have been used, that their market value has been reckoned; he notes the strangeness of them, even as he uncritically assimilates that strangeness to his own culture's repertory of objects (which include harness and bedspreads). But he also notes, in perceptions highly unusual for his own time, that these objects are 'much more beautiful to behold than prodigies'. Dürer relocates the source of wonder from the outlandish to the aesthetic, and he under

stands the effect of beauty as a testimony to creative genius: 'I saw amongst
them wonderful works of art, and I marvelled at the subtle *ingenia* of men
in foreign lands.'

It would be misleading to strip away the relations of power and wealth
that are encoded in the artist's response, but it would be still more misleading, I think, to interpret that response as an unmediated expression of those
relations. For Dürer gives voice to an aesthetic understanding – a form of
wondering and admiring and knowing – that is at least partly independent
of the structures of politics and the marketplace.

This understanding – by no means autonomous and yet not reducible to
the institutional and economic forces by which it is shaped – is centred on a
certain kind of looking, a looking whose origins lie in the cult of the marvellous
and hence in the art work's capacity to generate in the spectator surprise,
delight, admiration and intimations of genius. The knowledge that derives
from this kind of looking may not be very useful in the attempt to understand
another culture, but it is vitally important in the attempt to understand our
own. For it is one of the distinctive achievements of our culture to have
fashioned this type of gaze, and one of the most intense pleasures that it has
to offer. This pleasure does not have an inherent and necessary politics, either
radical or imperialist, but Dürer's remarks suggest that it originates at least in
respect and admiration for the *ingenia* of others. This respect is a response
worth cherishing and enhancing. Hence, for all of my academic affiliations
and interests, I am sceptical about the recent attempt to turn our museums
from temples of wonder into temples of resonance.

Perhaps the most startling instance of this attempt is the transfer of the
paintings in the Jeu de Paume and the Louvre to the Musée d'Orsay. The
Musée d'Orsay is at once a spectacular manifestation of French cultural
dépense and a highly self-conscious, exceptionally stylish generator of resonance, including the literal resonance of voices in an enormous vaulted
railway station. By moving the Impressionist and Post-Impressionist master-
pieces into proximity with the work of far less well-known painters – Jean
Béraud, Guillaume Dubuffe, Paul Sérusier, and so forth – and into proximity
as well with the period's sculpture and decorative arts, the museum remakes
a remarkable group of highly individuated geniuses into engaged participants in a vital, conflict-ridden, immensely productive period in French
cultural history. The reimagining is guided by many well-designed informa-
tive boards – cue cards, in effect – along, of course, with the extraordinary
building itself.

All of this is intelligently conceived and dazzlingly executed – on a cold
winter day in Paris, the museum-goer may look down from one of the high
balconies by the old railway clocks and savour the swirling pattern formed
by the black and gray raincoats of the spectators below, as they pass through
the openings in the massive black stone partitions of Gay Aulenti's interior.
The pattern seems spontaneously to animate the period's style – if not
Manet, then at least Caillebotte; it is as if a painted scene had recovered
the power to move and to echo.

But what has been sacrificed on the altar of cultural resonance is visual wonder centred on the aesthetic masterpiece. Attention is dispersed among a wide range of lesser objects that collectively articulate the impressive creative achievement of French culture in the late nineteenth century, but the experience of the old Jeu de Paume – intensive looking at Manet, Monet, Cézanne and so forth – has been radically reduced. The paintings are there, but they are mediated by the resonant contextualism of the building itself and its myriad objects and its descriptive and analytical plaques. Moreover, many of the greatest paintings have been demoted, as it were, to small spaces where it is difficult to view them adequately – as if the design of the museum were trying to assure the triumph of resonance over wonder.

But is a triumph of one over the other necessary? I have, for the purposes of this exposition, obviously exaggerated the extent to which these are alternative models for museums (or for the reading of texts): in fact, almost every exhibition worth the viewing has strong elements of both. I think that the impact of most exhibitions is likely to be greater if the initial appeal is wonder, a wonder that then leads to the desire for resonance, for it is easier to pass from wonder to resonance than from resonance to wonder. Why this should be so is suggested by a remarkable passage in his *Commentary on the Metaphysics of Aristotle* by Aquinas's teacher, Albert the Great:

> wonder is defined as a constriction and suspension of the heart caused by amazement at the sensible appearance of something so portentous, great, and unusual, that the heart suffers a systole. Hence wonder is something like fear in its effect on the heart. This effect of wonder, then, this constriction and systole of the heart, spring from an unfulfilled but felt desire to know the cause of that which appears portentous and unusual: so it was in the beginning when men, up to that time unskilled, began to philosophize. . . . Now the man who is puzzled and wonders apparently does not know. Hence wonder is the movement of the man who does not know on his way to finding out, to get at the bottom of that at which he wonders and to determine its cause. . . . Such is the origin of philosophy.[16]

Such too, from the perspective of the new historicism, is the origin of a meaningful desire for cultural resonance, but while philosophy would seek to supplant wonder with secure knowledge, it is the function of new historicism continually to renew the marvellous at the heart of the resonant.

Notes

1 Walter Cohen, 'Political Criticism of Shakespeare', in *Shakespeare Reproduced: The Text in History and Ideology*, ed. Jean E. Howard and Marion F. O'Connor (New York and London: Methuen, 1987), p. 33; Edward Pechter, 'The New Historicism and its Discontents: Politicizing Renaissance Drama', *PMLA* 102:3 (May, 1987), p. 301.

2 'The new historicists and cultural materialists', one typical summary puts it, 'represent, and by representing, reproduce in their *new* history of ideas, a world which is hierarchical, authoritarian, hegemonic, unsubvertable. . . . In this world picture, Stephen Greenblatt has poignantly asserted, there can be no subversion – and certainly not for *us*!' (C. T. Neely, 'Constructing the Subject: Feminist

Practice and the New Renaissance Discourses', *English Literary Renaissance*, 18 (1988), p. 10) Poignantly or otherwise, I asserted no such thing; I argued that the spectator of the history plays was continually tantalized by a resistance simultaneously powerful and deferred.

3 See my *Renaissance Self-Fashioning: from More to Shakespeare* (Chicago: University of Chicago Press, 1980), pp. 174–5: 'We are situated at the close of the cultural movement initiated in the Renaissance; the places in which our social and psychological world seems to be cracking apart are those structural joints visible when it was first constructed.'

4 Louis Adrian Montrose, 'Renaissance Literary Studies and the Subject of History', in *English Literary Renaissance*, 16 (1986), pp. 5–12; Don Wayne, 'Power, Politics, and the Shakespearean Text: Recent Criticism in England and the United States', in *Shakespeare Reproduced: The Text in History and Ideology*, ed. Jean E. Howard and Marion F. O'Connor (New York and London: Methuen, 1987), pp. 47–67; Catherine Gallagher, 'Marxism and the New Historicism', in *The New Historicism*, ed. Harold Veeser (New York and London: Methuen, forthcoming).

5 Jean E. Howard, 'The New Historicism in Renaissance Studies', in *Renaissance Historicism: Selections from 'English Literary Renaissance'*, ed. Arthur F. Kinney and Dan S. Collins (Amherst: University of Massachusetts Press, 1987), pp. 32–3.

6 Cohen, 'Political Criticism of Shakespeare', pp. 33–4.

7 Thomas Greene, *The Vulnerable Text: Essays on Renaissance Literature* (New York: Columbia University Press, 1986), p. 100.

8 Quoted in Linda A. Altshuler and Anna R. Cohn, 'The Precious Legacy', in David Altshuler (ed.), *The Precious Legacy: Judaic Treasures from the Czechoslovak State Collections* (New York: Summit Books, 1983), p. 24. My sketch of the genesis of the State Jewish Museum is largely paraphrased from this chapter.

9 Ibid, p. 36.

10 In effect that dream of possessing wonder is at once aroused and evacuated in commerce as well, since the minute the object – shoe or dress or soup tureen – is removed from its magical pool of light, it loses its wonder and returns to the status of an ordinary purchase.

11 Joinville, *Life of Saint Louis*, in *Chronicles of the Crusades*, trans. M. R. B. Shaw (Harmondsworth: Penguin, 1963), p. 315.

12 Quoted in J. V. Cunningham, *Woe or Wonder: The Emotional Effect of Shakespearean Tragedy* (Denver: Alan Swallow, 1960; orig. edn 1951), p. 82.

13 B. Hathaway, *Marvels and Commonplaces: Renaissance Literary Criticism* (New York: Random House, 1968), pp. 66–9. Hathaway's account of Patrizi is taken largely from Bernard Weinberg, *A History of Literary Criticism in the Italian Renaissance*, 2 vols (Chicago: University of Chicago Press, 1961).

14 It is a mistake then to associate the gaze of the museum-goer with the appropriative male gaze about which so much has been written recently. But then I think that the discourse of the appropriative male gaze is itself in need of considerable qualification.

15 Quoted in Hugh Honour, *The New Golden Land: European Images of America from the Discoveries to the Present Time* (New York: Pantheon Books, 1975), p. 28.

16 Quoted in Cunningham, *Woe or Wonder*, pp. 77–8.

ROBERT WEIMANN

Text, Author-Function and Society: Towards a Sociology of Representation and Appropriation in Modern Narrative

The first question that an historical approach to our subject seems to call for is, how can historical activities be viewed as constitutive of the uses of representation, including the uses of representational language? As this formulation may suggest, the answer should neither fall back on idealist methodologies of closure and homogeneity nor, for that matter, accept the antirepresentational dogma of the autonomy of the signifier. This is not to say that I think anyone today can afford to ignore or take lightly the postmodern revulsion from representation. I am not in the first place thinking of the critique of the concept as associated with a certain school of *Ideologiekritik* according to which 'representation' has come to be identified with an oppressive regime of social domination, some *Herrschaftseffekt* (as in the language of the German new Left a few years ago) or that, along similar lines, it is taken to provide an apology for a world packaged, as it were, for the convenience of the consumer, known and agreed upon in advance.

Actually, the poststructuralist critique of representation goes much deeper than this and is part of the post-Nietzschean revolt against the anthropocentric and logocentric standards of classical and modern humanism. In particular, the objection is against that logocentric and referential approach to signification, according to which the relationship between signifier and signified is conceived as representational rather than conventional or arbitrary in the sense that the lexical and semantic units of language respectively obey their own always already given differential. To ignore this differential and deferment (in the sense of Jacques Derrida's *différance*) and to compensate for the nonexistent order of the *Logos* by vicarious functions of *clôture* and plenitude is, so the argument goes, to indulge in the illusion of presence as re-presented in language. Hence, representationalism threatens to suppress or obliterate the discontinuity of textual production, naturalizes the sign, homogenizes narrative space and so voids it of contradiction, ranks its codes in a stabilizing hierarchy rather than permitting them to interrogate and contradict one another.

Although these charges must be taken very seriously indeed, when viewed from a historicizing perspective on 'representation' they appear to raise more questions than they can answer. The same holds true for Michel Foucault's brilliant archaeology of the rise and decline of representation, *Les Mots et les choses*, which contains some unforeseen element of paradox, some unsuspected inversion of teleology by which the narrative of the undoubted crisis of representation is turned into a privileged code which maps out a cyclic movement (not to say progress) of the scientific consciousness toward the *liberation* of language from its representational functions. Since Foucault's impressive scheme quite ignores what Stephen Greenblatt has called 'the cunning of representation: the resiliency, brilliance, and resourcefulness' of its strategies, are we not justified in assuming that we still need a good deal of knowledge and thought about the actual modes and functions of representation in literary history, especially after it was first uncritically taken for granted for so long and then so quickly proscribed almost out of existence?

In order to go beyond the deconstructionist position, it is of course impossible to fall back on any of the classical or romantic versions of representation. Although I do not intend to argue on an epistemological level, my position is that as against both the classical and the poststructuralist position an understanding of representational activity as radically historical is impossible on the presuppositions of either the hegemony of the subject or that of language itself. Michel Foucault's view of the ultimate hegemony of discourse leaves almost as much representational practice out of account as does the traditionally mimetic approach which, in the work of Erich Auerbach or Georg Lukács, continues to be associated with classical concepts of mimesis, continuity and the subject. Even more important, both these quite different approaches may be said to appear monistic in that the gaps and links between what is representing and what is represented are viewed dogmatically, *either* in terms of rupture and discontinuity *or* in terms of closure and continuity. But as I shall proceed to glance at some representational strategies in the modern period (I must confine myself to some late nineteenth- and early twentieth-century texts) it becomes obvious that it is precisely in these gaps and links, and in the way in which, simultaneously, the gaps are closed and the links are broken up, that historical activity can be seen to assert itself.

To situate historical activity within the (dis)integrating process and the (non)unified products of representation itself is to assume an open concept of history as a constellation of discursive as well as nondiscursive activities, a shifting conglomerate of social energies and conflicting interests which are taken to assert themselves within and without the text. To correlate the historiography within the text to the social history without the text is, at the crossroads of performance and function, to acknowledge the politics of representation as nothing external. Rather, the existential dimension (as involved in the legitimation or subversion of power, the appropriation of the means of subsistence, communication, and knowledge) so implicates language that the functions of signification and the effects of socialization constantly interact.

Hence, to talk about the sociology of literary representation is, first and foremost, to propose to historicize representational activity at that crucial point where its social and linguistic dimensions intersect.[1] The troublesome incongruity between these two dimensions need not be minimized, but it can be grappled with as soon as the presuppositions of either the hegemony of the subject or that of language itself are questioned. In this view, the position of Georg Lukács (like that of the more traditional sociologist of literary referentiality) tends to overlook the state of extreme vulnerability and recurrent jeopardy in which representation has always found itself, just as Michel Foucault's diametrically opposed view of the ultimate hegemony of discourse obliterates or displaces a lot of unbroken contemporary representational practice.

If, anywhere, the contradiction of system and event, predetermination and performance can be seen to affect representational activity, and if this contradiction can at all be formulated in terms of a sociological *Erkenntnisinteresse*, the issue of historicity must be discussed on more than one level: not only on the level of what is represented (which would reduce this project to some genealogy of the signified) but also on the level of who and what is representing. The point is to view these levels (the rupture between them as well as their interdependence) together and to attempt to interconnect the semiotic problematic of signification and the extra-textual dimension of representativity, as involving shifting relations of writing, reading, social reproduction and political power. In this view, the use of signs, although never quite reducible to a referential function, must be reconsidered and the question needs to be asked: under which conditions and in which respects would it be possible to talk of social history in that area of instability itself which marks the relations between signifier and signified, between the author's language and the reader's meaning?

Uses of Appropriation

This, of course, is a highly provisional and oversimplified chart of the theoretical question which has to be raised, but even so may perhaps suffice to introduce a concept of 'appropriation' (or expropriation) as denoting some social and temporal kind of activity which precedes the problematic of both the subject and the sign. As against both the classical-romantic view of the text as the purely referential activity of some 'reflecting' subject and the (seemingly opposite) view of the text as some autonomous locus of self-determining differentials or epistemes, the concept of appropriation may, I submit, help us to focus on the shifting constellations of the contradiction itself between whatever extralinguistic activity and whatever intralinguistic difference engage in the process of representation. Although, ultimately, the contradiction between discourse and production, linguistics and sociology, may turn out to be quite irreducible, the links even more than the gaps between them have not been sufficiently explored.

Thus, although the study of discourses as juridical '*objects* of appropriation'[2] is of the greatest importance, it must be complemented by their study as *Subjekte* of appropriation, that is, as historical agencies of knowledge, pleasure, energy and power. In other words, the question of appropriation must be studied not only in relation to the exchange value of an author's works, that is, their property status, but also and at the same time in terms of the use value of his *work*; that is, with reference to the changing functions and effects of his literary production as an appropriating agency. In terms of the functions of representation, then, appropriation would have to be defined at the intersection of both text-appropriating and world-appropriating activities, in the sense that the concept will, over and beyond its economic and juridical dimensions, encompass non-economical and non-juridical activities. These activities will be conceived in terms of *Aneignung*, of making things (relations, books, texts, writings) one's own. Hence it seems possible to say that both the world in the book and the book in the world are *appropriated* through acts of intellectual acquisition and imaginative assimilation on the levels of writing as well as reading. In this connection, the German term *Aneignung* has the advantage of not necessarily involving an ideologically preconceived idea of (private) ownership or (physical) property; instead, it allows for acquisitive behaviour as well as for nonacquisitive acts of intellectual energy and assimilation. Since, therefore, the term is not limited by juridical ideas of private property, the sense of 'making things one's own' can and, in fact, must be used *literally*, not as a metaphor of some juridical action or condition associated with a certain type of (bourgeois) society.

'Appropriation' so defined would provide us with a concept denoting an activity which, even while it can precede ideology and signification, is not closed to the forces of social struggle and political power or to the acts of the historical consciousness of the signifying subject. Linking the world of prehistory with that of historical activities, Marx was the first to define 'appropriation' in relation to *Arbeit* (work, labour). Defining *Aneignung* as a function of work, Marx related the varying modes of appropriation not only to the changing conditions of production and ownership but also to changing patterns of relationship between the individual and his/her community.[3] On a theoretical foundation such as this, appropriation may involve events and structures of homogeneity as well as heterogeneity, in the sense that the relationship between the appropriator and his property is not a fixed or invariable one but, historically, may allow for varying degrees of identification as well as distance, alienation and reification. The process of making certain things one's own becomes inseparable from making other things (and persons) alien, so that the act of appropriation must be seen always already to involve not only self-projection and assimilation but alienation through expropriation.

Author-function and Appropriation: The Epic and Beyond

To emphasize the potential contradiction between the process and the product of appropriation seems especially important as soon as we return to the task of historicizing the variegated uses of representation. In our context, the shifting nature of the space for (non)identity between what is representing and what is represented emerges perhaps most clearly when we compare representation in modern fiction with, say, that in the heroic and courtly epic up to and including Chrétien de Troyes, Hartmann von Aue, Wolfram von Eschenbach, Gottfried von Straßburg and even late, borderline cases like Sir Thomas Malory. In precapitalist societies the distance between the poet's act of appropriating a given text or theme and his own intellectual product and property is much smaller: the extent to which his *matière* is given, the extent to which 'sources', genre, plot-patterns, *topoi*, etc. are preordained is much greater. What is more, the poet's production never attains to a state of personal property or ownership. The amount of assimilating activity, the capacities for self-projection or alienation between the act and the product of representation remain limited. As long as the appropriator relates to the means and modes of his production as largely communal, as some unquestioned given, shared property, there is very little that *he can make his own*. Hence, the epic poet tended to take previously inscribed authority for granted: He affirmed the validity of the work of his predecessors more readily; he accepted as part of his own work the labour (as it were) already invested in the invention of a great story with widely known events and characters. But in doing just that, he subscribed to a literary mode of production that was in many ways correlated to a socially dominant mode of appropriation in which, as Marx notes, 'the chief objective condition of labour does not itself appear as a *product* of labour, but is already there'.[4] The discontinuity between the act and object of appropriation and its effects and functions is not all that considerable; the act of intellectual assimilation constitutes itself on the basis of the givenness of what is to be assimilated. The author's function is to assert known and publicly acknowledged ideas; it is not to appropriate any area of thought or experience that has not previously been appropriated in feudal society itself.[5]

Thus, the changing context of appropriation can be seen to affect or even help constitute shifting modes and functions of representation: In the absence of deeper divisions between the appropriator and his properties the functions of representation remained limited. In pre-modern narrative there was little need for that romantic and realistic mode of representation, where a deliberate act of self-projection came to interact with the intellectual assimilation of the world, and where the universality of the latter helped to intensify the particular expression of individuality in the former. In other words, the self-projecting uses of representation remained limited as long as appropriation was characterized not by dynamic contradictions between individual activities and given objects and relationships but by 'the *repro-duction* of *presupposed* relations'. As long as the appropriator related to his objects as, in the words of Marx, some 'inorganic part of his own subjectivi-ty',[6] the uses of representation were restricted.

But at the beginning of the modern period, the process of discursive *Aneignung* in representational form assumes a more highly dynamic and unpredictable quality; being less predetermined by the given state of communal property, the givenness of cultural materials, literary conventions and traditions, the act of representation emerges under conditions where the writer is faced with the growing need for himself to appropriate the means and forms of literary production itself; he has to make them his own, precisely because he confronts the conditions and means of literary production and reception as something alien, as produced by others, as something which he cannot unquestionably consider as part of the existence of his own social and self-fashioned intellectual self. Hence, the *representative* quality of his writing, the function of representativity itself becomes fraught with a burden. As the writer's and reader's distance from the means and modes of production (including the production of literary texts) grows, there develops new scope for his own individual point of view, for his own choice of productive strategies *vis-à-vis* the increasing availability of those means, modes, and materials which, self-consciously and self-fashioningly he can make his own.

Thus, ever since the Renaissance, the dimension of representativity in discursive utterances can no longer be taken for granted. The representative function of discursive action enters a state of vulnerability and unpredict-ability which, paradoxically, makes representation – in politics just as in literature – problematic as well as necessary. As Stephen Greenblatt notes, 'most great representational art in our culture seems to be generated' out of 'a healing of some loss or undoing'.[7] What, more than anything else, representational art presupposes and what it thrives on is indeed the loss, the undoing of the plenitude of that property in which the self and the social are mutually engaged and in which their engagement is unquestioningly given and taken for granted.

Flaubert and the Crisis in Discursive Appropriation

Since the modern dialectic of representation and appropriation cannot adequately be discussed on a purely theoretical plane, let me at this point introduce two or three narrative texts in which the modern aims and functions of representational discourse have – out of their fullness – entered that state of crisis which makes them particularly illuminating. Although unfinished at the time of the author's death, Gustave Flaubert's *Bouvard et*

Pécuchet deserves our special attention, because in it a new and highly critical function of representation appears to be closely associated with a radically negative version of the theme of appropriation itself. In fact, it may without exaggeration be said that this narrative comes close to being a *Zurücknahme*, a revulsion from those classical fictions like *Robinson Crusoe* and *Faust*, where the link between appropriation and representativity was particularly strong, where the hero (Robinson Crusoe or Faust), through and in the image of the act of appropriating the world, achieves a high status of representativity, where he becomes in fact the representative of a class or even of humanity precisely because of the way he copes with and conquers the forces of nature.

As against such representativeness on the levels of both social function and iconic signification, the new departures in Flaubert's narrative can best be characterized by saying that the traditional links between the representational quality of the signified and the social representativity of the signifying activity become tenuous to the degree that the writer's own mode of literary production tends to be isolated or to turn away from the material productions and the social mode of economic appropriation in bourgeois society. On the surface, Flaubert's narrative appears to recapitulate the whole sweep and variety of the parable of appropriation, but to an altogether different effect. Bouvard and Pécuchet, two Parisian copy-clerks, resolve to retire to a village in Normandy, in order to dedicate the rest of their lives to successive explorations into those areas of nature, experience and knowledge from which their previous bourgeois existence had effectively debarred them. But for them the challenge of appropriation results in a course of action marked by radical failure, with the effect not of representativity but social isolation. As the two bachelors diligently attempt to make their little world their own, as they set out to appropriate the arts of gardening, agriculture, viticulture, chemistry, medicine, geology, archaeology, literature, and even criticism, they neither extend the frontiers of knowledge and experience nor, even, confirm and reauthorize any previously appropriated body of knowledge and control over nature. Despite all their dedicated efforts Bouvard and Pécuchet permanently and increasingly 'enlarge the distance between what they are studying at any given moment and their ability to cope with the problems of daily life'.[8] As they read and read a vast literature of appropriation, as they proceed from authority to authority, the narrative widens the gulf between the signs of their reading and the symbols of their experience, between the acquired language of their theoretical knowledge and its actual meaning in iconic terms of subsequent actions and images.

There emerges an ever-widening dichotomy between what the words and figures of their reading are representing and what, in the course of following these learned significations, is actually achieved and represented in the narrative of their reception and application. What finally signifies is the narrative of how, in the act of its reception, the inscribed intellectual authority enters a state of crisis. What results is some loss in the applicability of authority, some decline in its validity, the defeat of its representativity. As the two bachelors begin to dabble in the arts of writing and reading, they come up against the 'aplomb', the 'entêtement', even the 'improbité' in the critical columns of their day; they are bewildered by 'les âneries de ceux qui passent pour savants et la bêtise des autres que l'on proclame spirituels'. Facing a deep crisis in authority, they themselves discuss the predicament of literary criticism in terms of the loss of its own representativity:

> C'est peut-être au public qu'il faut s'en rapporter.
> Mais des oeuvres applaudies parfois leur déplaisaient, et dans les sifflées, quelque chose leur agréait.
> Ainsi, l'opinion des gens de goût est trompeuse et le jugement de la foule inconcevable.[9]

> Perhaps one should consult the opinion of the public.
> But there were times when they disliked works which had won critical acclaim, and times when they found charm in works which were notoriously inferior.
> Thus the opinion of people of taste is unreliable and the judgement of the masses is impossible to take seriously.

Torn between the crumbling authority of intellectual experts and the unimaginable legitimacy of 'le jugement de la foule', Bouvard and Pécuchet themselves rehearse a crisis in authorizing some representative response and judgement. Their own failure and defeat is so startling, because they start out much like the traditional type of appropriating hero in fiction, but rather than assimilating the world that surrounds them so as to represent it – in Hegel's terms – 'as some outer reality'[10] of their own striving selves, they utterly fail in their attempt at both world-appropriating and text-appropriating action. Finally, at the end, when they have completely isolated themselves from their community (and this was Flaubert's own, unfinished design) the two inseparable friends end up as copyists at a double-sided desk. *Aneignung* has become an impossible task: to appropriate, to make one's own the world of nature and society, yields nothing but defeat and, finally, despair. Having despaired of appropriating, using, enjoying the knowledge and the ways of their world they content themselves with copying, i.e. rewriting, not the signified of their own experience, but the mere signifiers from the books which they so miserably failed to receive and translate into some meaning of their own.

Representations of Self and Society in Henry James

The early decline, in France, of discursive representativity provides a particularly revealing perspective on the more optimistic and, or so it seemed, democratic links between the American writer and his society. At a time when Baudelaire, Verlaine, Mallarmé and Rimbaud already exemplified some deep gulf between the verbal representations and the social representativity of the poet, the American writer was prepared, tragically as with Melville or comically as with Mark Twain, to shoulder the burden of representation on the levels of both textual signification and social function. In the transcendentalist tradition, the poet's version of his own representativity receives its most sustained affirmation in the writings of Ralph Waldo Emerson, who in one of his most influential essays declares the poet to be 'representative man'. Coming at the end of a European (largely German) romantic tradition of homogeneity and closure in the relation of text, history and subject, Emerson says: 'the poet is representative. He stands among partial men for the complete man, and apprises us not of his wealth, but of the common wealth.'[11] Characteristically, for Emerson, the poet's is 'the largest power to receive and to impart', he 'reattaches things to nature and the whole', and thus can 'raise to a divine use the railroad, the insurance office, the joint-stock company; our law, our primary assemblies, our commerce, the galvanic battery, the electric jar, the prism, and the chemist's retort; in which we seek now only an economic use'.[12] This reads as a positive representation of that world of economics, politics, nature and science which Flaubert had already surrendered as a space for appropriation in his more sceptical narrative. But in Emerson the poetic appropriation of the world is one in which the appropriator is still believed to be close to some universal and, hence, representative human property, which, in Emerson's definition, is 'the common wealth'. And since this 'common wealth' unites the representations of the poet with the appropriations of 'hunters, farmers, grooms, and butchers'[13] (not to mention the men of politics and business), the social impulse of the representer and the historical interests of the represented appear to be continuous rather than discontinuous, unified rather than heterogeneous. In other words, the authority of what is representing informs, and is informed by, the authority and legitimacy of what is represented: The verbal appropriations of the poet and the material appropriations of 'farmers, grooms, and butchers', chemists, joint-stock companies, and politicians are made to appear so close and mutually so self-supporting that they ultimately sustain a large space of homogeneity between them.

If this American picture of hope and illusion appears to project the very opposite of Flaubert's burden of representation it may appear ironic that one of the greatest of Emersonian disciples, Henry James, in setting out to revise the social connections of his own narrative, gradually but irresistibly arrives at a position which, after all, is not so far removed from Flaubert's. Since I have space only to choose from one of the great Jamesian themes, the most relevant in this context appears to be the one in which the writing represents the crisis of its own representativity. As in the work of Thomas Mann, the erosion of representativity itself is *represented* in its most immediate individual and psychological form: in the fiction and the figure of the artist himself, in his loss of social integration and bourgeois respectability, in the diminishing range of his own participation in the moral and political consensus. The crisis of representativity is turned into a theme, into a novelistic representation itself, and its most consistently mimetic form is, of course, the biographical *Darstellung* of characters, such as Tonio Kröger, Gustav Aschenbach and Adrian Leverkühn in Thomas Mann, or Neil Paraday (in 'The Death of the Lion'), Paul Overt ('The Lesson of the Master'), Ray Limbert ('The Next Time'), and of course Nick Dormer (*The Tragic Muse*) in Henry James.

In these fictional representations, the artist, far from being representative man, either renounces the claims of middle-class life or is already an outsider, standing (in the sense of Thomas Mann) in a queer, aloof relationship to the rest of humanity, out of harmony with at least some of the most broadly received middle-class values and attitudes. Although on the surface, in the reduced scope and mimetic form of novelistic subject-matter, the gulf between what represents and what is represented appears at least in part to be bridged once more, the underlying tensions in the identifications of self and society, the contradiction between self-projection and appropriation have vastly increased. This becomes obvious as soon as the Emersonian conception of the poet as the 'sayer' and 'namer' of the 'common wealth', as 'the only teller' of the news of the world is critically, not to say sarcastically, redefined in relation to such public forms of activity as, for instance, a career in journalism and politics involve.

As in Henry James's *The Tragic Muse*, the new perspective on the diminishing social representativity of art is exemplified in the antagonism between the status of the artist and the role of the politician – which conflict leads to a defiant emphasis on the independence, the self-respect and the uniqueness, if not the autonomy, of the function of art in society. The Emersonian concept of art as the most intensely representative vessel of life gives way to a sense of its autonomous or redeeming function, which resides precisely in its freedom from representativity. As Stephen Donadio has suggested in *Nietzsche, James and the Artistic Will*, this fiction shares 'the impulse to achieve a self-definition independent of one's own national or class origins, the impulse to be free of the limitations imposed by a particular time'.[14]

Such independence characterizes Nick Dormer, the central figure in *The Tragic Muse*, a promising politician, who begins to conceive of his future career as liberal Member of Parliament as 'talking a lot of rot' which 'has nothing to do with the truth or the search for it; nothing to do with intelligence, or candour, or honour'.[15] Authority, in other words (and Flaubert would have agreed), is not to be found in the public sphere of power and politics; henceforth, whatever common ground there was between the representation of politics and the politics of representation becomes tenuous and dissolves. So Nick Dormer the artist parts with his politically influential fiancée; he rejects 'the old false measure of success' and chooses to become a painter so as to be able to enjoy 'the beauty of having been disinterested and independent; of having taken the world in the free, brave, personal way'.[16]

The longing for a disinterested kind of independence, the preference for 'the free, brave, personal way' must be read as symptomatic, not only of the changing position of the artist in bourgeois society but of the new foundations on which James sets out to redefine the function and the art of representation. In that he comes close to the Nietzschean position (as formulated by Thomas Mann) 'that life can be justified only as an aesthetic phenomenon'.[17] If, up to a point, marked perhaps by the Joycean figure of Stephen Dedalus, the erosion of representativity is rendered in traditionally representational forms of novelistic mimesis, the reason is not of course simply that of their undoubted resiliency. There is, at the very moment of his social alienation, the artist's attempt (as Michael Fried has shown in the work of Courbet)[18] more resolutely than ever before to efface the distance between creator and art object and, in the teeth of its deepening contradiction, once more to fuse representation with what it represents. In this sense, these late endeavours in the traditional forms of realism do attempt that 'healing of some loss or undoing' on which some of the greatest representational activities seemed to have thrived.

However, if it is the gap, the lack of identity between what appropriates and what is appropriated which, in the first place, made representation necessary, this gap, once it is turned into an abyss, begins to affect and put strains upon representational form itself. The most immediate modernist link between the deepening crisis in representativity and the nascent erosion in representational form can be traced on the level of the writer's communication with his public. When, in *The Bostonians*, James satirically recoiled from the vulgar forms of commercialized publishing and when this major novel, just as *The Tragic Muse*, was ill-received and spitefully or, at best, indifferently reviewed, the author after the publication and unsuccessful reception of *The Bostonians* and *The Tragic Muse* began to experiment in and modify the traditional narrative conventions of representational form. The results are too well known for me to specify them here, but what needs to be emphasized is that there is a connection between the represented artist's option for 'the free, brave, personal way' and James's own redefinition of the representational strategy of the novel as a 'direct, personal impression of life'. The 'direct' and 'personal' quality of novelistic writing (just like the impressionism in contemporary painting) now serves as a distinguishing mark of the braveness with which the artist breaks away from that ideological authority which, in the form of a social and aesthetic consensus, had hitherto informed the standards of his representation. The 'brave, personal way' helps secure a new freedom from representativity; the very directness of the novel's impression guarantees the related freedom by which the signifying activity of the representer constitutes itself in relative independence of the given signified in the represented.

Thus, the loss in the artist's representativity is both redeemed and compensated for in terms of narrative technique; the emerging forms of narrative immediacy, the repudiation of omniscience, the stylized modes of point of view can all, in one important respect, be understood as a formally acknowledged relief from the traditional burden of authorial representativity. It is the 'direct, personal impression', the seemingly authentic flow of individual consciousness, the slice of life itself, which helps the author to leap over the crippling effects in the more homogeneous forms of representational closure, the ideological burden of determinacy in the public uses of language. This is what James in *The Tragic Muse*, coming now very close to Flaubert's *sottisier*, calls the 'ignorance', the 'density', 'the love of hollow, idiotic words, of shutting the eyes tight and making a noise'.[19]

Modernism and the New Economy of the Signifier

While the later fiction of Henry James reveals the precariousness of the links between the traditional forms of representation and the eroding relations of representativity, the elements of crisis reach their full force only in the flowering of modernist strategies of narrative. Although it is of course quite impossible here to project the full modernist problematic of narrative representation, let me at least suggest some of the gaps and moments of transition between the Jamesian and the post-Jamesian situation and explore the impact of diminishing appropriation on the rupture between what represents and what is represented (and representable). First, let me glance at Van Wyck Brooks' *America's Coming of Age* (written in 1913–14) where, shortly before the outbreak of the First World War, the language of the dominant culture is revealingly taken to task. What Brooks, in the following passage, articulates is the complaint that the public language of politics is both unrepresentable and unrepresentative and that 'ideals of this kind, in this way presented . . . cannot enrich life, since they are wanting in all the elements of personal contact.' Brooks notes the depth of the gulf, in language, between what represents personal consciousness and what is represented in public ideology:

> The recognized divisions of opinion, the recognized issues, the recognized causes in American society are extinct. And although Patriotism, Democracy, the Future, Liberty are still the undefined, unexamined, unapplied catchwords over which the generality of our public men dilate, enlarge themselves, and float (careful thought and intellectual contact still remaining on the level of engineering, finance, advertising, and trade) – while this remains true, every one feels that the issues represented by them are no longer genuine or adequate.[20]

The failure, then, in these signifying concepts of politics and morality was that 'the issue represented by them' had ceased to communicate any intellectual authority: The traditional signified had exhausted its capacity for legitimation, and the representational function of these signs was gravely impaired. What emerges from the writings of Brooks and those radical intellectuals who disowned the progressivism of the politicians is that the crisis in the representational function of language was primarily related to the erosion of a certain type of social, cultural and philosophical authority. Whatever stability had remained in the relation between what was representing and what was represented, in the light of this failed authority a good many public significations now appeared as 'undefined, unexamined, unapplied'. While in Van Wyck Brooks' view this crisis was diagnosed as mainly a rupture 'between university ethics and business ethics',[21] the latter still seemed to retain an element of representability: language on the 'level of engineering, finance, advertising, and trade' continued to appear intact and was not viewed as subjugated to that crisis in appropriation to which the public language of culture and politics had succumbed.

In early twentieth-century fictional discourse, the inroads into the traditional social function of representation can most conspicuously be traced where, during or shortly after the First World War, the erosion of authority led to a new political economy of signification, best known to us in Hemingway's writing. As an illustration let us look at a well-known passage in *A Farewell to Arms* which is revealing and perhaps unique because, paradoxically, what it represents is a crisis of representativity in the novelist's language itself. The first person singular is of course Frederick Henry's:

> I was always embarrassed by the words sacred, glorious, and sacrifice and the expression in vain. We had heard them, sometimes standing in the rain almost out of earshot, so that only the shouted words came through, and had read them, on proclamations that were slapped up by billposters over other proclamations, now for a long time, and I had seen nothing sacred, and the things that were glorious had no glory and the sacrifices were like the stockyards at Chicago if nothing was done with the meat except to bury it. There were many words that you could not stand to hear and finally only the names of places had dignity. Certain numbers were the same way and certain dates and these with the names of the places were all you could say and have them mean anything. Abstract words such as glory, honour, courage, or hallow were obscene beside the concrete names of villages, the numbers of roads, the names of rivers, the numbers of regiments and the dates.[22]

Hemingway's character is embarrassed by the collapse of any representational function on the part of some of his signifiers. But the embarrassment serves more than characterization; it transcends its fictional emitter, the first person singular instance, the 'I' as an iconic sign and narrative point of view, so as to embrace the discursive practice of this passage as some strategic economy of writing itself. The crisis in representation remains attached to the characterizing icon of the first person singular and yet goes beyond it; in other words, this crisis is both represented and representing at the same time. Since the problem is articulated so self-consciously, on the level of both iconic sign and narrative activity, representational product and representational process, this text can be read on at least two levels.

First, although my interests here do not point this way, it can be read in terms of the iconic constraints of the fictional product of representation which, most immediately, are revealed in the language of the Hemingway hero, his muteness, his modernist inability to assert himself anywhere except in the bar-room, the bedroom, the arena and on safari.[23] Secondly, the crisis in representation can be studied on the level of discourse, in terms of constraints and possibilities that this new rhetoric as some ideological and aesthetic economy of articulation implicates. On this level, our text reveals some extraordinarily articulate reluctance to authorize, let alone to appropriate the dominant language of politics. There is some stark discontinuity between the given spectrum of public significations and the actually usable, much more limited range of the novelist's signifier. When the use of this signifier appears conditioned by its increasingly tenuous relation to any 'abstract words', i.e. to any generalized mode of public signification, the consequences are of course more complex than a naively referential understanding of fictional discourse can ascertain.

This must be emphasized even when, as in other fictions of this period, the mimetically structured narrative of individual experience, especially in the love story, persists virtually unchallenged. As opposed to the as yet unbroken representational forms of this fictional figuration, the representational action on the level of discursive practice is so much more deeply affected. But there remains an uneasy connection between *histoire* and *discours* when this text goes out of its way to transcribe the dilemma of representational·discourse in terms of a soldier's image of a legitimation crisis as a spatial metaphor of the distance from, and the loss of authority in, the official language of war politics. What we have is a spatial icon of physical aloofness distancing the language of propaganda through the rain and the sheer distance (from those who stood there and were told to listen). In this image, just as in that of 'proclamations . . . slapped up . . . over other proclamations', the imperfectly achieved or redundantly handled process of communication serves as a metaphor of the inefficacy of the authority transported therein. When Frederick Henry heard these words, 'sometimes standing in the rain almost out of earshot, so that only the shouted words came through', the transcendental signified is, as it were, acoustically undermined, any claim of representativity is refuted, precisely because, in Van Wyck Brooks' phrase, 'ideals of this kind, in this way presented . . . are wanting in all the elements of personal contact'.

In Hemingway's text, intellectual contact and, of course, appropriation remained viable, if not 'on the level of . . . finance, advertising, and trade', at least perhaps on that of 'engineering, geography, and statistics'. In *A Farewell to Arms*, 'only the names of places' had 'dignity', and the irony in the use of a concept like 'dignity' must not detract from the fact that place names did retain some representational function and authority, so that 'dignity' here, presumably, was associated with a simple, unbroken sense of continuity between signifier and signified. Hence, it was 'the concrete names of villages, the numbers of roads, the names of rivers, the numbers of regiments and the dates' which allowed for what Van Wyck Brooks called 'careful thought and intellectual contact', and which did not sound 'obscene' as against the real obscenity in taking for granted continuity in the representational function of transcendental signifieds with so heavy an ideological liability.

Notes

1 For some theoretical presuppositions, see my critique of poststructuralist concepts of 'representation' in the 'Epilogue, 1984' to the expanded edition of *Structure and Society in Literary History* (Baltimore: Johns Hopkins University Press, 1984), pp. 267–323. At the same time, the present essay substantially draws on some of the historical materials and texts as first used in a contribution to a colloquium held at the University of California, Irvine (1984), published in *The Aims of Representation: History – Subject – Text*, ed. Murray Krieger (New York: Columbia University Press, 1987).

2 Michel Foucault, 'What is an Author?', *Textual Strategies: Perspectives in Post-Structuralist Criticism*, ed. Josué V. Harari (London: Methuen, 1980), p. 157.

3 See Karl Marx, *Grundrisse: Foundations of the Critique of Political Economy*, trans. Martin Nicolaus (New York: 1973), pp. 485ff.

4 Ibid., p. 485.

5 I have developed the problematic of appropriation in late medieval and Renaissance prose narrative in the first two chapters of *Realismus in der Renaissance, Aneignung der Welt in der erzählenden Prosa*, ed. Robert Weimann (Berlin and Weimar: Aufbau-Verlag, 1977), pp. 47–182. For an English summary and expansion of this approach see my article '"Appropriation" and Modern History in Renaissance Prose Narrative', *New Literary History*, 14 (Spring, 1983), pp. 459–96.

6. Marx, *Grundrisse*, p. 487.

7 Preface to *Allegory and Representation*. Selected Papers from the English Institute, ed. Stephen Greenblatt (Baltimore and London: Johns Hopkins University Press, 1981), p. ix.

8 Gustave Flaubert, *Bouvard and Pécuchet*, trans. with Introduction by A. J. Krailsheimer (Harmondsworth: Penguin Modern Classics, 1978), p. 10.

9 Gustave Flaubert, *Bouvard et Pécuchet* (Paris: Garnier-Flammarion, 1966), p. 167.

10 G. W. F. Hegel, *Ästhetik*, ed. Friedrich Bassenge (Berlin Aufbau-Verlag, 1955), p. 75 (my translation).

11 *The Complete Essays and Other Writings by Ralph Waldo Emerson*, ed. Brooks Atkinson (New York, 1950), p. 320.

12 Ibid., pp. 321, 328, 314f.

13 Ibid, p. 326.

14 Stephen Donadio, *Nietzsche, James and the Artistic Will* (New York: Oxford University Press, 1978), p. 90. See, in this connection, the cogent re-interpretation of Jamesian formalism by John Carlos Rowe, *The Theoretical Dimensions of Henry James* (Madison, Wisc., 1984), pp. 225–37.

15 Henry James, *The Tragic Muse* (Harmondsworth: Penguin Modern Classics, 1978), pp. 74f.

16 Ibid., p. 725.

17 Donadio, *Nietzsche, James and the Artistic Will*, p. 61.

18 Michael Fried, 'Representing Representation: On the Central Group in Courbet's *Studio*', in *Allegory and Representation*, ed. Greenblatt, pp. 94–127.

19 James, *The Tragic Muse*, p. 75.
20 Van Wyck Brooks, *America's Coming of Age* (New York, 1924), pp. 23, 166f.
21 Ibid., p. 7.
22 Ernest Hemingway, *A Farewell to Arms* (London, 1977), p. 133.
23 See Stanley Cooperman, *World War I and the American Novel* (Baltimore and London: Johns Hopkins University Press, 1967), p. 185.

Part III

Part III

MICHAEL RIFFATERRE

Undecidability as Hermeneutic Constraint

One of the most striking developments in recent literary criticism, especially deconstructive criticism, has been the growing popularity of the concept of undecidability.[1]

It has always been a truism that literature is an oblique form of communication that both demands a conscious effort of interpretation and hampers it, delaying it, or allowing for more than one interpretation, or preventing readers from preferring one over another, or even excluding any stable reading, any definitive solution to the problems it raises. Critics have traditionally isolated and catalogued devices aimed at jeopardizing interpretation: e.g. *obscurity*, defined as a block to the identification of the object the sign refers to (a block especially conspicuous in the case of symbolism); *ambiguity*, the inability to decide among a finite number of alternative meanings having the same phonetic form;[2] *syllepses*, that force us to attribute more than one meaning at the same time to a given phonetic form, etc. But there is now a tendency to generalize from these phenomena, and to question the very validity of any interpretation, which is seen as a preconception, arbitrarily imposed on the text, not reflecting textual facts but inventing them (this is Stanley Fish's position: 'it is from the perspective of [the reader's] assumptions that the facts [of the text] are specified'[3]. From this viewpoint, the interpretation of each segment of the text is deemed to deconstruct the interpretation of the previous one.

It seems to me that this view is untenable for two reasons. First because its advocates all share, perhaps unconsciously, a yearning for a quasi-mystical view of literary phenomena, an assumption that the essence of art must elude analysis. Secondly, the same critics who assume that the text itself deconstructs the interpretations it elicits, thus generating a theoretically continuous and practically multiple series of readings shifting between textual aporia and metalinguistic contradictions, also seem unable to prove the mobility of self-erasing interpretations except by presupposing a relative immobility of the textual aporias that cause them. I will address only this second problem, it being the one that can be discussed objectively on the evidence of the texts themselves. Aporias are consistently identified with firmly localized passages, where the problems arise from the lexicon itself. Undecidable signs are assumed to be the same words or phrases as opposed to the changing connections or functions critics try to make them fit. The dynamics of undecidable literary reading are paradoxically derived from a static concept of the sign, based unquestioningly on the same segmentation of the verbal sequence that I suspect is valid only for lexicographers.

It seems to me, on the contrary, that the literariness of literary texts does not reside in the fact that they contain specifically literary signs which would remain so in any context (e.g. tropes; markers of irony, parody, etc.; markers indicating the genre to which the text belongs etc.). If such permanent signs existed, we could not explain why they can be observed in non-literary texts (in a sophisticated conversation, for instance, or a newspaper editorial) while failing to innoculate such texts with literariness. Rather, signs pointing to or generating a text's literariness should be seen as allowing for two different readings. Separately and successively, as the eye spots them along the written lines they express whatever meaning, and suggest whatever connotation(s) our linguistic competence tells us they ought to convey within the restrictions the context may impose on our decoding.[4] From another, retrospective, viewpoint, upon reaching the end of the text as we look back and make comparisons and perceive connections, we discover among these signs similarities or relationships independent of grammar or of their usual associations within the lexicon. With the benefit of hindsight, we are thus compelled to renounce the segmentation of the text that was sufficient for our initial reading, the segmentation dictated by usage and that accounts for those features common to non-literary and literary texts alike, namely linguistic features. A different segmentation imposes itself upon us, that permits the alternative reading which substitutes for the discrete, successive meanings, first perceived and now found insufficient, significances represented by new signs. These new signs have no existence outside the text we are reading or they are only valid for our new reading of it. Together, these significances, born of the new segmentation, generate the text's overall significance, the substance of its literariness.

The model I am proposing thus posits two readings for any literary text. One is minimal, tentative and exploratory: this is the linguistic reading. The other is a retrospective, totalizing, revisionary scanning of the verbal sequence: this is the literary reading.

Reading retrospectively is enough for us to identify the new literarily relevant signs. There is, however, another factor at work, one that makes this revision a radical erasure of our initial interpretation, and that confers on the new sign system the durability we expect of a work of art. This other factor also confers on our reading of the literary text the repeatability that characterizes any experience of art.

This factor always, in one way or another, takes the form of a difficulty we experience in the first reading. What is called undecidability is simply an extreme case of difficulty, as the very finality of the word 'undecidable' suggests. The corollary of this view is that literariness resides in a hurdle that cannot be cleared, an assumption I find hard to reconcile with any definition of significance.

I propose instead to see undecidability only as what sets the stage for a second reading, the literary reading proper, as the first step towards recovering significance where meaning has failed. It seems to me that undecidability derives this capability from the fact that the elements of the text it affects are undecidable only in terms of linguistic segmentation, only in terms of a mistaken decision on the reader's part as to what constitutes a relevant sign in the text. As the reader's focus changes through rereading, so does the segmentation, and the formerly irrelevant signs become operative, that is, capable of significance, once they are reassembled to form new *ad hoc* signs of which they become components at the expense of their own discrete meanings, and to whose structures they are now subordinate. I shall call these products of the literary segmentation, these superordinate semiotic compounds, *hypersigns*.[5]

In accordance with this model, undecidability is the outcome of the linguistic segmentation of the text, and the literary segmentation the outcome of reader response to undecidability. This response therefore accounts for the common empirical perception of literary communication as richer, more complex, more elusive and yet more demanding of our participation. The paradoxical combination of elusive significance and of compelling effect results from the shift from one sign system to another. That shift is not, however, a solution or an end to undecidability, but rather a new focus pointing towards what the text is really about. This new focus, the literary significance proper, controls and guides reader response, constituting indeed a hermeneutic constraint that clearly informs our decision as to the significance and its aesthetic (and eventually ethical) values. It is perhaps no exaggeration to venture that this constraint is more powerful than that exerted by decidable signs, since it paradoxically inverts factors, forcing the undecidable to represent decidability elsewhere, either in an intertext or at a level different from that of the text (at the level of genre, for instance, or tropology). Three types may be distinguished: in the first, the undecidable is left entire but instead of pointing to a solution destined to remain unattainable, it becomes a representation of undecidability, and it is as such, not as a content, that it produces literariness. In the second, undecidability becomes a periphrasis or an implication of decidability, the latter being located in an actual or potential intertext. In the third, undecidability transfers significance from the text to intertextuality itself, rather than to an intertext.

My example for the first type is a familiar instance of ambiguity which Umberto Eco dusted off and proposed again a few years ago: 'Charles makes love with his wife twice a week. So does John'.[6] There is no doubt that this is an undecidable utterance if this utterance is perceived through the successive decoding of its discrete components (several words, two sentences, the first one explicit, the second referring implicitly to the first), for the listener or reader cannot decide whether three or four people are involved (two couples, or one couple and an interloper). But such a success-ive, piecemeal perception can never occur, because the whole utterance is perceived only as belonging to a genre expressing an intention on the speaker/writer's part, as well as describing a situation. The genre is that of the joke (or the subgenre of the *risqué* joke), the intention a ribald or malicious one. It is made not only possible but necessary by the sociolect intertext: as Christine Brooke-Rose[7] has pointed out, no ambiguity would arise (in Eco's terms) and therefore (in my terms), no pseudo or represented ambiguity would be resorted to, if the utterance were 'Charles walks his dog twice a day. So does John.' There is no intertext at work in the case of the dog. In the case of a wife, on the other hand, the word *wife* has a seme *monogamy* or *availability to one person only* in a love-making context, whether the seme is actualized positively or negatively (as *adultery* or *promiscuity*). Representation leaves no doubt that the sentence is intended to suggest that Mrs Charles is having an affair. It is an unambiguous represen-tation of a jocular innuendo.

Even if there *was* hanky panky going on, we would still have an unambigu-ous representation of a make-believe ambiguity – one that does not leave any doubt as to the purpose of the sentence. This purpose is not just to hint but to activate the comical potential of a hint, what makes a hint a verbal game, in other words, its literariness. It does not matter whether the triangle hinted at is fact or fiction. The point or intention is to make light of its implications. To that end, a comical variant of the *marriage* descriptive system has been selected over an equally possible tragic version. Equally possible but not equally treated in literature, let alone in the sociolect. Ever since medieval *fabliaux*, the husband's cuckoldry or woman's supposed treachery have been favourite themes. This preference is so pervasive and constant, that the more stereotyped the mimesis of matrimony, the more expected and predictable the comicality. But it is like a humorous bias in the statement of facts, not a factual statement *per se*. For comicality in representation remains unaffected whether or not the statement is true or false. This comicality is therefore independent of reality, non-verbal context, or circumstances. It is a way of saying built on an indifferently hypothetical or verified *disambiguation* of an ambiguity. The ambiguity has been presented only to be eliminated along the line of irony or of the pessimistic, malevolent conventional wisdom of the sociolect – part and parcel of a cynical stereotype of woman in its various but always comical versions (the shrew, the liar, the hot spot, etc.).

As a sentence the verbal sequence is referential and undecidable. As a text, it is self-sufficient and univocal.[8] And what gives the text its status as a unit of significance is the presence of the sociolect, of the intertext the relevance of which is activated by an essential seme of the sememe *wife*.

In the second type of undecidability as hermeneutic constraint, the ambiguous text is generated by a repetition of a verbal expansion on an undecidable given or matrix. Every iterating sign points to an implicit statement which it refers to while repressing or displacing it into the intertext. In fact, these insistent ambiguities presuppose the intertext. In that respect, they are synonymous with one another and thus tautological. Recovery of the presupposed item is therefore unavoidable and provides readers with a disambiguated equivalent of what the text has been stating ambiguously. The text unfolds as a paradigm of indeterminacies while the intertext this paradigm presupposes neither progresses nor changes. The intertext remains unmodified, serving as an explanatory counterpart to each component of the paradigm, and containing the key to our interpretation of all of them. The intertext thus is the deciding version that ends the repeated ambiguities of the text. It therefore makes sense to suggest as I did above that the undecidable text stands as a periphrasis for the decidable intertext.

Consider the conflicting trends in the interpretation of 'The Tyger'. For some critics, Blake's wild beast is an unambiguous symbol of pure evil and its creator cannot be God. Their opponents agree on the ferocity of the carnivore but they claim he is one of God's creatures none the less.[9] Still others have asserted that he is both good and evil. A commentator goes so far as to venture that the poem itself is the tiger and that it is Blake, or Blake's persona who smiles upon it. At the other end of the critical spectrum, the claim is made that the questions asked in the poem are not meant to be answered.[10]

The multiplicity of mutually contradictory interpretations would seem to establish undecidability. Moreover it looks as if formal undecidability is compounded with one of content, since most readers would recognize in the former a vivid mimesis, or hypotyposis, of man pondering a metaphysical and ethical mystery: what reasons may there be for the presence of evil in the universe and the part it plays in the scheme of things?

To be sure, some aspects of the poem can be readily decided, even though undecidability seems at first to affect these aspects as well. Whether or not we can identify the maker of the tiger, for instance, there is no doubt as to his function and as to the nature of the successive representations referring to him:

The Tyger

Tyger! Tyger! burning bright
In the forests of the night
What immortal hand or eye
Could frame thy fearful symmetry?

In what distant deeps or skies   5
Burnt the fire of thine eyes?
On what wings dare he aspire?
What the hand dare seize the fire?

And what shoulder, & what art,
Could twist the sinews of thy heart?   10
And when thy heart began to beat,
What dread hand? & what dread feet?

What the hammer? what the chain?
In what furnace was thy brain?
What the anvil? what dread grasp   15
Dare its deadly terrors clasp?

When the stars threw down their spears,
And water'd heaven with their tears,
Did he smile his work to see?
Did he who made the Lamb make thee?   20

Tyger! Tyger! burning bright
In the forests of the night,
What immortal hand or eye
Dare frame thy fearful symmetry?

We can safely put names on the references: Daedalus (line 7), Prometheus (line 8), Hephaestos or Tubalcain (lines 13–16). We may also safely assert that these are not the principals themselves, but metaphors. Each metaphor serves to complete the composite portrait of an inventor extraordinaire. Each is exemplary, maximal or hyperbolizing, and consecrated by the authority of a tradition.

Even though these mythological intertexts might someday vanish with the culture which generated them or with the canons of that culture, no ambiguity or indeterminacy would result from their disappearance. It would not, because the achievements of the mythical characters are narrative stereotypes anyway, exemplifying boldness in enterprise (ascension and playing with fire for the first two), or expertise and miraculous skills in the execution (from 'shoulder' and 'art', line 9, to 'dread grasp', line 15). The mythical heroes are but conventional embodiments of these narratives, translating them into personifying codes. The narratives endure even after their actualizations become obsolete. Indeed they are still active today, and keep producing variants, with science fiction substituting for mythology (e.g. modern inventors in Jules Verne and H. G. Wells, Mary Shelley's Dr Frankenstein, Thomas A. Edison fictionalized in Villiers de l'Isle-Adam's *Eve future*, etc.).

In any case, no single character could embody the talents of the maker of the Tyger unless he were a supernatural being. And that therefore is the first answer to the repeated queries. From one stanza to the next, the mythological metaphors add up to a periphrasis, the grammar of which is a sememe best represented by the word *demiurge*. The periphrasis constitutes a repetitive paradigm in which each tautological slot is filled out with a myth (either metaphorically when the smith himself is alluded to, or metonymically when his tools are mentioned instead of him). This paradigm is thus a hypersign that stands for: *who?* The hypersign is framed so that the answer to this metaphysical whodunnit can only be God or the Fiend.

Which of the two remains to be decided, and here again undecidability seems to interpose a screen. If we are to judge the smith by his work, is the tiger bad unconditionally, or bad and yet a thing of beauty? And can the Providence personated by the smith be good and produce the good *and* the bad? Logic would require that we asked the reverse question as well: can an *evil* Providence create the bad *and* the good? Literature, however, must arouse interest, thus privileging those contents and forms that have aesthetic and emotive potency. Literary indeterminacy cannot therefore have the range of logical indeterminacy, since the former tends to ignore undecidables evident at the cognitive level, but negligible or indifferent in their affective or aesthetic connotations. Thus either because mythologies are designed to assuage anxiety (the Devil is always short-changed, easily led, often a dupe etc.), or because the lamb is obvious and boring, no one ever wonders whether the Enemy could have wrought that antithesis of the tiger. Within these limits, however, another semanalysis, quite like the one we perform on *demiurge*, will solve this second riddle.

The fact that some critics fail to solve it should not cast doubts on my argument. They fail only when they stick to the wrong segmentation. A twin opposition defines Blake's beast: 'fearful symmetry', the oxymoron of the awful and the awesome, and the tiger versus lamb polarity. Critics insist on privileging one pole over the other, thus dissolving the oxymoron. They seize upon the word 'forest', because it sticks out in the context of 'night', and must therefore be reconcilable with that context only if it is figurative. One critic argues that 'forest' puts the stamp of evil on the tiger because Blake only uses that word in contexts referring to the 'fallen world'. Another retorts that 'forest' suggests tall straight tree trunks, and an analogue to the 'orderliness of the tiger's stripes, hence a tiger whose destructiveness is transfigured'.[11] But focusing on 'forest' combines the empirical but questionable belief that words are always natural meaningful units, and the critics' tendency to misuse anything conspicuous in context to shore up their interpretations of the whole text. There is in fact nothing in 'forest' that might be relevant to undecidability because the word is simply a component of the descriptive system of 'tiger', as 'lair' would be for a boar and 'eyrie' for an eagle. 'Forest' is derived from 'tiger', and so is its symbolism if any: bad if the big cat is also mean, good if he is a natural wonder. Here the word does not even seem to be a fully fledged marker, but simply a transform of an analogical conjunction, as if 'like' had been translated into 'tiger' code. If the tiger is the Tyger, that is if the fearsome beast is represented as a beautiful object through the metaphor of a constellation called the Tyger, then its modality of existence as an asterism is to burn as a light in the night. The actual carnivorous quadruped's life pattern is to surprise one in the midst of a forest. Analogically, then, the night is to the Tyger what the forest is to a tiger, and the metaphor makes the analogy-actualizing comparison by conflating the corresponding terms into one sentence. Instead of the 'like' or 'as' of a simile, the equation between tenor and vehicle of the metaphor is posited by the sentence weaving its thread from the jungle to the night, from the literal to the figurative.

In contradistinction to these irrelevancies, the pertinent segmentation is obviously the one delineated by the series of questions, both in terms of their form, and of what they aim at or imply. The answers are provided by our linguistic competence, and by an intertext so basic that knowing it pertains to linguistic competence as well.[12] The interrogative sequence is coterminal with the poem. Furthermore this parallelism is not allowed to pass for a mere coincidence since the first and last stanzas repeat each other save for one word ('dare', line 24, instead of 'could', line 4). Not only does this one word differentiate the clausula from the incipit, but it does so significantly with a last reference to the maker's distinctive wishfulness and high purpose. We could not dream of a more perfect adequation of form and content.

The undecidability of these questions, lacking as they do explicit answers, hovers between two possible definitions: either they admit of only one answer, so obvious it need not be expressed or they admit of none. If the former is true, they are rhetorical questions, in which case undecidability is but a momentary hurdle, hardly more than an emphasis on the question mark, the function of which is to elicit readers' participation. Undecidability is but an exercise we have to perform, a variant of suspense. Indeed they *are* rhetorical questions, as readers are compelled to recognize for three reasons, all three converging towards the same effect: generic, semanalytic and intertextual.

Generic: there exists a minor genre in which the teaching of basic truths and of articles of faith is carried out either through apodictic assertions or through rhetorical questions. This subgenre is the catechism, as taught in most religious communities. In Sunday school, the open-endedness of questions about metaphysical problems and principles is only a device to emphasize that there is only one proper answer, self-evident and unavoidable. In a system which tolerates neither doubt nor discussion, catechumens are asked who created creatures and made the wonders of the universe, studding it with mysteries to meditate on, and catechumens have no choice but to answer 'God'. The tenor of our poem's questions, all about evil, make it clear that they belong to that genre.

Semanalytic: the function of semanalysis is to indicate the obviousness of the reply to the rhetorical question. Since the subject matter is Creation, its engineer must be the Creator. Add to this that the essential seme of the sememe *creation* is *universality* since it inheres in the very concept of God that there cannot be anything before or outside of Him or that would not be born of his will. Evil cannot be excepted, and this is of course made explicit in line 20. One of the usual forms of the literary mimesis of *everything*, one that avoids the need for a catalogue that could not begin to list the components of any form of being, consists in representing *everything* with abbreviated paradigms. Instead of attempting to exhaust the possible components of a paradigm, literary description suggests the whole by opposing the lowest and highest rung of the paradigm. The animal world is thus represented by a phrase like 'from the mite to the elephant', the moral world by opposing extreme instances of good and evil, of meekness and pride, by opposing, as line 20 does, the lamb and the tiger. Any mutual complementarity that is polarized becomes a transform of *creation*, and the question about creation entails only one God.

Intertextual: a third component confirms and further controls reader response here, the very intertext that catechism brings to mind, Biblical authority. Line 19 makes the necessary connection: it is impossible for us to read 'Did he smile his work to see?' without bringing to memory the terms of God's self-satisfaction with his first week of work. Seven times, after making light, the seas, animals, etc., the Lord looked back and seven times the verse ends on 'and God saw that it was good'.[13] It is true that many intertexts' recovery may depend on the reader's luck, but not with this one, so central to our culture. Assuming that it might nevertheless go the way of other intertexts, the first two factors I listed would suffice to dictate the proper answer. But in fact, up to our day and age, the three factors have functioned together. Each of them having the same interpretant as the others, they combine to form one hypersign that happens to be indistinguishable from the poem as a whole. The poem's verbal sequence is no longer seen as a chain of sentences but as a single manifestation of textuality.

Undecidability of a third type leads readers to find a solution in intertextuality. Intertextuality is a reference to one or more text(s), the intertext, without which the text under our eyes could not make sense beyond what is allowed by its barest linguistic segmentation. For the same reason that reference must be distinguished from the referents it involves, intertextuality as a function must be differentiated from the intertexts that it affects. The reason for this is that, as we read a text, especially one made difficult by indeterminacy, the intertext with which we connect it is, because of that difficulty, now like an object to the text's hypersign. The relation is the same as that maintained between any linguistic sign and its object. Such a relation, however, cannot remain dyadic: C. S. Peirce has shown that it necessarily involves a third element, the interpretant, namely the idea(s) that the dyadic relation gives rise to. In the same way, intertextuality as a function assumes the role of the interpretant, and it accordingly can play a role in controlling or informing interpretation that neither the text nor the intertext could. In the case of the third type, intertextuality proffers a frame or model for looking at both text and intertext as two versions to be seen in their differences, rather than in their complementarity.

I chose my example, the last of Wordsworth's so-called *Lucy Poems*, because the many commentaries that have sprouted around it fall neatly into two irreconcilable tendencies, into two main reading trends that are polarized to the point of being mutually exclusive, so much so, in fact, that 'A Slumber did my spirit seal' is now a well-worn example for serious discussions of hermeneutics:[14]

> A slumber did my spirit seal,
> I had no human fears:
> She seemed a thing that could not feel
> The touch of earthly years.

No motion has she now, no force;
She neither hears nor sees,
Rolled round in earth's diurnal course
With rocks and stones and trees!

The disagreement separates those who believe that the two stanzas are hopelessly pessimistic, an elegy unremittingly sombre, from those who read the story of the young woman's untimely death as an uplifting optimistic tale of pantheistic fusion of the beloved with Nature. Cleanth Brooks nicely represents the first trend:

> [The poet] attempts to suggest something of the lover's agonized shock at the loved one's present lack of motion – of his response to her utter and horrid inertness. . . . Part of the effect, of course, resides in the fact that a dead lifelessness is suggested more sharply by an object's being whirled about by something else than by an image of the object in repose. . . [She] is caught up helplessly into the empty whirl of the earth which measures and makes time. She is touched and held by earthly time in its most powerful and horrible image.[15]

The opposite trend contradicts the above to such an extent that it almost sounds like a parody. This is by F. W. Bateson:

> The final impression the poet leaves is not of two contrasting moods, but of a single mood mounting to a climax in the pantheistic magnificence of the last two lines. . . . Lucy is actually more alive now that she is dead, because she is now part of the life of Nature, and not just a human 'thing.'

As before, the pertinent segmentation may once more settle the question by eliminating the wrong reading, and we would have one more instance of undecidability that remains confined to a corpus of critical metatexts. Such a segmentation clearly seems dictated by a transformation that occurs between the first and the second quatrains and coincides with the sudden narrative shift 'now'. This transformation textualizes a single word, positing as it does a semiotic equivalence that makes the second stanza a four-line periphrasis, and therefore a hyperbolic variant of 'thing' (line 3). The new attributes of Lucy (motionlessness, powerlessness, senselessness, mineral and vegetable inertness) spell out the semes of that sememe. We cannot escape the grim irony of fate (then she seemed a thing that life's wear and tear could not touch, now she is a lifeless thing indeed) thanks to this equivalence, which obtains only in this context, between a given (thing as metaphor) and its narrative consequences (the thing has turned literal), from trope and delusion (she seemed like) to literalness and stark truth (she is).

　　The poem therefore is utterly pessimistic and elegiac, although this reading does not exclude fusion with Nature, which Wordsworth critics of the historicist persuasion insist on calling pantheism, and which they assume to correspond to a positive and necessarily optimistic stance. This interpretation could make the presumed undecidability a temporary one, of the second type, one to which the shift from a linguistic to a paradigmatic segmentation puts an end.

There is however another undecidability at work in the poem, one that is built on the most remarkable word in its eight lines, a word that differs from all the others because of its technicality, its ostensible Latinate form in the midst of a lexicon that is just as ostensibly English, and also because of its phonetic difference (it is the only word with a hiatus in it): that adjective is 'diurnal'. Proof of its singular power is this explosion of divergent glosses collected by Norman E. Holland, who adds his own in conclusion:

> Hugh Kenner calls it an 'abstract, technical term,' and F. R. Leavis says the word has a 'scientific nakedness' but also 'evokes the vast inexorable regularity of the planetary motions.' By contrast, Cleanth Brooks finds in it a 'violent but imposed motion,' a 'whirl.' F. W. Bateson calls it a 'solemn Latinism' which contrasts with the other, simpler words, to set off 'the invulnerable Ariel-like creature' against her present 'lifeless and immobile' state. Elizabeth Drew finds this 'one long formal word in the poem' not lifeless at all, but contributing to 'a majestic affirmation.' Robin Skelton finds in it a fear that, if the poet unites his soul with nature, he will be turned daily like the earth, selfless and unthinking. Skelton also finds a 'subconscious effect of the syllable "di," which to the ear suggests that a word having reference to division, to the dichotomy of the world, is about to be spoken.' To whose ear? And yet, I hasten to admit, I hear in 'diurnal' the word 'urn' as saying another way the whole earth has been made Lucy's funeral vessel.[16]

The residual substance left after we clear out these interpretations, after we retain of them only the evidence of the word's potency, is twofold. First, 'diurnal' most powerfully expresses a transfer of motion from Lucy to the earth (with an implicit transition from the earth under which she is buried, and where she is an inert thing among others, to the planet Earth rolling round). Secondly, 'diurnal' translates this notion from the discourse of human time to that of cosmic time.

The first stage is but an instance of the most common intertextual mechanism: a given textual component derives from the intertext powers it could not acquire simply from usage or from its own context. The intertext the word is activating refers to or describes the opposite of that word, proposing images or symbols whose authority and weight the word now has to buck in order to make sense: thus motionlessness is here described in terms of the motion it cancels and displaces somewhere else. Wordsworth often resorts to such images of immobility in *motion* code, as in his reminiscences about ice-skating in 'The Prelude'; the skater stops making circles (lines 458–60):

> yet still the solitary cliffs
> Wheeled by me, even as if the earth had rolled
> With visible motion her diurnal round;

But of course the pertinent intertext here is Shakespeare, because Claudio's anguished fear of death in *Measure for Measure* (III, i, 114) so closely resembles our narrator's, save for Claudio's focusing on his dear self, and our speaker on his dear other:

> Ay, but to die, and go we know not where
> To lie in cold obstruction and to rot;
> This sensible warm motion to become
> A kneaded clod; . . .   (11. 116–17)

> To be imprison'd in the viewless winds,
> And blown with restless violence round about
> The pendant world!   (11. 122–4)

As for the second stage, it is a shift from 'diurnal', referring to the earth's rotation, to 'diurnal' meaning 'daily' with astronomical connotations. Lucy's existence is no longer measured in life's years, but in days – in the time of the planet. There is however another intertext pertinent to our text, the poem 'Three years she grew', which Wordsworth repeatedly printed side by side with 'A Slumber did my spirit seal' in the successive publications of his work, while at the same time separating this pair from the other texts we moderns arbitrarily place under the rubric of the Lucy poems (the others were relegated to the so-called *Poems Founded on the Affections*):

> Three years she grew in sun and shower,
> The Nature said, 'A lovelier flower
>   On earth was never sown;
> This Child to myself I will take,
> She shall be mine, and I will make   5
>   A Lady of my own.
>
> 'Myself will to my darling be
> Both law and impulse, and with me
>   The girl, in rock and plain,
> In earth and heaven, in glade and bower,   10
> Shall feel an overseeing power
>   To kindle or restrain.
>
> 'She shall be sportive as the fawn
> That wild with glee across the lawn
>   Or up the mountain springs;   15
> And hers shall be the breathing balm,
> And hers the silence and the calm
>   Of mute insensate things.

'The floating clouds their state shall lend
To her; for her the willow bend;   20
   Nor shall she fail to see
Even on the motions of the storm
Grace that shall mould the maiden's form
   By silent sympathy.

'The stars of midnight shall be dear   25
To her; and she shall lean her ear
   In many a secret place
Where rivulets dance their wayward round,
And beauty born of murmuring sound
   Shall pass into her face.   30

'And vital feelings of delight
Shall rear her form to stately height,
   Her virgin bosom swell,
Such thoughts to Lucy I will give
While she and I together live
   Here in this happy dell.'   30

Thus Nature spake – The work was done –
How soon my Lucy's race was run!
   She died, and left to me
This heath, this calm, and quiet scene,   40
The memory of what has been,
   And never more will be.

The two texts do complement each other: the story they tell is the same.
Lines 1 to 5 of 'Three years she grew' correspond to our first stanza, and the last stanza of this long poem is the benign equivalent of 'now' in 'A Slumber'. The absorption of the maiden into nature is more gradual (lines 7 to 30), but especially explicit in lines 29 to 30, 7 to 11, and lines 17 to 18 where 'mute insensate things' are but another wording for our 'rocks, and stones, and trees'. Above all, the longer poem clearly expresses the same transfer of motion we have been discussing: 'Myself will to my darling be/Both law and impulse' (cf. lines 13 to 15 and 19 to 24). Furthermore, even though Nature speaks the language of love, even though her intent seems good, and this idyllic optimism indeed makes the piece a triumph of what Wordsworthians call pantheism (animism might be better), it must be obvious that nature's embrace is as deadly, at least in human terms, from the viewpoint of the lover, in 'Three years' as it is in 'A Slumber'. The last stanza of 'Three years' conveys the same bereavement as in 'A Slumber'. But 'Three years' is long and allegorical and it personifies Nature and disguises through metaphors and similes the dissolution of the maiden into Nature's shapes, while our poem is literal, and altogether plain vernacular.

It would be too simple to say that the pantheistic piece disambiguates 'A slumber' into a clearer message. Rather, the two poems are parallel versions expressing the same train of thought in two different styles.

Undoubtedly, their being side by side may nail down an interpretation readers already privilege, enabling them to confirm what appeared only probable (obviously if the pantheistic piece leads to the speaker's pessimistic conclusion, the octet will be pessimistic *a fortiori*).

But the procedure that makes content probable – what comes close to disambiguating the ambiguous – is a simultaneous, half-actual/half-mnemonic reading of two versions of the same story. The procedure is a comparative game, an exercise as we speak of piano exercises. The recovery of decidability therefore does not take place in the intertext, but in the interpretant common to the two sign systems, to the two hypersigns, textual and intertextual, a model that remains abstract and potential, halfway between two actualizations that separately would be undecidable (or one of which would be undecidable).

Consequently, disambiguation takes two steps. First, comparison enables readers to spot those elements that are not affected by differences (here, the elegiac invariant). Secondly, comparison thus enforced becomes the literary event. Similarly, an art collection may contain various versions of the same picture displayed next to each other, in which the artist may have attempted to repeat the same message in different moods. Museum visitors' artistic experience in such a situation is not derived from enjoying separately each version of the picture, but from the back and forth viewing pattern they must follow, and from the composite image that now forms itself in their minds and that exists nowhere else. Intratextual segmentation is no longer operative here: because texts are the basic units, nothing can take place, and no message be conveyed, within one text, since a sequence of texts or at least a pair is necessary for them to be units, and no unit can be perceived as such without the paradigm of which it is a basic constituent. Literariness then is not experienced in the textual units themselves, but in a new awareness, triggered by undecidability within these units when read separately – the awareness that there exists a paradigm comprised of them. As a frame or pattern, the paradigm must be read as a variation on a message. Undecidability is not eliminated, but replaced as the locus of literariness by the paradigmatic pattern, and its constant semiotic features – the interpretant. The pleasure of the text is now the pleasure of variations played on a paradigm of texts, here the pleasure of comparing elegy in the bucolic mode and elegy in its funereal mode, or again the pleasure of comparing a positive and a negative treatment of the same theme. Variation is thus a paradoxical instance of a model or template that we have to abstract from its variants in order to read them as literary. I cannot think of anything else in literature demanding that reading procedure, except of course literary genres which are likewise perceived in the light of an imagined model. Undecidability of this type thus achieves the extremest conceit or verbal artifice, since whatsoever indeterminacy it represents is marshalled to target with utmost precision a model that in itself must remain invisible.

If we now cast a final global glance at the three types, undecidability would seem indeed to control, limit and guide interpretation. It puts constraints on it, instead of causing it to fail. It does so because undecidability in the text is not undecidability itself but a sign that stands for it, a representation of undecidability. Its perception yields decidability, because the object of that sign is elsewhere, in a different way of segmenting that leads to a perception of a model for reading (the genre or the whole text in the first type, a trope and a sememic matrix in the second, a paradigm in the third). In each sense, undecidability is temporary, a kind of initiatory step, but one that must be repeated with each rereading, and one that cannot be taken unconsciously. Undecidability therefore makes for the kind of active and even strenuous, but disciplined commitment that, more than anything else, characterizes literary response to perceived literariness.

Notes

1   See Jonathan Culler, *On Deconstruction* (Ithaca, NY: Cornell University Press, 1982); Paul de Man, *The Rhetoric of Romanticism* (New York: Columbia University Press, 1984), and *Resistance to Theory*, (Minneapolis: University of Minnesota Press, 1986). Also M. Riffaterre, 'Interpretation and Descriptive Poetry', *New Literary History*, 4 (1973), pp. 229–56; 'Interpretation and Undecidability, *New Literary History*, 12 (1980–1), pp. 227–42; and 'Prosopopeia', *Yale French Studies*, 69 (1985), pp. 107–23.

2   This is Max Black's felicitous definition of ambiguity, in *Language and Philosophy. Studies in Method* (Ithaca, NY: Cornell University Press, 1949), p. 42, n.33).

3   Stanley Fish, *Is There a Text in This Class? The Authority of Interpretive Communities* (Cambridge, Mass.: Harvard University Press, 1980), p. 340.

4   At any rate the restrictions dictated by the context *preceding* each such sign.

5   *Segmentation* refers to an operation performed by linguists and critics alike, and also, more or less intuitively, by ordinary readers. It consists in discovering what the minimal signs are that convey meaning in the verbal sequence. Prefixes, for instance, may or may not be separable from the words they modify (*disgust* is an elementary sign, *discharge* contains two) at the linguistic level, but they may be treated as elementary signs in a tautological series at the literary level, when their repetition causes them to be perceived as a multiple hypersign with its own significance. I define the *hypersign* as a sign valid only within a text (such as the incipit-clausula, or the prolepsis-analepsis, rhyme pairs, etc.). The hypersign cannot be accounted for by linguistics since it is not a word, phrase or sentence, nor can it be understood as a sentence component, nor described by the methods of sentence analysis as a predication. It is a compound sign the pertinent components of which must be at least two, and such that our understanding of the first is modified by the second. The second certainly can be said to be made more significant by a recollection of the first, but this yields only one reading. The first, however, has now two readings and only

the second reading is literary, having to do with the one feature that distinguishes literary texts from others, i.e. its unity. See M. Riffaterre, 'Hypersigns', *The American Journal of Semiotics*, 5 (1987), pp. 1–12.

6 U. Eco, *The Role of the Reader. Explorations in the Semiotics of Texts* (Indiana University Press, 1979, pp. 24–5).

7 Quoted by Eco, *Role*, pp. 41–2, n.12.

8 Most texts are of course comprised of more than one sentence. In the case of a one-sentence text (i.e. a maxim, an aphorism, an epitaph, a monostich, a proverb), the same verbal stretch can be read as a mere sentence, but once it is recognized as a member of a class, i.e. of a genre, it is perceived as a text.

9 For a convenient overview of the hermeneutic polarization that plagues the interpreters of Blake's "Tyger", see Fish, *Is There a Text*, pp. 259–63 and especially pp. 339–42.

10 Also that we cannot even know who is asking the questions. These latter attempts seem to me wholly irrelevant. They are motivated not by the texts but by the clear polarity of the hermeneutic metatexts. This polarity alone has fuelled the craving for an alternative: a third, intermediate option, or else a refusal of all options. The implicit model for such attempts in this case appears to be the reasoning that produced non-Euclidean geometries by positing that more than one parallel can be drawn from a point outside a straight line, or no line at all. But the complete, exhaustive testing-out of all logical choices that is possible where you start from postulates presupposing a *tabula rasa*, such a testing-out is inevitably a logical perversion, or failure of common sense, where you are starting from the given of a text. The text is emphatically not a *tabula rasa*.

11 The first is Kathleen Raine, the second, E. D. Hirsch, quoted by Fish, *Is There a Text*, p. 339.

12 Linguistic competence refers, of course, to the instinctual or native ability of speakers to recognize the well-formedness (as linguists say) of an utterance they may hear for the first time ever. We should include in this concept the sociolect, a mnemonic familiarity with the themes, motifs and stereotypes that form the body of mythology shared by all speakers of a language at a given time in a given social class (or even by all classes, at the level of national consciousness), and representing their conventions and their consensus about reality.

13 *Genesis* 1:4, 10, 12, 18, 21, 25 and 30, the seventh day being upgraded to *very good*.

14 At least since E. D. Hirsch elevated the debate from a mere discussion on a poem to the theoretical level, *Validity in Interpretation* (New Haven: Yale University Press, 1967), pp. 227–30, 239–41).

15 Quoted by Hirsch as well as the Bateson piece, *Validity*, p. 228.

16 Norman N. Holland, 'Literary Interpretation and Three Phases of Psychoanalysis', in Alan Roland (ed.), *Psychoanalysis, Creativity and Literature* (New York: Columbia University Press, 1978), p. 238.

ANN JEFFERSON

Literariness, Dominance and Violence in Formalist Aesthetics

A recent spoof on modern critical theory has presented it as a kind of hagiography in which the major theorists appear not as the secular thinkers we take them for but as saints engaged in a holy crusade.[1] This comic parallel draws attention by negative implication to one rather striking difference between these latter-day holy men and their Christian forebears: namely that the moderns are saints without lives. The lives of literary theorists normally figure only in the meagre forms of the occasional date of birth alongside the ISBN of the books which they author, or the condensed *curriculum vitae* that appears on the dust cover. In this the theorists – and of course their publishers – are merely complying with the conventions of the academic institution in which lives necessarily take the generic form of the *curriculum vitae*, which functions as a token in trade for the strictly earthly rewards of promotion, professional advancement and financial reward.

In a somewhat less cynical perspective, though, this biographical reticence is also in line with the fundamental anti-biographism of most twentieth-century theory. Indeed, whatever the other differences that divide theorists, and whatever their underlying principles, the attack on biography in literature has been the issue on which theory has been most consistently and resolutely united. The formalists were the first but some of the most vehement in their opposition to biography and Osip Brik was voicing a characteristic formalist hostility to the notion of biographically based authorship when he wrote, 'Had Pushkin not existed *Evgeny Onegin* would all the same have been written. America would have been discovered even without Columbus.' This highly provocative claim merely makes explicit the formalist view that as far as literature is concerned '*there are no poets or literary figures, there is poetry and literature.*'[2]

There is therefore an element of heresy in using biography as a basis for re-evaluating some aspects of formalist theory as I intend to do in this essay. But I believe that I might nevertheless have had the blessing of my main biographical victim, Roman Jakobson. On the one hand Jakobson's own treatment of his life in the *Dialogues* with Krystyna Pomorska is austerely and single-mindedly restricted to the intellectual sphere.[3] Thus, of his childhood we learn that his passion for metrics first manifested itself when he was a nine-year old school boy; and the Second World War impinges on his life only as the reason why the Fifth International Congress of Linguists had to postpone the meeting at which Jakobson was to have delivered a paper on the phonic laws of child language in Brussels in September 1939 (p. 36). However, on the other hand, when he comes to comment on the principle of anti-biographism in his own work, Jakobson acknowledges the necessity of recognizing some overspill between life and literature in the cases of writers such as Mayakovsky and Pushkin because, he explains, there are instances where one can detect an 'internal relation between life and creativity' (p. 144). It is with just such an 'internal relation' that I shall be concerned here.

Or rather, in the case of Jakobson I shall be dealing in the first instance more with the apparent *absence* of any such link than with the disovery of such a structural similarity. My excursion into Jakobson's life will be brief, and it is not my wish to intrude upon his privacy nor to glamorize his intellectual achievements by providing a biographical narrative for them. The bare outline of Jakobson's career will be enough to make the point.[4] He was born in Russia in 1896 and died in the USA in 1982. He studied at the Lazarev Institute of Oriental Languages and graduated in 1918 from Moscow University – in other words, his student days coincided with the First World War and the Russian Revolution. He was a founder member of the Moscow Linguistic Circle, but in 1920 he left the Soviet Union to settle in Czechoslovakia where he was active and influential in the Prague Linguistic Circle, and from where he had to flee when the Nazis arrived in 1939. He spent some time working with linguists in Scandinavia before moving to the United States, and for the last 30 or more years of his life he taught at Columbia, Harvard and MIT – a far cry from the Soviet Union in which the formalism to which he made such a significant contribution, flourished and perished in the 1920s. This brief biographical sketch is chiefly intended to hint at two of the themes which have prompted the approach I am adopting in this essay: first, Jakobson's life spanned a marked cultural and linguistic diversity; and second, it coincided with and was affected by enormous political changes and considerable political violence (the Russian Revolution, the Nazi invasion of Czechoslovakia, not to mention the fact of two world wars as mere historical background).

The significance of these themes is made all the more prominent by the broad structural similarities and contrasts between the life of Jakobson and that of his near-contemporary Mikhail Bakhtin, whose influence on modern literary theory has been of similar importance to Jakobson's but whose life shows up as a kind of inverse image of Jakobson's. (There, but for the grace of God . . .) Bakhtin's is one of the few lives of the theorist-saints to have been written and the biography by Katerina Clark and Michael Holquist provides a thorough and amply documented account.[5] Bakhtin was born a year before Jakobson in 1895 and died in 1975, seven years before Jakobson's death. After a provincial childhood, Bakhtin studied at the University of what became Petrograd and graduated (in classics) in 1918, the same year Jakobson graduated in Moscow. Apart from the common experience of the war and the Revolution, both came under the cultural influences first of symbolism and then of futurism. Bakhtin never became a member of any formalist group, but his critique of formalist theory, written under the name of P. N. Medvedev (and perhaps also to some extent with him)[6] displays a thorough acquaintance with formalism; and his work appears sufficiently formalist in general character and approach to have caused Victor Erlich to regret his omission of Bakhtin from the original edition of his *Russian Formalism*.[7] Bakhtin was arrested for his religious activities in 1929 and released into exile (rather than being imprisoned) on account of his bad health. The main part of his working life was spent teaching in obscure provincial colleges of higher education until his belated recognition enabled him to move to Moscow in the late 1960s.

Bakhtin's life is both a parallel and, as I have said, an inverse image of Jakobson's, in which the similar intellectual development of their respective youths gives way to a contrast between the provincialism and obscurity of Bakhtin's maturity and the international fame and recognition of Jakobson's.[8] This structural comparison is not just a gratuitous aestheticizing of lived experience, but is designed to emphasize the contrast in intellectual preoccupation between the two, for it is Bakhtin who theorizes the cultural diversity and the political and social conflicts which Jakobson's life seems to illustrate so much more dramatically than his own. And the comparison has provoked me to go back to formalist theory, not with the intention of revealing strict historical and genetic connections between events and ideas, but in search of the sort of structural similarities that Jakobson found so illuminating in Mayakovsky.

In doing so I hope to be doing formalist thinking, and Jakobson in particular, the service of making them readable again – in however limited a way. As things stand at the moment Jakobson has the status of a respected but largely irrelevant figure in contemporary literary theory. He continues to feature on reading lists, but mainly as a kind of intellectual teething-ring the purpose of which is to equip students with the necessary analytic edge for their encounters with more solid and theoretically nutritious stuff. The 'Linguistics and Poetics' article is regularly if cursorily plundered by students and their teachers for the six-function model and its attendant terminology, because it's useful to have terms like 'phatic' or 'conative' to hand whatever you might be up to, and because the model itself has great pedagogical value in introducing students to twentieth-century ideas about language. Similarly the 'Two Types of Aphasia' essay remains a current reference (though I suspect that it is rarely read) since it contains the by now classic distinction between metaphor and metonymy which has gone on to find further theoretical fortune in more closely studied theorists, most notably Jacques Lacan.[9] Terms like 'shifter' and 'dominant' which Jakobson helped to give currency to are vaguely associated with his name but tend to conjure up a world which is rapidly being lost to present-day literary theory. The

bulk of Jakobson's voluminous output has long since been handed back to
the experts in linguistics and stylistics who are left to make of them what
they will. In short, Jakobson's moment seems to have passed. No-one even
does him the courtesy of disagreeing with him any longer, and even the
critiques outlined in the 1970s by Jonathan Culler and Mary Louise Pratt
are themselves gradually passing into history.[10]

In re-reading formalism in the light of the themes suggested by Jakobson's
life and Bakhtin's thought, I shall be looking at the connotations and
metaphors associated with the overt theoretical content rather than at the
prima facie content itself. Peter Steiner has already paved the way for such
an approach in his *Metapoetics* which proposes a reading of formalism
through a set of characteristic metaphors. However, his concerns are *meta*-
theoretical rather than what – for want of a better word to describe what I
shall be doing – I shall call merely quizzical.[11] Although I shall try to avoid
the usual rehearsal of the largely familiar and self-explanatory theoretical
ideas of formalist theory,[12] a certain amount of recapitulatory exposition
will be unavoidable. I shall begin with formalism proper with the aim of
drawing attention to the way in which the violence so obviously associated
with their lives and times also emerges as an aspect of their thinking, even
though that thinking was not explicitly intended to theorize violence.[13] I
shall go on to discuss Jakobson's work in its own right, still keeping an eye
out for these violent undercurrents. And finally, I shall conclude by comparing Jakobson's linguistic and literary theory which ignores the violence it
nevertheless implies, and which also focuses largely on poetry, with the
linguistic and literary theory of Bakhtin, whose preoccupation with conflict
is central and whose concerns are largely with the novel.

Formalism is and is not something of a misnomer. Boris Eikhenbaum,
one of the formalists' most articulate spokesmen, claimed that they weren't
formalists as such, but what he called *specifiers*. The big issue for the
formalists wasn't form *an sich* but 'literariness' – the specifics that distinguish
literature from any other material.[14] They wanted, as it were, to clean up
literary studies, and to establish them as an autonomous discipline with its
own methods and its own object. The study of literature was to become a
'literary science' that rejected the 'gratuitous mixing of [the] different scientific disciplines' which had previously characterized literary studies; history,
biography, psychology, philosophy, aesthetics, sociology, ethnology, and so
on had been drawn on in what the formalists evidently saw as a totally
indiscriminate and unprofessional way by literary critics.[15] Jakobson has a
rather striking metaphor for these practices which incidentally – but
tellingly – introduces the question of violence. Literary studies, says Jakobson, have behaved rather like the police who, when they go to make an
arrest will round up everybody who happens to be in the apartment and
even the odd passerby in the street.[16] Jakobson raises the issue of violence
but attributes it to practices that are about to be superseded. The cleaning
up proposed by formalism is presumably going to be rather different from
the random cleaning up practised by the police. However, the logic of the

metaphor does leave one wondering whether, even if innocent bystanders are not going to be subject to wrongful arrest, there will still be arrests, by the police and of at least one suspect. But this aspect of the question will have to be left on one side for the time being.

The procedural method of the new literary science of formalism consisted largely in adopting a negative or contrastive approach to the distinctiveness of literature. It was not a question of drawing up a list of the inherent characteristic features of literature (as Northrop Frye does, for example), but of defining literature on the basis of differential discriminations. Literature was constituted in opposition to everything with which it had hitherto been so *in*discriminately lumped: literature quite simply was everything that history, philosophy, ethnology, psychology and so on, were not. Thus the way was opened quite naturally to metaphors of incipient aggression, as Shklovsky's account of the differential principle of *defamiliarization* already begins to show:

> Art exists that one may recover the sensation of life; it exists to make one feel things, to make the stone *stony*. The purpose of art is to impart the sensation of things as they are perceived and not as they are known. The technique of art is to make objects 'unfamiliar', to make forms difficult, to increase the difficulty and length of perception because the process of perception is an aesthetic end in itself and must be prolonged.[17]

The value of the literary is in the obstructive way in which it systematically works against one of the most powerful forces at work both in life and in art – what the formalists called *automatization*. The defamiliarizations of literature de-automatize the automatization that afflicts stones, language and also literature itself. 'Habitualization', says Shklovsky using another term for automatization, 'devours works, clothes, furniture, one's wife, and the fear of war' ('Art as Technique', p. 12). Literature counters this insidious and deadening process by creating difficulty, in a manner which often carries its own counter-violence. This, to begin with, may be no more than a matter of vocabulary, but its effects can also include reminders of the existence of violence itself – the passion and the fear of war which Shklovsky alludes to.

Conflict and aggression are repeatedly demonstrated in the examples that the formalists choose to discuss. For instance, in illustrating the effects of literary defamiliarization, Shklovsky takes Tolstoy's story 'Shame' where, says Shklovsky, flogging is defamiliarized by being described but not named: flogging is conveyed by a periphrasis that makes explicit the violence that it entails ('to strip people who have broken the law, to hurl them to the floor, and to rap on their bottoms with switches', 'Art as Technique', p. 13). Similarly, Shklovsky praises *War and Peace* for the way in which Tolstoy defamiliarizes battles, and thus restores and renews one's sense of the fear of war which everyday existence inevitably erodes. So that defamiliarization is implicitly defined as a violence directed against habitualizations that affect even violence itself.

However, since neither form nor language is exempt from the process of habitualization/automatization, the major thrust of the formalists' enterprise eventually became concentrated on the defamiliarizing effects of literature upon language, leaving stones and the fear of war to fade into the background. Literature was seen primarily in its relation to language, and its defamiliarizations were first and foremost defamiliarizations of language. The defamiliarizations of literature operate by separating signifier from signified, especially by focusing perception onto the material, phonic nature of the signifier. But for all the abstraction implied in this linguistic formulation, defamiliarization is still seen primarily as a kind of aggression in which the severing of signifier from signified is an act of violence performed by literary language against the habitual forms of what the formalists called 'practical language'. Shklovsky proclaims that 'The language of poetry is a difficult, roughened, impeded language' ('Art as Technique', p. 22), and the formalists are delighted to find an anecdote in Pushkin describing the stiff jaw suffered by one General Ermolov after an evening spent reading works of the early nineteenth-century writer Griboedov. Poetry, says Jakobson in a nutshell definition, is 'organized violence committed on ordinary speech'.[18] This formulation suggests that even in the purely linguistic sphere (a sphere that has nothing to do with either flogging or the fear of war) defamiliarization entails a notable degree of conflict and aggression.

In formalist theory the chief means whereby this violence can be committed is provided by form in general, and the device in particular. As Jakobson said, 'the device' was to be 'the sole hero' in this new anti-psychological, and generally anti-mimetic approach to literature.[19] The effect of literary devices was to defamiliarize the signifiers of language: language was regarded as the 'material' of poetry whose devices transformed it (language, that is) from the automatized state of practical usage to the jaw-breaking defamiliarizations of poetry. And it may well be that it is precisely the apparent abstraction of the linguistic from other spheres of human activity, and the apparently purely formal nature of the device which prevented the formalism from taking on board at an explicitly theoretical level the implications of the violence that seems inevitably – but only ever implicitly – to accompany defamiliarization in all its manifestations.

In addition, the formalists put themselves in a position where they would be unlikely to pursue this kind of issue by adopting the linguistic presuppositions that tended to make formalism a theory of poetry rather than a theory of prose or of literature in general. Or, rather, in so far as it was a theory of literature in general, it was a theory according to which some genres were bound to appear more literary than others. And in so far as the formalists had a theory of prose (actually the title of one of Shklovsky's books) it was grafted onto what was at bottom a theory of poetry. On the one hand, their views about prose extended the scope of the problem of conflict that I have been discussing; but on the other, the fact that prose was seen as broadly analogous to poetry meant that the possibilities for facing up to the problem (so enthusiastically embraced by Bakhtin in his concern with the novel – as we shall see later on) remained just as remote.

In dealing with prose the principle of defamiliarization remained the overriding criterion of literariness. And the concepts of device and material found their equivalents in narrative terms. *Fabula* [the 'story'] provides the 'material' which is then defamiliarized and made literary by the devices that constitute the *syuzhet* [the 'plot']. What is foregrounded (to use another formalist term to refer to the results of defamiliarization) in prose is not language in its material reality, but form itself. But despite the linguistic analogy and the formalism of the basic principle of prose, violence proves to be an integral characteristic of the prose scenario too, although – once again – in a manner which fails to achieve explicit theorization. It shows, for example, in the comments that Shklovsky makes about *Tristram Shandy* (for him 'the most typical novel in world literature'): 'By violating the form, he [Sterne] forces us to attend to it . . . Awareness of the form through its violation constitutes the content of the novel.'[20] It is these repeated violations which, in Shklovksy's eyes, make *Tristram Shandy* an exemplary instance of the genre of fiction. The violence that poetry perpetrates against language is directed by prose against itself, or rather against its own formal components.

The self-directed violence of prose (which of course applies in equal measure to poetry) points to a second phase in formalist thinking where the violence that made possible the differentiation between literature and non-literature becomes located within literature itself. And yet in this move conflict seems to be even more liable to be ignored rather than recognized. The site of conflict shifts from outside to inside the literary work in this way because it turns out that not all devices can be good devices (not all of them are heroes). This in turn is because literary forms and literary devices are necessarily just as susceptible as anything else to the forces of automatization: heroic devices too may fall from grace and lose their capacity to make it strange. Literature needs to be turned against itself in order to counter the anti-literary processes of habitualization. It is this view that generates the formalist concept of literary history as a sequence of defamiliarizations of form and convention.

It also generates the concept of the *dominant*, which Jakobson eulogized as 'one of the most crucial, elaborated and productive concepts in Russian Formalist theory' (in his essay on the subject written in 1935).[21] It continued to function as a key concept in his own subsequent work and proved in the process (as I shall be showing) to be one of the most important strategies whereby conflict is both integrated into the literary and simultaneously screened off from any recognition. The dominant becomes important when literariness is constituted not by just any device (because a device may be rendered useless through habitualization), but by the dominant device, and the dominant becomes the key to the definition of the literary. Rather than see the literary work as a collection of devices which all work to defamiliarize language or narrative sequence, it comes to be conceived as a structure which derives coherence and integrity from a dominant device. As Jakobson puts it: 'The dominant may be defined as the focusing component of a work of art: it rules, determines and transforms the remaining components. It is the dominant which guarantees the integrity of the structure.' In short, 'The dominant specifies the work' ('The Dominant', p. 41).

This leads to a rather tautologous definition of art according to which 'a poetic work is defined as a verbal message whose aesthetic function is its dominant' (ibid., p. 43). But what this means is that a work can have other, non-literary components, and other linguistic functions, notably a referential function and/or an expressive function (functions which earlier formalism ascribed exclusively to practical language). And yet it is still a work of literature because where the aesthetic function is dominant, the other functions are *transformed* by this dominant. Jakobson uses a rather curious simile to describe the operations of the dominant when he compares the aesthetic function to oil in cooking – not something that can be eaten as a dish in its own right, nor just an extra ingredient that may be optionally added to a dish,[22] but something which transforms all the other ingredients, sometimes beyond recognition. And he goes on to prove the point etymologically, if not gastronomically, by citing the fact that in the Czech language a fresh sardine and a sardine in oil have two completely different names.

This image is curious for two reasons. First there is its quaint homeliness which is rather out of step with the more heroic or futurist quality of the majority of formalist metaphors. But the more striking feature is the complete absence of any hint of the violence associated with the earlier descriptions of the relations between the literary and the non-literary. As that violence is moved from the boundary of the literary work to its inside, the language of violence disappears from formalist prose (and Jakobson's prose in particular). Gone are the dislocated jaws, the violations, deformations, struggles, floggings and sex (about which I have said less but there are repeated allusions to sex in early formalist writing), and in their place we have the humble sardine, innocuously proclaiming its innocence. The domination of the dominant appears to be achieved without violence as it unctuously transforms other elements for the greater integrity of the literary work of art.

Nevertheless, Jakobson's vocabulary cannot conceal the fact that there are still power relations involved: the dominant, says Jakobson, 'rules', 'determines' and 'transforms' simply by 'exerting influence upon other linguistic forms'. What has changed is that, whereas the early formalist emphasis on defamiliarization implied that the literary was a contestatory force challenging the authority of habit and demanding separate recognition, the later, more characteristically Jakobsonian view implies that authority is automatically granted to the literary, whose power operates in a more imperialistic way, subjugating and subsuming all potential differences and resistances. For where the dominant is an aesthetic dominant it acquires rights and functions denied to non-aesthetic dominants. The aesthetic function is not cancelled or negated in an extra-literary context, in the way that expressive and referential functions are subordinated and ambiguated in literary works. The aesthetic dominant simply neutralizes the alternative forces of the other linguistic elements in a given utterance.

The 'Linguistics and Poetics' paper takes this line of argument even further, offering a fuller and more complex account of this view. By 1960 Jakobson had distinguished *six* components of a linguistic utterance with six corresponding linguistic functions. (In 1935 there were only three, the expressive, the referential and the aesthetic.) Any verbal utterance, says Jakobson, involves six factors: a speaker, or ADDRESSER who sends a MESSAGE (i.e. the utterance itself) to a receiver or ADDRESSEE. In order for communication to be effective, addresser and addressee require a CONTEXT to be referred to (i.e. a referent), a common CODE (i.e. a language or idiolect that both parties understand) and a CONTACT or channel (physical or psychological) that allows communication to be maintained.[23] These are the constitutive factors of Jakobson's famous model, each of which has a corresponding function: the emotive, the poetic, the conative, the referential, the metalingual and the phatic. All utterances involve all six functions, but in any given utterance, only one of them will have priority or dominance. However, by 1960, in spite of the increase in the number of functions in play, dominance is achieved so easily, that the word itself is replaced by other, even more innocent-looking words: 'set', 'orientation' or '*Einstellung*' (attitude).

There is nothing in this discussion about even the milder – or at least milder-looking – forms of power attributed in the earlier article of 1935 to the dominant. The 'set' or 'orientation' towards the poetic function (still the one which interests Jakobson the most) is not apparently achieved by influence, transformation, rule or determination, let alone by violation, deformation or dislocation. Dominance of the poetic is the result of a 'set' towards the MESSAGE component of the poetic utterance, and this in turn is achieved by the process that Jakobson neatly formulates as follows (the italics are his): '*The poetic function projects the principle of equivalence from the axis of selection into the axis of combination.* Equivalence is promoted to the constitutive device of the sequence' ('Linguistics and Poetics', p. 71). The quasi-formulaic quality of the principle is rather apt is discourage one from exploring the argument which underpins it, but it is worth the brief digression it will entail.

The assumption behind Jakobson's formula is a broadly Saussurean view of language as a store of *langue* on which individual instances of *parole* may draw. In Jakobson's use of this model the emphasis is not so much on any implicit distinction between *langue* and *parole*, but rather on their interdependence. He stresses that the passage from the one to the other (*langue* to *parole*) reveals the existence within language of two complementary axes: the 'paradigmatic' and the 'syntagmatic'. The paradigmatic involves *selection* amongst *equivalences* and *similarities* and is therefore allied to the *metaphoric* (because similarity is its underlying principle). The syntagmatic, on the other hand, involves *combination* and *contiguity* and is therefore allied to the *metonymic* principle. These two axes are not just what permits the transformation of *langue* into *parole*, but are essential to the proper workings of all utterances. What happens in utterances where the poetic function is dominant, or rather where the set is towards the message, is that the paradigmatic or metaphoric axis is not just limited to the latent, but is deployed along the syntagm itself.

If one pursues Jakobson's formulation, and reads his account of the interdependency of the two axes in his paper on aphasia ('Two Aspects of Language and Two Types of Aphasic Disturbances'),[24] one can get some sense of just how much is at stake in this mutual complementarity of the two axes, and how devastating are the effects of any imbalance. In the process I hope to suggest how the apparently strictly formal and non-combative definition of poetry proposed in 'Linguistics and Poetics' ('*The poetic function projects the principle of equivalence from the axis of selection into the axis of combination*'), is actually tantamount to saying that poetry courts linguistic disaster through the imbalance, or excessive domination by one linguistic axis over the other.

I should stress that this is not quite the spirit in which Jakobson presents his discussion. Indeed his account of the two different types of aphasia is designed to confirm his view that language is composed of these two axes, the metaphoric and the metonymic. He does this by pinpointing two types of speech disorder, each of which involves a malfunction of one of these axes: a similarity disorder where patients have difficulties with selection, and a contiguity disorder where patients have difficulties with combination.

He discusses the similarity disorder first and incidentally reveals what violence is done to the language of speakers when one axis secedes to the dominance of the other. Patients with a similarity disorder are capable of adding to a syntagm but cannot initiate one, and the more a word is dependent on syntax, the better able they are to use it – witness the heart-rendingly inarticulate example of one German patient (which I shall quote from Jakobson's original before attempting an English translation):

> *Ich bin doch hier unten, na wenn ich gewesen bin ich wees nicht, we das, nu wenn ich, ob das nun doch, noch, ja. Was Sie her, wenn ich, och ich wees nicht we das war ja . . .*

> But I'm down here, well when I've been I dinna ken, how that, well when I, whether after all, still, yes. What you here, if I, oh I dinna ken how it was here, yes . . .[25]

These patients are unable to produce synonyms or equivalents, and given the word 'bachelor', for example, have no trouble adding the word '-flat' to it, but find it impossible to define it as 'unmarried man'. Nor are they able to name, and when asked to produce a word for knife, can only shift metonymically to name the contiguous fork.

The problems for patients with a contiguity disorder are equally disabling, and are a mirror image of the similarity disorder. These patients lose all grasp of grammar, and this agrammatism reduces their sentences to 'word heaps', as Jakobson puts it. They lose all words that have a purely grammatical function (the ones that propped up the empty sentences of the patients with similarity disorders), such as pronouns, conjunctions, prepositions, and so on. They too have difficulty in naming things, but they use metaphorical substitutes rather than the metonymic ones resorted to by the similarity disorder patients. So that, for instance, a microscope is metaphorically defined as a 'spyglass', a gaslight as 'fire'.[26]

One way or the other then – although, as I have suggested, this is not the moral that Jakobson derives from his sad tale of aphasia – dominance of one axis over the other produces effects that are so disabling, and so devastating, that the language of victims of aphasia is effectively destroyed. Jakobson is using these pathological cases to support his hypothesis about the two axiological components of language, but in the process, and entirely unintentionally, he reveals this other moral to his tale, and hints at the presence of repression and pathology in all language use. It is not just aphasics who are threatened by imbalance but everybody and in all spheres.

In the conclusion to his paper Jakobson claims that for personal and/or cultural reasons, everyone will reveal an imbalance by giving preference either to the metaphoric axis, or to the metonymic. Moreover, he says, while any symbolic process will involve both axes, one will always be given priority over the other. Here he refers briefly first, to Freud's distinction between *condensation* and *displacement* in dream images, and second to Frazer's categorization of magic rituals into 'imitative magic' and 'contagious magic'. He argues that each element of these contrasting pairs displays an affinity to one or other of the two main poles of language (condensation and imitative magic are metaphoric in structure, while displacement and contagious magic are metonymically organized). Finally, he suggests that poetry and prose can be matched to the same distinction, poetry being built on the principle of similarity, while prose follows the metonymic principle whereby things are connected by relations of contiguity. Thus the prose author

> follow[s] the path of contiguous relationships [and] metonymically digresses from the plot to the atmosphere and from the characters to the setting in space and time. He is fond of synecdochic details. In the scene of Anna Karenina's suicide Tolstoy's artistic attention is focused on the heroine's handbag ('Two Aspects of Language', p. 111)

This distinction incidentally concedes once and for all – if only *en passant* – that prose and poetry are antithetical principles, rather than complementary components of an overarching literariness. But more important is the fact that, given the theme of the paper to which these remarks provide the conclusion, this is tantamount to saying that prose is a sort of similarity disorder in language, and poetry a contiguity disorder. The similarity with the speech disorders of aphasics suggests that there must be some kind of 'deformation', 'violation' or 'dislocation' operating within the linguistic system even if Jakobson does not openly acknowledge it. And the fact that dreams and rituals, and indeed individual idiolects involve similar distortions implies that perhaps *all* language-use entails distortion and deformation.

Now a brief recapitulation before embarking on the final part of the argument: what the history of formalist thought in its various guises and phases seems to suggest is that there is a direct but inverse correlation between the acknowledgement of violence in language and literature and its actual extent. The early stages used a vocabulary of aggression and associated it with the need to separate the literary from the non-literary: violence was a necessary strategy in the process of decontamination. You might say that the early formalists were freedom fighters for whom aggression provided the only means of achieving autonomy and independence for literature and literary studies. As the critical vocabulary was toned down in the gradual move away from 'violation', to 'dominance' to 'set', so literature itself – rather than its boundaries – increasingly became the site of conflict, but it was one whose conflictual nature was masked by a simultaneous belief in the authority and power of the aesthetic. If impure elements crossed the border, they could supposedly be co-opted and subsumed under the aegis of the poetic dominant. Finally, linguistic theory (which is what both the aphasia paper and the 'Linguistics and Poetics' essay purport to be) in which the vocabulary consists of 'axes', 'poles' and 'principles' unwittingly reveals imbalance and conflict in all language use, not just poetic use, and an imbalance which is all the more disquieting for not being explicitly acknowledged as such. The strategic aggression of defamiliarization, and the unshakeable authority of the aesthetic dominant were at least restricted forms of violence, but in the final stage imbalance seems to testify to uncontrolled and unlimited conflicts everywhere in language.

This account has deliberately played up the themes of violence and aggression, but I have allowed myself to indulge this emphasis because it seems to me to be both provoked and justified by the extraordinary number of parallels between the terms of Jakobson's thought and the thought of his biographical *alter ego* Bakhtin. The parallel of the lives is in some senses repeated in the thought, although on the face of it nothing could be more different than the work of these two thinkers. But for all their differences (differences which I have no interest in seeking to diminish), they prove to be extraordinarily and very revealingly comparable.

The chief difference consists first, in Bakhtin's explicit theoretical preoccupation with conflict, and second in his profound suspicion of linguistic universality of the kind exemplified by structural linguistics. Language, or rather discourse (as he calls it), is for him a plural thing because it is always language in action, that is to say in the service of a particular interest or set of interests, which are necessarily in conflict with other interests and therefore with other discourses. Linguistic unity of the kind that Jakobson takes for granted as a kind of extension of Saussurean *langue*, is for Bakhtin only a semblance of unity. In a 'dialogic' system of discourse such as the one he conceives of, unity is necessarily the product of discursive dominance and can only be achieved by some kind of repressive violence directed against alien language types.

He thinks in this way because he has a totally different concept of language from that of Jakobson and the formalists. In Bakhtin's view 'verbal discourse is a social phenomenon – social throughout its entire range and in each and every one of its factors, from the sound image to the furthest reaches of abstract meaning'.[27] According to him the social character that the formalists might have acknowledged as an element of what they called 'practical language' is not shed either by a defamiliarizing focus on the material quality of the signifier (the 'sound image'), nor by the abstractions of Jakobson's later interest in what he called 'the fundamentals of language' (the title of the book written by himself and Morris Halle and in which his paper on aphasia originally appeared). In Bakhtin's view, even the metaphoric and metonymic axes would not escape the social condition of language.

Within this overall and thorough-going difference of approach, there are, nevertheless, some striking points of particular comparison and contrast. Both are agreed that language is composed of multiple elements. For Jakobson these are the six formal components of an utterance: Addresser, Addressee, Message, Context, Code and Contact. For Bakhtin, however, the multiple character of discourse is rather differently construed. All national languages, he claims, (i.e. Russian, English, French, etc.) are internally stratified into what he calls different 'social speech types' by which he means (in his own words):

> social dialects, characteristic group behaviour, professional jargons, generic languages, languages of generations and age-groups, tendentious languages, languages of the authorities, of various circles and of passing fashions, languages that serve the specific socio-political purposes of the day, even of the hour. ('Discourse in the Novel', p. 263)

The relation between these different speech types is fundamentally one of conflict, unlike the six functions of the Jakobsonian model which comply co-operatively with whichever one of them happens to be the dominant.

Bakhtin's is a model of discursive conflict largely because of the effects of the two main forces which he sees at work in language – forces which he calls *centripetal* and *centrifugal*. The centripetal force in language seeks to 'reign over', 'supplant', 'enslave', and 'incorporate' other languages (ibid., p. 271). It directs attention 'away from language plurality to a single proto-language'. It imposes itself as a unitary language, a language of authority. The centrifugal force, by contrast, works to undo linguistic unity and unseat linguistic authority; it fights enslavement and incorporation. Every utterance, says Bakhtin, is crossed by both forces, on the one hand 'participating in the "unitary language", and at the same time partaking of social and cultural heteroglossia' (ibid., p. 272). This view of the dual tendencies in all utterances is uncannily reminiscent of Jakobson's theory of the two

linguistic axes manifest 'in all symbolic processes', even if his theory neglects
to consider the possibility of any problem – let alone the possibility of
conflict – in their relationship.

Finally, although Bakhtin is primarily concerned with the novel and
Jakobson with poetry, they share the same underlying assumptions: first
that literature is instructive about the nature of language; and secondly,
that the function of literature (whether 'literature' be taken to mean poetry
or prose) is, to paraphrase Jakobson, to focus attention on the message
itself. In Bakhtin's view, the function of the novel is to create a heightened
awareness of the heteroglot nature of language, or discourse, to intensify
what he calls the 'dialogism' of social discourse in a manner which includes
an awareness of its own nature as discourse. Or as he puts it himself:
'Language in the novel not only represents but itself serves as the object of
representation. *Novelistic discourse is always criticizing itself.*'[28]

Thus Bakhtin and Jakobson would appear to be working with broadly
similar assumptions: (1) language has multiple components; (2) language
is constructed according to two counterweighted principles; (3) literature is
a self-referential use of language. These similarities are extraordinarily
precise, even though the significance that the two theorists attribute to those
assumptions is very different: social for Bakhtin, structural for Jakobson.
The closeness of the theoretical parallel invites a comparison that allows
one to see what is left unsaid and unaccounted for by each of them when
viewed in the light of the concerns of the other.

In particular – and perhaps I should admit in advance that I am giving
the whip hand to Bakhtin – Jakobson's failure to theorize the conflicts and
the power relations that are entailed in his views about language and about
literature seems, in the light of what Bakhtin has to say about these things,
to be an unfortunate and rather glaring omission. Bakhtin's theory allows
one to read another tale in Jakobson's poetics, so that, for example, when
he characterizes poetry as organized violence committed on everyday language, he appears to be ascribing to literature a centrifugal function that
emphasizes heteroglossia and resists the unitary. But when he speaks of the
aesthetic dominant 'ruling, determining, transforming and influencing' other
linguistic factors, the semantic similarities with the characteristic actions of
Bakhtin's centripetally directed languages of authority (which 'reign over,
supplant, enslave, incorporate'), create the suspicion that literature is being
constructed by Jakobson as another language of authority.

In other words, the autonomy of literature that the formalists and Jakobson were seeking to establish in the various ways that I have described,
may work in formal terms (and these aren't terms which I should want
entirely to jettison), but the susceptibility of their arguments to translation
into a Bakhtinian approach rather suggests that autonomy can't necessarily
be achieved in social terms, and that the character of literary language
cannot be exhaustively described by a purely formal linguistic analysis.

In concluding I see that old rhetorical habits die hard and that I have
come very close to turning my comparison into a pitched battle between

one theorist and another in which – such are the stakes of literary theory – the less fashionable one (currently Jakobson) is bound to lose out to the more fashionable one (currently Bakhtin). But, as I suggested at the beginning, it was not my intention to engage in this kind of exercise, but rather to see if Jakobson could be salvaged for a different kind of reading, and in the process to ask what it means to read theory. Jakobson himself makes some suggestive comments about this in the opening remarks of 'Linguistics and Poetics' where he claims not only that 'disagreement generally proves to be more productive than agreement', but more specifically that the advantage of disagreement is that it 'discloses antinomies and tensions within the field discussed and calls for novel exploration' (p. 62). The 'disagreement' between Jakobson and Bakhtin which I have sketched out was conceived with the aim of just such an exploration in mind.

The hope was not to do Jakobson down (again), nor yet to rehabilitate him with his old paraphernalia, but to retrieve him from the archives of literary theory and to make it possible to read him afresh. And if it does now seem possible to undertake such a reading, one way to do it would be in the light of problems which Bakhtin discusses explicitly and he does not. In other words, I would like to suggest that far from offering a self-explanatory but largely uninteresting repertoire of technical terms, Jakobson (and indeed formalist aesthetics as a whole) is saying more than he appears to realize. This is a suggestion which in turn raises questions about the status of theory itself. Engaging with theory does not just oblige us to ask who is right and who is wrong, and who deserves our allegiance and who our contempt (although the dialogic nature of all discourse, including theoretical discourse makes these questions inevitable), but to consider how we might be reading theoretical discourse in the first place.[29]

Notes

1 John Harwood, 'From "The Annotated Gospel According to Jacques" ', *English* (Spring 1985), pp. 44–50.
2 Osip Brik, 'The So-called Formal Method', trans. Ann Shukman, *Russian Poetics in Translation*, 4 (1977), edited by L. M. O'Toole and Ann Shukman, pp. 90–9 (p. 90). Brik's emphasis.
3 Roman Jakobson and Krystyna Pomorska, *Dialogues*, trans. Christian Hubert (Boston, Mass.: MIT Press, 1983). Pomorska was Jakobson's wife, so she would have none of the professional interviewer's normal curiosity about her husband's life since she shared it with him.
4 Information culled from *Russian Poetics in Translation*, vol. 4, p. 4, and Victor Erlich, *Russian Formalism: History–Doctrine*, 3rd edn. (New Haven, Conn.: Yale University Press, 1981). My interest in Jakobson's biography has not taken me beyond the most readily available critical sources.
5 Katerina Clark and Michael Holquist, *Mikhail Bakhtin* (Cambidge, Mass.: Harvard University Press, 1984). My biographical information about Bakhtin is derived entirely from this book.
6 See P. N. Medvedev/M. M. Bakhtin, *The Formal Method in Literary Scholarship*,

trans. Albert J. Wehrle (Baltimore, Md.: Johns Hopkins University Press, 1978). For a discussion of the authorship of this book see Wehrle's Introduction, and Clark and Holquist, *Mikhail Bakhtin*, pp. 146–60.

7   See his preface to the 3rd edn, p. 10 where, although he concedes (quite correctly) that 'Bakhtin . . . could not be labelled a Formalist', he argues that 'the essentially structural and metalinguistic thrust of *Problems of Dostoevsky's Poetics* attests to a strong affinity for the mature phase of Formalist theorizing'.

8   It is not all just a matter of contrast and parallel: their paths actually crossed when Jakobson came to Bakhtin's help in the growing attempt to get his (Bakhtin's) work proper recognition in the 1950s, first by using his (Jakobson's) position as a member of the International Committee of Slavists to mention Bakhtin's work at a meeting in Moscow in 1956, and second by referring to Bakhtin in a review (written in Russian) of a book by Shklovsky in the first number of the *International Journal of Slavic Linguistics and Poetics* in 1959. See Clark and Holquist, *Mikhail Bakhtin*, pp. 331–2.

9   See especially Jacques Lacan, 'The Agency of the Letter in the Unconscious', in *Ecrits: A Selection*, trans. A. Sheridan (London: Tavistock Press, 1977). Maria Ruegg's article 'Metaphor and Metonymy: The Logic of Structuralist Rhetoric', *Glyph*, 6 (1979), pp. 141–57 offers a useful account of the fortunes of these terms in structuralist theory.

10 See Jonathan Culler, 'Jakobson's Poetic Analyses' in *Structuralist Poetics* (London: Routledge and Kegan Paul, 1975), and Mary Louise Pratt, *Toward a Speech Act Theory of Literature* (Bloomington, Ind.: Indiana University Press, 1977).

11 See Peter Steiner, *Russian Formalism: A Metapoetics* (Ithaca, NY: Cornell University Press, 1984). Steiner offers a reading of formalist writing under three metaphorical headings – the machine, the organism and the system.

12 There are straight-forward expository accounts of all aspects of it – and of Jakobson and Bakhtin – in *Modern Literary Theory: A Comparative Introduction*, ed. A. Jefferson and David Robey (2nd edn London: Batsford, 1986).

13 This was not because the formalists were above it or indifferent to the question – witness the non-theoretical account in Victor Shklovsky, *A Sentimental Journey. Memoirs 1917–22*, trans. Richard Sheldon (Ithaca, NY: Cornell University Press, 1984).

14 Boris Ejxenbaum, 'The Theory of the Formal Method', in *Readings in Russian Poetics*, ed. Ladislav Matejka and Krystyna Pomorska (Ann Arbor, Mich.: Michigan Slavic Publications, 1978), pp. 3–37 (p. 7).

15 The inclusion of biography in this list of the contents of the 'gratuitous mix' of disciplines is characteristic of the formalists' anti-biographism.

16 Quoted from Roman Jakobson, 'The Latest Russian Poetry. First Draft. Viktor Khlebnikov' (1921), in O'Toole and Shukman (ed.), *Russian Poetics in Translation*, vol. 4, p. 17.

17 Victor Shklovsky, 'Art as Technique', in *Russian Formalist Criticism: Four Essays*, ed. L. T. Lemon and M. J. Reis (Lincoln, Neb;: University of Nebraska Press, 1965), pp. 3–24 (p. 12).

18 From 'On Czech Verse' (1923), quoted by Victor Erlich, p. 219.

19 From 'The Latest Russian Poetry', quoted in O'Toole and Shukman (ed.), *Russian Poetics in Translation*, p. 37.

20 Viktor Shklovsky, 'Sterne's *Tristram Shandy*: Stylistic Commentary', in Lemon and Reis (ed.), *Russian Formalist Criticism*, pp. 25–57 (pp. 30–1).

21 'The Dominant', in Roman Jakobson, *Language and Literature* (Cambridge, Mass.: Harvard University Press, 1987), pp. 41–6.

22 'Qu'est-ce que la poésie?', trans. from Czech by Marguerite Derrida, in *Huit Questions de poétique*, ed. Tzvetan Todorov (Paris: Seuil, 1977), pp. 31–49 (p. 46).

23 See 'Linguistics and Poetics', in Jakobson, *Language and Literature*, pp. 62–94.

24 In Jakobson, *Language and Literature*, pp. 95–114.

25 P. 101. I am grateful to Elizabeth Wright and Anthony Glees for advice and suggestions for the translation.

26 One can't help noting that Jakobson's examples contrive to 'date' him in a manner that has perhaps not been to his advantage. The concept of a 'bachelor' has become nearly as archaic as the 'gas-light' is antique.

27 Mikhail Bakhtin, 'Discourse in the Novel' in *The Dialogic Imagination*, ed. Michael Holquist, trans. Caryl Emerson and Michael Holquist (Austin, Tex.: University of Texas Press, 1981), pp. 259–422 (p. 259).

28 Mikhail Bakhtin, 'From the Prehistory of Novelistic Discourse' , *The Dialogic Imagination*, pp. 41–83 (p. 49), my emphasis.

29 It is a pleasure to record my gratitude to Tony Nuttall, Willie van Peer, Angela Williams and Elizabeth Wright who offered fruitful comment and advice on the foregoing essay.

SARAH KOFMAN

Conversions: *The Merchant of Venice* under the Sign of Saturn

Translated by Shaun Whiteside

The Apotrope Against Atropos

In *The Motif of the Choice of the Caskets* (*Das Motiv der Kästchenwahl*),[1] examining the myths, stories and fairy-tales that involve a choice between three women, an ancient theme whose interpretation and derivation he seeks, Freud concludes that the final choice of the most beautiful, the most desirable, the wisest, the most faithful, the best or the most adorable woman is the result of a fiction (*Schöpfung*) produced by desire. Paradoxically operating a double reversal (*Wunschgegenteil, Wunschverkehrung*), replacing one thing by its opposite, desire masks the necessity of death. By means of this ruse, reaction-formation (*Reaktionsbildung*), or *apotrope*, desire triumphs over the Invincible, *Atropos*, the third of the three Fates, the Inexorable: 'Choice stands in the place of necessity, of destiny. In this way man overcomes death, which he has recognized intellectually. No greater triumph of wish-fulfilment is conceivable. A choice is made where in reality there is obedience to a compulsion; and what is chosen is not the Terrible, but the fairest and most desirable of women.'[2]

Freud corroborates his regressive interpretation, which reveals a 'prim-aeval identity' which is more or less concealed, more or less distorted, but which never completely disappears from myths or literature, by relying, as ever, on a few revealing details or traces (*Resterscheinungen*) which, beyond the differences of eras, civilizations and genres, lead towards a hidden universal meaning.

The comparative, or indeed structural, thematic reading undertaken by Freud thus enables him to compare, in an unusual way, the anonymous Greco-Roman myths or stories (the story of the choice which Paris has to make between the three goddesses, the myth of the three Fates), with certain stories from the *Gesta Romanorum*, an Estonian poem, the *Psyche* of Apuleius, the story of *Cinderella*, certain of Grimm's tales (*The Six Swans, The Twelve*

This essay was first published as 'Conversions. Le Marchand de Venise sous le signe de Saturne' (Paris: Galilée, 1988).

Brothers), the libretto of Offenbach's *La Belle Hélène,* and finally *The Merchant of Venice,* the starting-point of the analysis, and *King Lear.* These two plays, each in its own way, one of them rather unserious (*heiter*), the other more tragic, each producing a particular effect, one comic, the other crushing, sublimely affecting, or, in Freud's word, overwhelming (*ungeheuer*), are also held to take as their essential subject a choice between three women, and to harbour the same universal meaning.

But if, from identical material or an identical motif, one 'story-teller' (*Dichter*) may draw very different effects, if all of his art consists precisely in being able to 'guide the current of our emotions, to dam it up in one direction and make it flow in another',[3] does not isolating one motif from the rest mean losing the essence of art or poetic creation? And how can Freud invoke the 'primaeval human identity' to explain the moving dramatic effect of *King Lear* if, arranged and composed in quite a different way, it can produce a quite different effect, a 'lighter' one for example?

The answer to this objection consists, for Freud, in tracing the difference in effects – and therefore in genres – back to a difference in degrees of repression of the 'primitive content'. Of the examples chosen, *King Lear* is seen as the work in which the poignant meaning of the primitive myth, weakened by later distortions, returns, and, by means of the reduction of the distortions, exerts its profound power over us. *The Merchant of Venice* owes its greater 'lightness' to a more thorough concealment of the primitive meaning.[4] That is why, in this case, it takes all of Freud's ingenuity to discover it or rather, from the distortions of the manifest content, to manage to 'construct' the latent content. The postulate of such a method is that one must understand the literary text as one listens to the discourse of a neurotic on the couch, discreetly devoting suspended attention to anything that appears to sound strange if not uncanny, or at least revealing. Thus, with regard to Bassanio, who, in seeking to glorify lead, finds few things to say, and because this 'is little and has a forced ring' (*ist wenig und klingt gezwungen*), Freud writes: 'If in psychoanalytic practice we were confronted with such a speech, we should suspect that there were concealed motives (*geheimgehaltene Motive*) behind the unsatisfying reasons produced.'

So, listening to *The Merchant of Venice* with a detective's suspicious ear, armed with the magic wand of the model of the interpretation of dreams, Freud successively strips the manifest (*scheinbar*) content of the text of all of its supposed disguises. This method allows him to dismiss both the most usual astral interpretation[5] and the one which is most obviously manifest and banal: 'one should no more trust flattery (a lesson to be drawn from *King Lear*) than appearances (*Schein*)'. Freud therefore acts like the good suitor Bassanio who, in making his choice, is able to resist the brilliance of gold and silver. But, paradoxically, it is by obeying the lesson to be drawn from the manifest text that he precisely distinguishes the manifest meaning from the latent meaning, and rejects the former in favour of the latter, as Bassanio rejected gold and silver in favour of lead. At the very point where he considers it necessary to neglect the manifest text, Freud obeys its imperative: far from inventing the distinction of the 'latent' and the manifest, and 'applying' it to literature from without, Freud borrows it from literature, more powerful than psychoanalysis, since it secretes this inherent distinction and consequently also secretes the demand for a certain decoding.

To strip the text of its gold-mail garments which, with all their loud jangling, muffle the leaden silence of the latent content, Freud resorts essentially to dream symbolism. He first resorts to it (a recourse which will bear the entire weight of the interpretation) in order to convert the choice of the three caskets into a choice between three women; a conversion which in itself allows him to include *The Merchant of Venice* within the thematic series under examination, and particularly to compare it to the Estonian poem and the story from the *Gesta Romanorum*. This is on condition, however, that he resort once more to the dream model and its process of reversal, since in these latter cases it is a young girl who must decide between three suitors, while in the first case it is a young man who must choose between three women magically replaced by caskets which are supposed to represent them in a symbolic and metonymic fashion. This is a substitution legitimate only for those who see literature as functioning like a dream, a typical dream whose interpretation dispenses with any need to turn to the associations of the dreamer:

> If what we were concerned with were a dream, it would occur to us at once that caskets are also women, symbols of what is essential in woman, and therefore of a woman herself – like coffers, boxes, cases, baskets, and so on. If we boldly assume that there are symbolic substitutions of the same kind in myths as well, then the casket scene in *The Merchant of Venice* really becomes the inversion we suspected. With a wave of the wand, as though we were in a fairy tale, we have stripped the astral garment from our theme; and now we see that the theme is a human one, *a man's choice between three women*.

One detail – neglected by Freud, who almost mechanically resorts to dream symbolism as the key to the text – could confirm this apparently arbitrary reading: the first time Portia mentions the caskets, she uses, as if in a lapsus, the word 'chest',[6] which also means a woman's breast; everywhere else the less polysemic 'casket' is used;[7] and this, translated into German as *Kästchen*, is the only one used by Freud, even in the title of his text. In the course of the interpretation, on the other hand, Freud once more resorts to dreams in a rather 'forced' way in order, this time in a way that is crucial to his reading, to equate lead with death, which is constantly symbolized by the third woman, silent, dumb, 'inconspicuous', hidden, 'unrecognizable', strikingly pale, all characteristics which, as clinical experience has proven – are supposed, from a symbolic viewpoint – to be equivalent. In fact, the substitution of death for lead is possible only if, on the one hand, with Freud, one decides in favour of one variant of the text, that of the *paleness* of lead ('Thy paleness moves me more than eloquence', 3, ii, 106), the other variant being that of 'plainness'; and if, on the other hand, one ignores the fact that this paleness is also a characteristic of silver: 'Thou pale and common drudge, Between man and man' (line 103), as Bassanio says of it.

Finally, one might assert that lead is less 'loud' than gold and silver, whose manners are shrill – and that it is therefore really 'dumb' like Cordelia who 'loves and is silent' and represents death, or like Aphrodite in *La Belle Hélène,* or discreet like Cinderella – as long as one forgets that the lead, like the gold and the silver, bears a formula, a motto, with at least a double meaning, which is designed to guide or mislead the choice, and is eloquent enough to those who can decipher and interpret it; as long as one also forgets that, like the other two caskets, the leaden casket bears an inscription which contains and sums up the fortune of the person who has chosen it. Strictly speaking, we cannot then say that it is dumb. It will only be seen as dumb by those who hear in Bassanio's discourse a weird and strange association, when in fact they themselves are following the thread of their own associations and the path of seductive analogies, creating, through this ruse, connections between the most heterogeneous texts.

The Ambivalence of Love

The dream model therefore seems to dictate the entire Freudian reading of the theme of the choice of the caskets. And yet – and as far as I know, no-one until now has pointed out the importance of this – at a crucial turning-point of the text, when he cites the dual reversal operated by desire in converting necessity into choice and death into love, Freud, stressing this, abandons this model:

> However, contradictions of a certain kind – replacements by the precise opposite – offer no serious difficulty to the work of analytic interpretation. *We shall not appeal here to the fact that contraries are so often represented by one and the same element in the modes of expression used by the unconscious, as for instance in dreams.* But we shall remember that there are motive forces in mental life which bring about replacement by the opposite in the form of what is known as reaction-formation; and it is precisely in the revelation of such hidden forces as these that we look for the reward of this inquiry. [My italics.]

This operation of a reversal, designed to satisfy our desire – to free man from the inexorable law of death and leave him with the illusion that he is an exceptional creation within nature, 'an empire within an empire' – is caused, for Freud, by the activity of the imagination (*Phantasietätigkeit*) the essential function of which is precisely to satisfy those desires which reality frustrates. However, to substitute for the third of the sisters – death – the goddess of Love or human figurations resembling her, the imagination does not, for Freud, borrow from the unconscious its processes and the technique of reversing something to create its opposite; on the contrary, it uses an old and more or less forgotten truth, an ancient ambivalence of Love, closely related, indeed identical to Death:

Nor was this substitution in any way technically [*technisch*] difficult: it was prepared for by an ancient ambivalence, it was carried out along a primaeval line of connection [*Zusammenhang*] which could not long have been forgotten. The Goddess of Love herself, who now took the place of the Goddess of Death, had once been identical with her. Even the Greek Aphrodite had not wholly relinquished her connection with the underworld, although she had long surrendered her chthonic role to other divine figures, to Persephone, or to the tri-form Artemis–Hecate. The great mother-goddesses of the oriental peoples, however, all seem to have been both creators and destroyers – both goddesses of life and fertility and goddesses of death. Thus the replacement by a wishful opposite [*Wunschgegenteil*] in our theme harks back to a primaeval identity.

This appeal to ambivalence as the *ratio essendi* of the splitting and division of a figure is not unique in Freud's work. In *The Uncanny*, dealing with *The Sandman*, it is cited as the explanatory principle of the breakdown of the paternal figure into two opposites: a good father and a bad, diabolical father (Coppelius, Coppola-Spalanzani). It is ambivalence yet again which, in *A Seventeenth-Century Demonological Neurosis*, is made responsible for the splitting into two figures with opposite and violently contrasted attributes (that of God, that of the devil) of a single personality, God, who, in the beginning, 'in the earliest ages of religion . . . still possessed all the terrifying features which were afterwards combined to form a counterpart of him.' In both of these cases, division intervenes to preserve the paternal figure from a mixture which would be made all the more intolerable by being the reflection of Oedipal ambivalence 'which governs the relation of the individual to his personal father'.[8]

So what is original about the *Theme of the Three Caskets*? On the one hand, in this case, the ambivalence is that of a maternal figure, and, on the other hand, the reason for this ambivalence is no longer Oedipus but the original identity of Love and Death, an identity which is to some degree structural. As the identity of the symbolized and the symbolizer in primitive language is, according to Sperber, the reason for their symbolic equivalence in dreams, [9] as the presumed identity of the two sexes in childhood authorizes their symbolic substitution,[10] so the structural identity of love and death is the *real* principle and the precondition behind the splittings, divisions, reversals, substitutions and conversions operated under the effect of the intolerance of our desire.[11]

The break with the dream model in favour of the notion of ambivalence – and of a structural ambivalence – strikes me as being of prime importance. With this break, in fact, a logic completely different from that of dreams is established; a logic of paradox which is unlike the oneiric or neurotic logic of ambiguity or compromise. While ambiguity, in an equivocal fashion, may equally well signify one meaning *or* another, ambivalence *simultaneously* asserts two opposite meanings, sense *and* non-sense; not love *or* death but love *and* death. The structure of ambivalence is the uncompromising structure of a two-faced *Janus*, precisely that, according to Freud, of the joke.[12]

If, in order to explain the substitution of the figure of Love for that of Death, Freud abandons the oneiric model and does not mechanically resort to the process of reversal in dreams, it is because this process does not necessarily refer to an original identity of opposites, since its use can lead to compromise formations permitted by the dream. However, in literature, as in jokes, both eminently social products addressed to the conscious man, the process at work must if possible satisfy – uncompromisingly – *both* desire which is frustrated by reality *and* thought which knows reality, in this case the necessity of death. The trick of the imagination – a faculty which, in a traditional way, plays, for Freud,[13] the role of intermediary, of 'binding agent' between the opposites which it reconciles – its technical feat is, paradoxically, that of inventing nothing but rather of exploiting a *real* relation, the close connection (*Zusammenhang*) of love and death recognized by thought, in order to magic it away by dissociating them and substituting one for the other: because they are closely linked and interdependent, it allows itself to put one in the role of the other at the risk – and this is what, in its duplicity, it is seeking to do – of allowing the one to be forgotten in favour of the other. In this duplicitous game of the imagination, the winners are both thought which can always, behind the face of love, sense that of death, and desire, which can fail to recognize death because it does not appear in its own guise but in the guise of its double. It is in this *simultaneous* recognition and misrecognition that pleasure lies: it is always accompanied by a sense of the uncanny, more or less slight, more or less intense according to whether recognition or misrecognition is dominant, according to the degree of distortion of the primitive myth, that is, according to the greater or lesser degree of the success of the 'creative' work, not that of the unconscious in its use of modes of expression from the primary process but entirely that of the double-faced imagination.

If, by means of its 'creations', the latter allows us, on the one hand, to triumph over death, nevertheless on the other hand and at the same time it never ensures the complete success of our desire: the pharmaceutical function of literature cannot be substituted for that of the dream or of psychosis. Its 'apollonianism' is only the other side and the more or less obvious reflection of its 'dionysianism'.

In *King Lear*, the effect of a powerful, e-norm-ous affect which grips the viewer is, for Freud, the sign that the original identity of love and death is more recognized than misrecognized in that play, while in *The Merchant of Venice*, a lighter play, it is misrecognition that is dominant.

Towards a General Ambivalence

At the end of *The Theme of the Choice of the Caskets*, as if he is still prey to the overpowering effect of *King Lear*, and also perhaps because he sees this tragedy as holding the 'truth' and the key of the comedy,[14] Freud seems to have completely forgotten the much more comic *Merchant of Venice*. This forgetfulness reveals a sort of theoretical insufficiency, which the reader at least perceives: if the creations of the imagination can do without the modes of expression of the unconscious, might one not read *The Merchant of Venice*, unlike Freud, without referring to the dream model? The typical dream model which leads to an almost mechanical symbolic[15] decoding of the text and to a thematic reading which isolates one theme from all the rest? Indeed, if one accepts this latter explanation in terms of the ambivalence of love, the theme of the three caskets does not in fact appear to be isolable, but rather to be a simple and perhaps paradigmatic case of the more general 'theme' of ambivalence which is put on display, as we shall see, in *The Merchant of Venice*.

The ambivalence of Portia and the choice of the caskets

The Freudian interpretation of the scene of the three caskets can be reduced to a statement that the leaden casket, as attested by its pallor and silence, represents death which no one chooses. The unbearable necessity of death therefore, according to this interpretation, is disguised by the choice of the fairest, most desirable, richest and wisest of women, Portia, whose portrait is contained in the leaden casket. It is true that there are many signs in the text which indicate a certain correlation between Portia and death and stress the ambivalence of her figure which permits this substitution: beautiful and intelligent, she is also perfidious and cunning, and is capable of using disguises in order to mislead people as to her sex. Her conquest, compared to that of the golden fleece (Act 1, Scene 1), implies, for all her suitors, a risk of symbolic death, since their possible failure leads to a definitive renunciation of love and marriage. When Bassanio opens the leaden casket and finds the portrait of Portia inside it, he compares her golden hair to a fatal spider's web.

> Here, in her hairs
> The painter plays the spider, and hath woven
> A golden mesh to entrap the hearts of men
> Faster than gnats in cobwebs. (Act 3, Scene 2)

Are these manifest connections between Portia and death features which, in her, approach the uncanny? Are they revealing details through which the figure of Death reappears behind the figure of Love? Do they not simply indicate the ambivalence of the figure of woman? The fact that the fairest of women is, in the eyes of men, always also the most dangerous, the most castrating woman? But it is precisely this *manifest* ambivalence of the figure of Portia that prevents her from playing the role of a reassuring figure capable of using the expedient of fiction in order to conquer the fear of the Invincible. Choosing Portia (Love) means *manifestly* choosing Death, not because, in order to satisfy our desire, the one is substituted for the other, but rather because, as a woman, she is deadly to the man who chooses her.

Similarly, the choice to which the suitors must submit cannot, as such, disguise the *necessity* of death: choice, by its very essence, implies luck, whether good or bad, and more particularly the risk, as in the golden casket (and not the leaden casket) of finding a skeleton in place of love. In any case it implies, once more in a *manifest* way, the risk of death, the only proof of a real love: that is why the will of the dead father which deprives the will of the living daughter of a free choice (cf. Act 1, Scene 2) in accordance with his wishes, in order apparently to subject her to a random and senseless lottery, is, *despite appearances* (as the maid Nerissa observes) a virtuous and wise will, because: 'the lottery that he has devised in these three chests of gold, silver and lead, whereof who chooses his meaning chooses you, will, no doubt, never be chosen by any rightly but one who you shall rightly love' (Act 1, Scene 2). If Bassanio gets the better of the other suitors – in accordance with Portia's vows and desires – it is because he alone, in making his choice, has been guided by love, his own love and the love of Portia that goes with it: 'If you do love me, you will find me out' (Act 3, Scene 2), she says.

Both the princes of Morocco and Arragon, on the other hand, cite not their love but their merits, and when making their choice they are guided by nothing but blind fortune, which is, however, less blind than they think:

> 'If Hercules and Lichas play at dice
> Which is the better man, the greater throw
> May turn by fortune from the weaker hand:
> So is Alcides beaten by his page;
> And so may I, blind fortune leading me,
> Miss that which one unworthier may attain . . .'
> 'Come, bring me unto my chance.'
> 'Good fortune then.'

> 'Fortune now
> To my heart's hope.' (Act 2, Scene 1)

Seen from this point of view – that the choice implies, as proof of a real love, the risk of death – the theme of the three caskets is comparable not so much to those fairy-tales or myths in which a choice must be made between three women, but to the story of Atalanta as told by Ovid.[16] In order to win her hand, Atalanta's suitors must accept the risk of death by taking part in a race in which the only winner will be he who can beat her, the Invincible, on pain of the loss of his life, thereby proving his love: 'he loves me, and thinks it worth while to risk death in order to marry me – for death is the price, if cruel fate deny me to him'. As in *The Merchant of Venice*, fate favours the suitor towards whom she herself is inclined, Hippomenes, who is only successful thanks to a trick: he throws golden apples into the race-track, golden fruits which, by their brilliance, seduce Atalanta and thrice distract her from the race, allowing Hippomenes to catch up with her. This reflects precisely the way the seduction of the gold and silver of the caskets turns the first suitors from the correct choice, that of the leaden casket, thus leaving Bassanio his chance.

Bassanio alone refuses to be seduced, refuses to 'trust appearances', and therefore conforms to the law secreted within each of the three caskets. Thus, the skeleton's eye enclosed within the golden casket contains a scroll on which is written the following inscription:

> All that glisters is not gold;
> Often have you heard that told;
> Many a man his life hath sold
> But my outside to behold;
> Gilded tombs do worms infold.
> Had you been as wise as bold,
> Your answer had not been inscroll'd. (Act 2, Scene 7)

The prince of Morocco, however, with his swarthy complexion, knows that his physical appearance is not the sign of a blackness in his heart – and warns Portia not to be taken in 'by appearances':

> Mislike me not for my complexion,
> The shadow'd livery of the burnish'd sun,
> To whom I am a neighbour and near bred.
> Bring me the fairest creature northward born,
> Where Phoebus' fire scarce thaws the icicles,
> And let us make incision for your love,
> To prove whose blood is reddest, his or mine

Yet this black prince – dressed all in white – chooses the golden casket, apparently the best, to his cost.

Similarly Arragon, who rejects the golden casket so as not to behave like the 'fool multitude', not to associate with vulgar minds in choosing by appearance, still chooses the silver casket, in which he finds not Portia's portrait but that of a grimacing idiot, his own image which means his dismissal because, not having tempered his judgement seven times as fire tempers silver, he can kiss nothing but a shadow, foolishly trusting 'silver'd' surfaces (Act 2, Scene 9).

Bassanio, on the other hand, in his words as well as his actions – the choice of the leaden casket rather than the flashing gold, 'hard food for Midas', and the silver, 'pale and common drudge / 'Tween man and man' – in an entirely Platonic fashion condemns 'outward shows' and 'ornament', 'The seeming truth which cunning times put on / To entrap the wisest', and is able to distinguish Portia's 'shadow', her portrait, from the real Portia of flesh and blood.[17]

Because he alone has not chosen appearance, his fortune is good and his choice a happy one – as the inscription in the leaden casket which delivers his verdict declares; he makes the right choice, that of Portia: a simple girl, but one who will not be guided by the superficial impression of the outward gaze (Act 2, Scene 1), by skin colour or brilliance of garb, who knows, as she will show, that the habit does not make the monk, since she will disguise herself as a man and in doing so deceive even the most ingenious.

The ambivalence of metals and their convertibility

In his examination of the scene of the three caskets, Freud's error is the converse of that of the first suitors: his eyes are for the leaden casket alone, which leads him rapidly and ironically to reject the lesson, banal as it may be, that what he calls the manifest meaning of the play, 'one should not trust appearances', is inscribed on all *three*. If one were to go no further than this, one would certainly not go very far; but there is nevertheless no reason to seek a latent content. Focusing one's attention on the *three* caskets, or more precisely on the *three metals* of which they are constituted, one will notice that all three teach the same lesson because they are actually indissociable, all three are profoundly ambivalent; and this ambivalence is the precondition of the 'false appearance' that they assume, seducing and misleading everyone who misrecognizes it; and also the condition of their convertibility or transmutability.

Despite appearances, *gold*, flashing and royal, solar and divine, is not the opposite of pale and base lead. Its perfection is the result of a slow gestation, a transformation of low metals. It is only this base origin of gold that explains its symbolic equivalence with the basest thing of all, excrement, and all the efforts of alchemists to convert lead into gold, merely achieving the natural transmutation of the base into the perfect by accelerating this process: to make gold the symbol of perfection, to trust the brilliance of its appearance, is to see only a result while forgetting its genesis.[18] It is to forget the time factor in any transmutation: the Age of *gold*, a mythical and paradisiacal age, is also the age of Saturn, of Time, associated with lead, a revealing association of the profound structural ambivalence of gold, of its two-faced nature, which gives rise to a dual evaluation: on the one hand it is the metal of wealth, of domination, and because it is the result of a slow gestation within the bowels of the earth it is the symbol of esoteric know-ledge. A source of light and radiance,[19] it is the symbol of fertility, and as a result of this characteristic it is associated with the ram, the emblem of generative potency. The golden fleece is the insignium of the master and of initiation. This is the golden, solar and appolonian face of gold, which *also* presents, on the other hand, a shadowy, dionysiac, demoniac or saturnine face, which makes it the symbol of the perversion and the impure exaltation of desires. No longer a weapon of light, but a burden which breaks your bones and your neck, transforming you, if your choice attaches to it, you who believe you are of divine origin and unperishable, into a base skeleton, perhaps enclosed within a gilded tomb, but no less gnawed by worms than if that tomb were of base lead. This duplicity on the part of gold, its two-faced nature which indicates, to anyone able to decipher it, the ambiguity of the formula designed to guide the act of choice: '*Who chooseth me shall gain what many men desire*', proves to be the fateful moment of choice, the moment of dramatic 'suspense', the moment of the suspension of time, as Portia is well aware when she seeks to defer the moment when Bassanio will have to make his choice,

> 'tis to peise the time,
> To eke it and to draw it out in length,
> To stay [him] from election (Act 3, Scene 2)

This suspense is a prelude to the catastrophic reversal, the conversion of positive to negative, the transition from the euphoric, manic phase to the depressive, melancholic phase, in which the man who could hope that the conquest of the golden fleece would be accompanied by the conquest of immortality is reduced to nothing. The moment of choice is the moment of the convertibility of gold into lead, which is always possible because, far from being its opposite, gold derives from lead; and it is to lead that it owes that very property which enables it, beyond its apparent perfection, to be transmuted into its supposed opposite.

The alchemists, in particular Paracelsus, are actually aware of this: *lead* is the water of all metals; anyone aware of its content would swiftly have abandoned all other materials to work with lead alone, for white lead implies the possibility of transmuting the properties of one body into that of another and the general properties of matter into the quality of mind. Lead symbolizes the most humble base from which a transforming evolution can emerge. By means of the transmutation of lead into gold, the alchemists sought symbolically to escape individual limitations in order to attain collective and universal values. A 'binding agent' between all metals, it is also – and this is its other face – the symbol of unshakeable individuality, and is therefore linked to Saturn, the god of separation whose scythe cuts through all bonds, all ties. Lead, like Saturn, is therefore the condition both of all connection, transformation, creation, *and* of all mortal separation, division and dissociation. Choosing lead therefore means, as the phrase on the casket says, choosing to 'give and hazard all [one] hath', for it means opting for the choice that involves the risk of catastrophic death, while the choice of gold – or of silver – for anyone who misrecognizes their profound kinship with lead, is an illusory choice of incorruptibility, a refusal of risk and hence a refusal of choice.

Silver, like gold and lead, is also a dual metal – and Arragon's failure is due to his ignorance of this ambivalence. An agent of mediation and exchange between men, it is also an intermediary between gold and lead. Base and pale like lead (which is why the version of the paleness of lead seems to me better than that of its plainness), it nevertheless possesses a certain brilliance, less than that of solar gold, whose female or lunar face it represents to a degree.[20] Like gold, it is subject to a dual evaluation. Pure and divine, it nevertheless gives rise to all forms of cupidity and produces the misfortune of anyone who chooses it through not having taken time to think, through not being aware that silver is also time, through having chosen time (lead) within silver while wrongly, narcissistically, trusting to their own good fortune and merit. Making the right choice primarily means essentially *taking one's time* as Bassanio does, doubly aided, both by Antonio's recommendations:

> Slubber not business for my sake, Bassanio,
> But stay the very riping of the time (Act 2, Scene 8)

and by Portia who, for fear of losing him, attempts to delay his choice, to slow down time, to let Bassanio *take his time* (Act 3, Scene 2).[21]

Thus, gold, silver and lead are all ambivalent, with an ambivalence that is concealed by their being split into three different, even opposite metals, which disguises their profound kinship, their common derivation from the metal which is supposed to be the most base: lead or Saturn; a split which masks the fact that each of them, and not lead alone, secretes time, the risk of transformation, of deterioration, of transmutation in one direction or the other, and conceals, beneath gilded and silvered surfaces, genesis, development and death. The three metals are therefore structurally homologous to the three Greek Aphrodites of which the third, the chthonic, identical with death, misrecognized and repressed, is present within the other two, the Uranian and the Pandemic Aphrodites. Is this homology on its own enough to allow us, without employing the key of dreams, to join Freud in making the transition from goddesses to caskets? The theme of the choice between three metals cannot actually be replaced by that of the choice between three women because the three metals are not merely components of the caskets, the supposed symbols of women; each of them, with its ambivalence, is embodied in one of the three main characters: Antonio, Bassanio and Shylock, whose dual faces are likewise concealed by division, and because one of them, Shylock the Jew, like lead (although he represents silver), like a real scapegoat, is burdened with all of the baseness.

Antonio/Bassanio, or the Dual Face of Saturn

Antonio and Bassanio, who are each other's doubles, each represent one of the faces of the double-faced Janus, Time.

Janus, close kin of Saturn, is invoked from the very first scene, by Solanio, in order obliquely to express, beyond obvious division, the dual face of all things, the real 'theme' of the *Merchant of Venice*:

> Now, by two-headed Janus,
> Nature hath fram'd strange fellows in their time:
> Some that will evermore peep through their eyes
> And laugh like parrots at a bag-piper,
> And other of such vinegar aspect
> That they'll not show their teeth in way of smile,
> Though Nestor swear the jest be laughable.

Solanio, in fact, is intrigued by Antonio's bottomless sadness: nothing can explain it, neither the pain of love nor the loss of money; the sadness of the melancholic, afflicted with *Acedia*:

> I do not know why I am so sad:
> It wearies me [. . .]
> But how I caught it, found it, or came by it,
> What stuff 'tis made of, whereof it is born,
> I am to learn.

Antonio represents the 'sad face', the face of death[22] of all the things he represents:

> I hold the world but as the world [. . .]
> A stage where every man must play a part,
> And mine a sad one. (Act 1, Scene 1)

Bassanio represents the other face; the living, gay and laughing face: in his first words he invites his friends to laugh: 'Good signiors both, when shall we laugh?' (Act 1, Scene 1), as he later urges them to put on their 'boldest suit of mirth' (Act 2, Scene 2). He is constantly accompanied, as if by his shadow, by Gratiano, who would rather play the role of fool than that of the wise man, and see mirth and laughter wrinkle his face rather than have a reputation, like Antonio, for depth and gravity, at the cost of a stagnant immobility and a leaden, deadly silence.

A dual reading of Antonio – the melancholic, Saturnian face with the leaden complexion – is possible, corresponding to the dual evaluation of *Acedia*. A negative evaluation: melancholy is connected with sadness, the coldness of ice, the immobility of death, solitude, sterility, dryness, a lack of vitality. This is the evaluation provided by Bassanio's entourage, by Solanio and Gratiano or by Shylock, close to the 'modern' psychoanalytic evaluation: Antonio is left with only a 'shrunken' ego because he has unloaded all of his narcissistic and homosexual libido onto his double; he has 'poured himself from his purse' and is ready to give his life for Bassanio, the only person who connects him with existence, because he has given him all of his existence: 'I think he only loves the world for [Bassanio]', says Solanio in Act, Scene 8:

> My purse, my person, my extremest means,
> Lie all unlock'd to your occasions [. . .]
> And out of doubt you do me now more wrong
> In making question of my uttermost
> Than if you had made waste of all I have. (Act 1, Scene 1)

He is prepared to give him his flesh and his blood, his life, on condition – and, beyond his total, flaunted 'disinterest', this reveals his deeper instinctual motivation – that the double be present at the sacrifice, that he see with his own eyes both his love and the payment for his love (Act 3, Scene 4).

Seen from this perspective, which accentuates Antonio's 'psychotic' character (hence his beautiful indifference, his beautiful disinterest), one might say that it is easy for him to agree to the sacrifice of his flesh as demanded by the Jew because he has already accomplished this sacrifice: he has already cut himself, castrated himself to the advantage of his double Bassanio. Saturn's scythe (associated, as we should not forget, with lead) has intervened – before the Jew's knife – and cut him off from any interest in material goods, setting him in pursuit of the loss of himself, of his ego and his loves – since by lending Bassanio his money, or at least his credit, he places Bassanio at a distance from himself, allowing him to set off to conquer Portia, who, taking his place from that moment onwards, becomes 'half' of Bassanio (as she emphasizes in a lapsus);[23] it also sends him to the loss of his boats and his fortune. From this negative point of view, Antonio represents Saturn's evil aspect, the man of ill luck and reversals of fortune who, in order to punish himself for some unnamed crime, runs headlong into catastrophe.

However, a different, positive reading is possible, the reading that Bassanio and, to a certain extent, Antonio and his friends give of this character: Antonio is the 'moral' man *par excellence*, the man of self-effacement, detachment and disinterested sacrifice, not through a lack of interest in life and a want of vitality, but through generosity and love; a Christian character, entirely spiritual, the opposite of Shylock the Jew with his basely materialist instincts. While the latter hoards his money to make it bear fruit, cautiously, anally locking it away in its box, Antonio spends and wastes it unreservedly and in conditions that entail risk, having no hesitation in gambling his entire fortune on the sea, that aporetic place *par excellence*.[24]

In his positive traits, notably his prodigality, it could be said that he bears within himself the traces of his double, of the golden, laughing and happy face of Saturn, outwardly projected in the figure of Bassanio.

Bassanio is, in fact, inordinately prodigal. As the euphoric, manic face of time, he represents its devouring and cannibalistic aspect: keen for pleasure, even at the cost of the resources and even the life of his double (and in this he has something in common with Shylock the Jew who at least has the honesty to declare not that he loves Antonio but that he hates him). The euphoric Bassanio is merely the converse of Antonio the melancholic, and the fates of these two divided faces of Time, unbalanced by their very essence, are closely linked. Bassanio's fortune depends on Antonio: it is only thanks to the credit of his double that he can try his fortune and set off, thanks only to his double, for the conquest of the golden fleece. His happiness finds a strict counterpart in Antonio's misfortune: at the very moment when Bassanio is winning his prize, Antonio is losing all his ships, as if the happiness of one necessarily involved the ruin of the other. To Gratiano, who announces to him 'We are the Jasons, we have won the fleece', Salerio replies 'I would you had won the fleece that he hath lost' (Act 3, Scene 2), and these bad tidings 'steal the colour from Bassanio's cheeks', as they had drawn blood from the body of his friend.[25] This arrival of a messenger announcing Antonio's misfortune – in the manner of classical drama – is therefore not the astonishing and arbitrary *coup de théâtre* of some *deus ex machina*; it is rather a blow dealt by the god Time,[26] two-faced, the condition of all catastrophic reversals, of all conversions of good fortune into ill and vice versa. Thus, at the end, a new 'reversal' of fortune allows Antonio's ships to come safely into port and Antonio to regain his fortune: to regain *himself*. Here again, the reversal is not arbitrary but is closely linked to the fate of his double: when the latter marries and, moreover, marries a rich woman, the homosexual link breaks down: it is then that Antonio can recover his narcissistic libido, as well as his money, and also reconstitute *himself* – the return of good fortune is the return of the ships loaded with Antonio's very life. The play therefore ends 'happily' for both doubles: but nothing ensures a 'definitive' happiness since *with time*, as at sea, all risk remain open, and since Gratiano, the fool who is wiser than sad Antonio, has metaphorically predicted, by associating them with one another, a return of both Bassanio's good fortune in love and Antonio's in trade:

> who riseth from a feast
> With that keen appetite that he sits down?
> Where is the horse that doth untread again
> His tedious measures with the unbated fire
> That he did pace them first? All things that are,
> Are with more spirit chased than enjoy'd.
> How like a younker or a prodigal
> The scarfed bark puts from her native bay,
> Hugg'd and embraced by the strumpet wind!
> How like the prodigal doth she return,
> With over-weather'd ribs and ragged sails,
> Lean, rent, and beggar'd by the strumpet wind! (Act 2, Scene 6)

With and through time, which is fundamentally ambivalent, all conversions remain possible.

The Ambivalent Figure of Silver: Shylock the Jew

This is a lesson that we also learn from Shylock the Jew; Shylock who, contrary to all expectations, while he has a visceral hatred of Christians, finally converts to Christianity (although under duress).

What Antonio is to lead and Bassanio to gold, Shylock is to *silver*: 'pale and common drudge / 'Tween man and man', yet necessary – and this is its other face – among other things, to Bassanio in his conquest of Portia, and to the prosperity of the Doges of Venice, who are forced to treat this dog, the Jew, with due care and to see justice done to him in spite of everything.

Shylock's kinship with the silver casket is shown obliquely by his attachment to his own casket (using the same word) in which he locks away all
his treasures, and whose theft by his daughter Jessica to the advantage of
a Christian will lead him to the same despair as the betrayal of his own
flesh. As he will proclaim at the end of the trial which opposes him to
Antonio, to take his money is to take his life:

> Nay, take my life and all; pardon not that:
> You take my house when you do take my prop
> That doth sustain my house; you take my life
> When you do take the means whereby I live. (Act 4, Scene 1)

The figure of Shylock, which is, like that of silver, ambivalent, is also
susceptible to a double reading, although the Christian protagonists stress
only its negative side. From their point of view, which opposes him to
Antonio, the figure of spirituality and disinterest, he is the absolute embodi-
ment of 'evil', a pleasure-seeker, a basely materialistic creature who lends
with interest and who, filled with hate for Christians, would not hesitate,
if necessary, like some wretched cur, to feed on their flesh. But, to their
accusations of insensitivity, Shylock has no difficulty in replying that his
behaviour is in accordance with the figure of the Jew that they themselves
have formed, and that it is contradictory of them to expect emotion, feeling
or friendship from a dog, to believe that the man whom they have reduced
to usury could, duped by their sudden goodwill, agree to dine with them,
to enjoy relations with them other than that of creditor and debtor: 'I will
buy with you, sell with you, talk with you, walk with you, and so following;
but I will not eat with you, drink with you, nor pray with you' (Act 1,
Scene 3). And again:

> Signior Antonio, many a time and oft
> In the Rialto you have rated me
> About my moneys and my usances:
> Still have I borne it with a patient shrug,
> For sufferance is the badge of all our tribe.
> You call me misbeliever, cut-throat dog,
> And spet upon my Jewish gaberdine,
> And all for use of that which is mine own.
> Well then, now it appears you need my help:
> Go to then; you come to me, and you say,
> 'Shylock, we would have moneys:' you say so;
> You that did void your rheum upon my beard,
> And foot me as you spurn a stranger cur
> Over your threshold: moneys is your suit.
> What should I say to you? Should I not say,
> 'Hath a dog money? Is it possible
> A cur can lend three thousand ducats?' or
> Shall I bend low, and in a bondsman's key,
> With bated breath, and whispering humbleness,

Say this:-
'Fair sir, you spet on me on Wednesday last;
You spurn'd me such a day; another time
You call'd me dog; and for these courtesies
I'll lend you thus much moneys?'
ANTONIO: I am as like to call thee so again,
To spet on thee again, to spurn thee too. (Act 1, Scene 3)

To the illogicality of the Christians, their contradictions even with regard to themselves and their faith (which will, for example, lead Bassanio and Gratiano to break the promises they made to their wives that they would never part with their rings, while the Jew would not have sold the ring given him by his wife for all the gold in the world, 'for a wilderness of monkeys' (Act 3, Scene 1), Shylock constantly opposes logic, rationality, the legitimacy of his acts in accordance with the letter of the law. His acts conform to the justice of his country (which, thanks to the trickery of Portia, disguised as an expert lawyer, will push this literalness as far as it will go, to his cost, in order to triumph over him), and in particular, according to him, they observe the law of God, the Jewish law which he sees as legitimating his profits; or 'his interests' (Act 1, Scene 3), as the others say, in order to mock him, failing to acknowledge that God himself commanded men to increase and multiply, and that this is a law of life and time: the law of fertility and reproduction which holds goods to be living creatures just as much as what Antonio, in his own barrenness, wrongly calls 'the barren metal'.[27] The biblical history of the trick invented by Jacob to derive a profit from his uncle Laban's sheep is held to confirm this:

SHYLOCK: When Jacob graz'd his uncle Laban's sheep, –
This Jacob from our holy Abram was,
As his wise mother wrought in his behalf,
The third possessor: ay, he was the third, –
ANTONIO: And what of him? did he take interest?
SHYLOCK: No; not take interest; not as you would say,
Directly interest: mark what Jacob did,
When Laban and himself were compromis'd,
That all the eanlings that were streak'd and pied
Should fall as Jacob's hire, the ewes, being rank,
In end of autumn turned to the rams;
And, when the work of generation was
Between these woolly breeders in the act,
The skilful shepherd peel'd me certain wands,
And, in the doing of the deed of kind,
He stuck them up before the fulsome ewes,
Who, then conceiving, did in eaning time
Fall parti-colour'd lambs, and those were Jacob's.
This was a way to thrive, and he was blest:
And thrift is a blessing, if men steal it not.
ANTONIO: This was a venture, sir, that Jacob serv'd for;
A thing not in his power to bring to pass,
But sway'd and fashion'd by the hand of heaven.

> Was this inserted to make interest good?
> Or is your gold and silver ewes and rams?
> SHYLOCK: I cannot tell; I make it breed as fast:
> But note me, signior. (Act 1, Scene 3)

For Antonio, this is a diabolical parable which would only help 'An evil soul (produce) holy witness' – 'O, what a goodly outside falsehood hath!'; Shylock, 'a villain with a smiling cheek', 'A goodly apple rotten at the heart', is behaving, in this story, like the devil citing the Scriptures for his own ends.

In Shylock's eyes, it at least justifies the permanent association between his daughter[28] – the offspring of his flesh – and his profits, the offspring of his money, those two most precious 'goods' that he will lose simultaneously when Jessica leaves with his coffer. An association ridiculed by Salanio in his account of it, mocking the laments of the Jew as those of a madman:

> My daughter! O my ducats! O my daughter!
> Fled with a Christian! O my Christian ducats!
> Justice! the law! my ducats, and my daughter!
> A sealed bag, two sealed bags of ducats,
> O double ducats, stol'n from me by my daughter! (Act 2, Scene 8)

These laments prove that if, unlike Antonio, Shylock is familiar with the creative face of time, aware that 'time is money'[29] – and that anyone borrowing 3,000 ducats from him should be immediately asked: 'For how long?' – he cannot accept the converse and correlate of this positive face, the risk of ruin that time *also* implies, the risk that time, which does not belong to him and of which he is both trader and thief, does not only cause his flesh and his money to bear fruit, but can also act against him: that his offspring can leave him, his daughter can marry, taking his profits with her, that his own flesh can turn against him. And because he cannot bear to be cut off from his own flesh, in order to avoid falling into melancholy, like Antonio, after his double loss, of that which he had until then 'locked away' in his caskets without spending it, and of his daughter whom he has always hoarded and saved at home, all for himself, he seeks more than ever to avenge himself on the Christians:

> a diamond gone, cost me two thousand ducats in Frankfort! . . . Two thousand ducats in that; and other precious, precious jewels. I wish my daughter were dead at my feet, and the jewels in her ear! would she were hearsed at my foot, and the ducats in her coffin! . . . loss upon loss! the thief gone with so much, and so much to find the thief; and no satisfaction, no revenge. (Act 3, Scene 1)

Because his flesh has been doubly cut from him he will wish – an eye for an eye, a tooth for a tooth – to cut the living flesh from Antonio, Antonio who imprudently risked his entire fortune on the venturous sea, the plaything of a thousand chances and vicissitudes, permitting Shylock by this very fact, because of all these risks incurred over three months, to seek a supplementary guarantee of his solvency: the right to take from him – and this will be a matter of the strictest law and justice – a pound of his flesh if the debt is not repaid at term.

From then on one can say that the 'logic' of the Jew and his constant reference to the legitimacy of his acts only conceal, with their apparent rationality, a quite different logic: that of desire and compensation, the logic of the fatal supplement and cruelty, a logic of madness, which, no longer relying on strict equivalence and justice, silences all calculation, all reason, and means that Shylock the Jew, despite his assumed avarice, prefers – out of hatred, to everyone's astonishment, and despite their successive appeals to his cupidity and to the clemency of his heart – a pound of flesh to 3,000 ducats (just as Antonio, for love in this case, and in a reversal of Shylock's logic but just as 'unreasonably', in the terms of the same strange logic, prefers death to life):

> You'll ask me why I rather choose to have
> A weight of carrion flesh than to receive
> Three thousand ducats: I'll not answer that:
> But say it is my humour: is it answer'd?
> What if my house be troubled with a rat,
> And I be pleas'd to give ten thousand ducats
> To have it baned? What, are you answer'd yet?
> Some men there are love not a gaping pig;
> Some, that are mad if they behold a cat;
> And others, when the bagpipe sings i' the nose,
> Cannot contain their urine: for affection,
> Mistress of passion, sways it to the mood
> Of what it likes, or loathes. Now, for your answer:
> As there is no firm reason to be render'd
> Why he cannot abide a gaping pig;
> Why he, a harmless necessary cat;
> Why he, a wauling bagpipe; but of force
> Must yield to such inevitable shame
> As to offend, himself being offended;
> So can I give no reason, nor I will not,
> More than a lodg'd hate and a certain loathing
> I bear Antonio . . . (Act 4, Scene 1)

Shylock prefers the torture of Antonio to his money, for that is the basis of this strange and subterranean logic:[30] watching or causing suffering brings pleasure, and this pleasure is intensified by the fact that the debtor is a master who is hierarchically superior to the creditor who, throughout this unexpected spectacle – the duration of a Saturnalia – can thus, reversing the roles, assume the role of master, assume, that is, a right to cruelty, exert his power over a person reduced to powerlessness and voluptuously enjoy this dish, particularly flavoursome to one who, until that point, has been ridiculed and humiliated, treated more badly than a dog.

In operating this reversal of mastery, Shylock not only fully satisfies his will to power but, in showing that he prefers revenge to money, he reveals his 'spirituality' to those who have denied it and, beyond established social and racial differences, proclaims the universality of instincts, notably that of cruelty, and hence the unity of the human species:

> I am a Jew. Hath not a Jew eyes? hath not a Jew hands, organs, dimensions, senses, affections, passions? Fed with the same food, hurt with the same weapons, subject to the same diseases, healed by the same means, warmed and cooled by the same winter and summer, as a Christian is? If you prick us, do we not bleed? If you tickle us, do we not laugh? if you poison us, do we not die? and if you wrong us, shall we not revenge? If we are like you in the rest, we will resemble you in that. If a Jew wrong a Christian, what is his humility? Revenge. If a Christian wrong a Jew, what should his sufference be by Christian example? Why, revenge. The villany you teach me I will execute, and it will go hard but I will better the instruction. (Act 3, Scene 1)

In his speech, Shylock thus converts the Christian into a Jew, and the Jew into a Christian, permitting and justifying, in the name of this mutual equivalence in cruelty, his own 'conversion', which is ironically announced in Scene 3 of Act 1: 'This hebrew will turn Christian: he grows kind', a conversion, however, that the modern viewer finds unbearable, since it does not indicate that universality and natural community between men, the condition of all convertibility, and because, imposed under duress, as a punishment, it marks the end of the Saturnalias, a new reversal of mastery in favour of those who have the power; the final humiliation of the Jew, who has not only lost his money and his daughter to a Christian, but finds himself forced to espouse a despised faith, this catastrophic reversal in an extreme dramatic moment is the counterpart of the 'reversals' of fortune undergone by Antonio, for whom, in the end, that fickle and two-faced goddess rights her wheel.

A question that has been much discussed is whether *The Merchant of Venice* is an 'antisemitic' play, and because its protagonists reflect ambient antisemitism Shakespeare himself has been held responsible for that antisemitism: however I do not see the author's 'sympathy' as being more with Antonio or Bassanio. He merely reveals the dual face, the ambivalence of each of the characters, the condition of their convertibility, which is the same – and exists for the same reasons – as that of the metals, of gold and silver into lead, and vice versa.

A Baroque Drama

To join Freud in privileging the theme of the three caskets, and to stress only the ambivalence of love, is therefore to misrecognize the more general 'theme' of ambivalence, the double face of time, the condition of all conversions, of all reversals. A theme which cannot be substituted for any other, which is not a theme like any other: it is a structural part of the theatre and of the *coup de théâtre*, especially in baroque theatre, in which the double face of Saturn is responsible for those catastrophic reversals which, in a moment – a moment of suspense, of choice – turn good fortune to ill and vice versa. Seen from this point of view, *The Merchant of Venice* – a drama of conversion in all its forms – is not a lighter play than *King Lear*. Neither a tragedy nor a comedy, but somewhere in between, a baroque drama the conditions of whose possibility *The Merchant of Venice* puts on show in a paradigmatic way. Using human vanity to express the vanity of all simple oppositions, by the same gesture in which, with his fools, he locates folly in the heart of wisdom and comedy within tragedy,[31] Shakespeare, in *The Merchant of Venice*, reveals, beyond the divisions carried out by desire, the close interdependence of sadness and laughter, the two faces, melancholic and manic, of Time.

If the Freudian reading had to be salvaged – but has it? – one might still say that the generalization of the theme of ambivalence and hence of conversion is still placed at the service of desire: that it provides a better disguise for the essential thing, the only thing that finally matters to us, the ambivalence of love (its identity with death), exactly as the generalization of anguish makes it easier for us to bear and repress any particular anguish. One might actually say this, but only by impoverishing the text and resorting, in a somewhat forced and unconvincing way, to the oneiric model that Freud himself disturbs – and for me this is the major contribution of the *Theme of the Three Caskets* – by introducing the category of a structural ambivalence, albeit without reaching this conclusion: the invalidation of a psychoanalytical reading of literary texts, at least in the most usual sense of that term.

Notes

1 And not *The Theme of the Three Caskets* in the Hubback/Strachey translation, or *Le Thème des trois coffrets*, in Marie Bonaparte's French rendering, both of which strangely shift the emphasis away from the Freudian reading. G. S. Freud, *Das Motiv der Kästchenwahl* (1913), 'The Theme of the Three Caskets', in *Art and Literature*, vol. 14 (Harmondsworth: Pelican Freud Library, 1985), pp. 233–47.
2 Translator's note: This translation has been somewhat modified at the suggestion of Sarah Kofman.
3 Cf. 'The "Uncanny" ' (Harmondsworth: Pelican Freud Library, 1919) vol. 14, p. 375.
4 If we had to date the latter work in relation to the former, we might be almost certain that it predates it. In *Leonardo da Vinci and a Memory of his Childhood*, Freud uses the criterion of the degree of repression to speculate that the *London Cartoon* is an earlier work than the *St Anne with Two Others*. Cf. my *The Childhood of Art* (New York: Columbia University Press, 1988).
5 The interpretation of myths borrowed from O. Rank allows him to dismiss the astral interpretation of E. Stucken: 'The question is not exhausted, for we do not share the belief of some investigators that myths were read in the heavens

and brought down to earth; we are more inclined to judge with Otto Rank that they were projected on to the heavens after having arisen elsewhere under purely human conditions. It is in this human content that our interest lies' *The Theme of the Three Caskets*, p. 236.

6   'The lottery that he hath devised in these three chests of gold, silver and lead' (Act 1, Scene 2, line 27).

7   In other texts, Shakespeare frequently uses the word, coffer, casket or closet, in a metaphorical sense, but this word never represents 'woman' or 'the essence of woman'. In Sonnet 46 it is the metaphor of the *heart*:

> My heart doth plead that thou in him dost lie, –
> A closet never pierc'd with crystal eyes, –

The same metaphor appears in Sonnet LII: 'So is the time that keeps you as my chest'.' In Sonnet LXV, it represents time itself, in which death preserves and keeps the jewels which he or she hides away from life:

> O fearful meditation! where, alack,
> Shall Time's best jewel from Time's chest lie hid?
> Or what strong hand can hold his swift foot back?
> Or who his spoil of beauty can forbid?

In all these cases the casket is something that guards, hides away and conceals, whether to preserve from death or to preserve from life. Similarly, the 'three caskets' contain either life or death. It is notable that the word 'casket' is not used in the Sonnets.

8   In *Freud and Fiction* (Cambridge: Polity Press, 1990), I have shown that the idea of Oedipal ambivalence alone cannot explain the infinite multiplication, and not merely by a factor of two, of the figures of evil in *The Sandman*. And also that ambivalence can only be effective if it encounters, in reality, a more original division which is the condition of its possibility: the double, as a bad father, refers in its possibility to a more original diabolism, the principle of all division and all things negative, which Freud will later call the 'death instinct'.

9   Cf. Sigmund Freud, *The Interpretation of Dreams* (Harmondsworth: Pelican Freud Library, 1976), vol. 4, p. 468: 'Things that are symbolically connected to-day were probably united in prehistoric times by conceptual and linguistic identity. The symbolic relation seems to be a relic and a mark of former identity.'

10 'It is true that the tendency of dreams and of unconscious phantasies to employ sexual symbols bisexually betrays an archaic characteristic; for in childhood the distinction between the genitals of the two sexes is unknown and the same kind of genitals are attributed to both of them. But it is possible, too, to be misled into wrongly supposing that a sexual symbol is bisexual, if one forgets that in some dreams there is a general inversion of sex, so that what is male is represented as female and vice versa. Dreams of this kind may, for instance, express a woman's wish to be a man.' (ibid., p. 476).

11 In Plato's *Symposium*, the dialogue between Diotima and Socrates which sees love as being based on an essential poverty (the mother of Eros is Penia, symbol of aporetic distress and indigence), thus surreptitiously introduces the chthonic Aphrodite, who is identical with death and repressed by Pausanias, who divides this ambivalent figure into two opposing figures, that of the Uranian Aphrodite, entirely valorized, that of the pandemic Aphrodite, whom he disqualifies entirely

as he does the female sex. Cf. my 'Beyond Aporia?' in *Poststructuralist Classics*, ed. A. Benjamin (London: Routledge, 1988).

12 Cf. Sigmund Freud, *Jokes and their Relation to the Unconscious* (1905) (Harmondsworth: Pelican Freud Library, 1976) vol. 6, and my reading of this text in *Pourquoi rit-on?* (Paris: Galilée, 1986).

13 Cf. particularly *Two Principles of Mental Functioning* (Penguin Freud Library, vol. 11), and my *The Childhood of Art*.

14 In the relationship that he establishes between these two plays and myths and literature, Freud works in an Aristotelian or Hegelian way: the end result contains the key to that which precedes it. On the other hand, however, it breaks with that linear or dialectical model because later development can only reveal the truth of the founding process in terms of a disguise effected by division or repression.

15 'It might be described as the *"decoding"* method, since it treats dreams as a kind of cryptography in which each sign can be translated into another sign having a known meaning, in accordance with a fixed key.' 'The essence of the decoding procedure, however, lies in the fact that the work of interpretation is not brought to bear on the dream as a whole but on each portion of the dream's content independently, as though the dream were a geological conglomerate in which each fragment of rock required a separate assessment' (Freud, *Interpretation of Dreams*, pp. 171–2).

16 *Metamorphoses*, Book 10.

17   yet look, how far
       The substance of my praise doth wrong this shadow
       In underprizing it, so far this shadow
       Doth limp behind the substance. (Act 3, Scene 2)

18 'Furthermore, everything that is complete and perfect is admired; everything evolving is underestimated . . . wherever we can see the evolution, we grow somewhat cooler', F. Nietzsche, *Human, All Too Human*, trans. Marion Faber (Lincoln; London: University of Nebraska Press, 1984), p. 162; see also 145, 252.

19 '[T]he colour gold is the most noble of colours, [Bartolo] says, because light is represented by it; if someone wished to represent the rays of the sun, the most luminous of bodies, he could not do it more properly than by rays of gold; and it is agreed that there is nothing more noble than light', Lorenzo Valla quoted by Michael Baxandall in *Painting and Experience in Fifteenth Century Italy* (Oxford: Oxford University Press, 1972).

20 'If you put the sun first, then you ought to make the moon second, and if you call the one golden you should call the other silver and next after the sun, just as silver comes second after gold . . .', (ibid.).

21 For the alchemical meaning of the three metals, cf. the *Dictionnaire des symboles*, by Jean Chevalier and Alain Gheerbrant (Paris: Seghers, 1973).

22 In Act 1, scene 2, Portia compares one of her melancholic suitors to Heraclitus, the weeping philosopher, and to a death's-head with a bone in its mouth.

23   Beshrew your eyes,
       They have o'erlooked me and divided me:
       One half of me is yours, the other half yours,
       Mine own, I would say; but if mine, then yours,
       And so all yours. (Act 3, Scene 2)

24   My wind . . .,
       Would blow me to an ague, when I thought

What harm a wind too great might do at sea.
I should not see the sandy hour-glass run
But I should think of shallows and of flats (. . .),
And not bethink me straight of dangerous rocks,
Which touching but my gentle vessel's side
Would scatter all her spices on the stream,
Enrobe the roaring waters with my silks;
And, in a word, but even now worth this,
And now worth nothing. (Salarino, Act 1, Scene 1).

25   Here is a letter, lady;
The paper as the body of my friend,
And every word in it a gaping wound,
Issuing life-blood. (Act 3, Scene 2)

26 Time as an all-powerful *deus ex machina* that allows all catastrophic reversals is put on stage in *The Winter's Tale*, in which it plays the part of the *Chorus* at the beginning of Act 4:

I, that please some, try all, both joy and terror
Of good and bad, that make and unfold error,
Now take upon me, in the name of Time,
To use my wings. Impute it not a crime
To me or my swift passage, that I slide
O'er sixteen years, and leave the growth untried
Of that wide gap; since it is in my power
To o'erthrow law, and in one self-born hour
To plant and o'erwhelm custom. . . .
                Your patience this allowing,
I turn my glass and give my scene such growing
As you had slept between.

27 The thesis of the 'barrenness' of metal is not Antonio's own, but is a generally held Christian belief. The condemnation of usury by the Church is based, among other things, on the confusion that the Jew was held to make between living matter and metal.

Saint Thomas said that 'money does not reproduce'. To make money breed is therefore an illegitimate phenomenon that goes against nature. Money on its own is unproductive, infertile. 'Money . . . was principally invented for exchange. Consequently it is unjust to receive a price for the use of loaned money; that amounts to usury'. (*Summa theologica*).

'Usurers sin against nature in seeking to beget money from money as one would beget a horse by a horse or a mule by a mule. Also, usurers are thieves because they sell time which does not belong to them' (thirteenth-century manuscript).

Texts quoted by Jacques Le Goff in *La Bourse et la vie* (Paris: Hachette, 1986), to which we refer for the position of the Church towards usury in the Middle Ages, a position which, for Le Goff, delayed the advent of capitalism, at least until the Church gave the usurer the hope of escaping hell thanks to purgatory.

The Old Testament, on the other hand, permits loans with interest to strangers (Deuteronomy, 23: 20), and hence to Christians: from this perspective, the position of Shylock is in accordance with Jewish law which only condemns lending with interest to other Jews.

28 This attachment to descent becomes all the more understandable if one bears in mind that for Shakespeare (if we return to the Sonnets), it alone is a means

of obtaining immortality, that is, of truly conquering Time and its scythe: Cf. for example Sonnet XII:

> And nothing 'gainst Time's scythe can make defence
> Save breed, to brave him when he takes thee hence.

29 As early as the fifteenth century, Leon Battista Alberti defines time as money. Quoted by Le Goff in *La Bourse et la vie*.

30 Cf. F. Nietzsche: 'the debtor made a contract with the creditor and pledged that if he should fail to repay he would substitute something else that he "possessed", something he had control over. . . . Above all, however, the creditor could inflict every kind of indignity and torture upon the body of the debtor. . . . Let us be clear as to the logic of this form of compensation: it is strange enough. An equivalence is provided by the creditor's receiving, in place of a literal compensation for an injury (thus in place of money, land, possessions of any kind), a recompense in the form of a kind of *pleasure* – the pleasure of being allowed to vent his power freely upon one who is powerless, the voluptuous pleasure *"de faire le mal pour le plaisir de le faire"*, the enjoyment of violation. This enjoyment will be greater the lower the creditor stands in the social order, and can easily appear to him as a most delicious morsel, indeed as a foretaste of a higher rank. In "punishing" the debtor, the creditor participates in a *rightness of the masters*: . . . The compensation, then, consists in a warrant for and title to cruelty', *On the Genealogy of Morals*, trans. Walter Kaufmann and R. J. Hollingdale (New York: Vintage Books, 1969), 2nd Essay, section 5.

31 Cf. Walter Benjamin, *The Origin of German Tragic Drama* (London: New Left Books, 1977).

JULIA KRISTEVA

Identification and the Real

Translated by Shaun Whiteside

Listening to Jean Oury,[1] it occurred to me that an 'identificatory process' had unconsciously enveloped us, for I intend to deal with a number of the themes which he has touched upon: as if a community of ideas or of clinical concerns had been established without our knowledge. I wondered whether it was not due to a ghost (certainly discussed a great deal, and I too shall return to it but in relation to Shakespeare), the ghost of Lacan and the need which he formulated, to study the notion of identification in terms of the symbolic, and of the paternal function.

In particular that leads us to recall a trait indicated by Freud under the name of *primary identification* with the 'father in the personal prehistory' (*The Ego and the Id*), a degree zero of identification which mobilizes affects, instincts and a certain image of the body of the analyst and the body of the patient at the moment of transference and that of counter-transference. To take up Schotte's argument,[2] it is clearly less the discourse of hysteria or melancholy that is at work here than that of psychotic or so-called *borderline* identification, which obliges us to re-examine primary identification. This is also true, in a less anthropological and more cultural way, of certain cultural phenomena: the sacred, or indeed our contemporary imaginary realm which, from the psychedelic to modern art, exhibits permanent fluctuations of identification.

I should like first of all to emphasize the necessary intensity that the term identification implies for me. Far from being a simple equivalent of the signifier or of symbolic schemas, it involves the real, and particularly the body. The symptom may be an identification made flesh, through refusing to submit to the demand for identity dictated by frustration and language. An identification such as this is a refusal of identity: it opts for pleasure and denies division, distinctness. A question arises: when the cure has better established identity and has classified identifications, it spares the subject a certain pleasure [*jouissance*], in favour of the delights of non-being; but is this tolerable, liveable, possible? One thinks, once more, of the 'future', perhaps of the necessity, of *illusion*. But to return to the topic at hand . . .

A 'fuzzy set'[3]

The psychoanalytic term *identification* covers various stages in the process of the creation of the subject: narcissistic identification, hysterical identification, projective identification, primary identification, ego-ideal ... If I admit that I am never ideally One under the Law of the Other, my entire psychical adventure is made up of failed identifications, impossible autonomies which become invested by narcissism, perversion, alienation. However problematic it may appear because of its polyvalence, the term *identification* nevertheless deserves to be maintained in analytic theory and practice, for at least two reasons.

Firstly, whatever the variants of identification, the generic term *identification* presupposes the tendency specific to the speaking subject to assimilate, *in symbolic and real terms*, another being separate from itself. Let us note that two processes of representation are required within this dynamic: one of them *verbal* and the other *trans-* or *preverbal*. Moreover, in counter-transference, identification operates as an instrument of knowledge and interpretation of the other. Finally, in the economics of writing, and more specifically in the case of Joyce, the problematic of identification has the advantage of shifting the emphasis from the Oedipus complex (of which several authors have indicated the minimal pertinence for a Joyce attracted less by Greek murderers, such as Oedipus and Orestes, than by wanderers such as Telemachus and Ulysses)[4] on to a different intra-psychic adventure, which precedes and intersects the Oedipus complex and eludes our conventional label of psychic 'structures', which, in the last instance, are imposed by psychiatry.

Let us therefore understand identification as meaning this *movement* by which the subject comes into being, through a process where he or she becomes one with another, identical to him- or herself. I am not saying that the subject models him- or herself on the other, which would be a characteristic of the formal plastic uncertainty of mere comparison. On the contrary, transferred to the Other, in identification, *I* becomes One with the Other throughout the whole range of the symbolic, the imaginary and the real. Freud evokes the intensity of an *Einfühlung*, an empathy appropriate to certain amorous, hypnotic or even mystical states. He also indicates that the primary identification of the subject occurs with a primitive figure which he calls a 'father in the personal prehistory' (*Vater der persönlichen Vorzeit*), and which, he argues, possesses the sexual attributes of both parents.

In contemporary analytic practice, the emergence in analysis of narcissistic, '*borderline*', or even psychosomatic structures calls much more on the analyst's powers of *Einfühlung* – that transverbal identification which doubtless derives from primary identifications – as a fundamental moment of the cure. The problematic repressions of these new patients move from '*word presentations*' through to *instinctual psychical representatives*, with transference provoking both the language and the affect of the analyst. To take my language to the psychical place where my patient has convulsive fits, for example, I must accompany my patient *in affect* in her suffering, but also make the leap into the *language* of signs, and give a name to our common affect, which has for a time been unnameable.

'Crossed' identifications

I must accompany my patient who has convulsive fits only when she is *en route*: I must accompany her affectively, with empathy, in her suffering as a little girl abandoned by her mother and separated from a father who has rejected the mother, while recognizing her progeniture as long as she lives ... far away. I am in full counter-transference of narcissistic and doubtless amorous, hysterical identification, which remains the unspoken part of the interpretation. However, an identification such as this is the underlying motor behind the interpretation that I propose to her, when she evokes, in the course of a session, the memory (or fantasy? – she is never sure), of a railwayman who attempted to seduce her ('but, perhaps, it was a ghost, someone I imagined', the patient hesitates) during a journey, on the way back from her father's house. I understand and see, in this 'ghost', that in place of frustrated incest the young girl has substituted identification with her father's whole body, identification with the phallic pleasure of the father who has literally *taken* the mother to make her come, but also to make her disappear, to make her die in a way, or in any case to make her disappear from the patient's representation.

My counter-transferential identification reproduces the incomplete dynamic of what I would call *crossed identification* in the case of this patient. Christine identifies with both her father and her mother, pleasure and disappearance, rigidity and absence, phallic power and death. It is because it is thus constituted by multiple incomplete and interwoven identifications that the identification of this patient fails to achieve ... identity.

In the true sense of the word it is a failed identification, prevented by an unnameable narcissistic hostility, but also by a fierce Oedipal jealousy. It may be suggested that, whatever the neurobiological determinations of her illness, the wasteful pleasure of the convulsion is integrated within her psychical apparatus, and may be unconsciously used to mime, reproduce and fix precisely that *identificatory conglomerate* which bars the way to *one* identity. Doubtless a fiction, always more or less problematic, *identity* presupposes the subject's choice of *one* identification and renunciation of all others, acceptance of his or her separation, a break. Analytic interpretation attempts to re-establish precisely this distinctness, this discreteness. Our interpretations place identifications in series, disentangling the identificatory conglomerate. And, at the price of a removal of pleasure, they indicate to the patient that *here*, they have taken themselves for *this*, and *there*, for *that*; *before*, for *this*, *now*, for *that*. Thus time and space plot their regained identity.

But to return to my interpretation. After her story about the railwayman seducer, I say to my patient: 'Take me, daddy, or there will be nothing for it but to take ourselves for daddy or disappear like mummy. While in the arms of this man, you can imagine being both him and her reunited.' Christine immediately continues: 'It's strange, that's exactly what happened. I told him, I think I told him to take me in his arms, but he thought I meant something else and I lost consciousness, I disappeared . . . '

'Daddy' who 'takes in his arms' meant, coming from me, and doubtless also for the patient who heard me, a conglomerate of pre-Oedipal mother and object of Oedipal desire. A pole too heavily charged with crossed identities, the paternal figure repeated in the almost hallucinatory image of the railwayman made one sole identification impossible. The auto-erotic discharge of the convulsion was probably used to fill this breach, this impossibility of distinctness, of identity. On the other hand, *naming* the crossed identifications can lead to a dissociation of the logical chains and also of the condensation of traces of contradictory affects, and help towards the dissolution of the convulsive symptom.

I insist on the counter-transferential movement of identification with this psychosomatic patient, as will have been guessed, in order to suggest a diachronic fiction: a hypothesis concerning the conditions of the structuring of the subject. Identification, in terms of metaphor rather than comparison, must be understood in the strong sense of a transport mobilizing instinctual representatives *and* word-presentations. If metaphor is involved, it is not rhetorical, but something closer to what Baudelaire meant by a 'mystical metamorphosis'.

However, it is this movement which is the *sine qua non* of the emergence of the subject. That is, metaphor in the sense of a transport of instinctual representatives and word-presentations, rather than another who makes me become One with him: body and soul.

Narcissistic duplication (I *repeat* mummy – not yet a stabilized identificatory metaphor, but a simple repetition) or a projective identification (I do not want to know that I hate her, so it must be she who detests me) are elements of a series which will conclude (temporarily, never completely) in the metaphorical movement of identification with the imaginary Father which Freud calls 'primary identification' and which is the degree zero of the autonomy of the subject. As in Christian *agape*, this identification comes to us from above, from a third party (who, for the analyst, is the object of maternal love), but the child does not have to elaborate it. Delights and appeasement, ghostly debt and the ultimate goal of existence: this will be the Joycian filial *agape*, judging by his Shakespeare, Bloom, Rudy, Dedalus . . .

The dominance of instinctive representatives over verbal representatives remains greater in narcissistic identification and projective identification, but it underlies all identification. For, according to its logic, identification is always instability and movement (a 'fuzzy set'), while in its economy it is ambiguous: both symbolic and real. It is a 'transcorporation'. At the moment of the cure's maturation, my body *is* the body of my patient, apart from the symptom: the source of my fatigue, also of my rejuvenation, my rebirth. However, interpretation, for me, and thus, for my patient, the verbalization enriched by our relationship, replaces the symptom from which my patient has been suffering. Apart from that – and it is fundamental – we live beneath the same identificatory sign, transference and counter-transference.

Transsubstantiation

So this *agape* leads us from identification to transsubstantiation. Is the Father consubstantial with the Son? Or is the Son perhaps merely in the image of the Father? Is the eucharist the real body of Christ with which I identify by absorbing it, or is it only a representation, or even, as the very Jansenist *Logique de Port-Royal* very logically states, was it a bread and a wine *before*, and *now* the body of Christ? I shall not give you the details of this discussion which divides Christianity until the Council of Trent (1545–63), and which is nevertheless at the heart of our examination of the psychic range of identification. I shall approach it from two secular angles: Joyce, obviously, but before him . . . Galileo.

You will not be surprised to learn that this debate about transsubstan-tiation has been revived, and actually allowed to lapse, by modern science, in particular by Galileo (cf. Pietro Redondi, *Galileo Eretico* (Turin: Einaudi, 1983)). The major element of the Church's case against Galileo does not seem to have been Galileo's Copernican heliocentrism, but rather his concep-tion of matter in which (particularly in his *Saggiatore*, 1623) they suspected an atomism. Indeed, if all matter is identically atomic, it is clear that there can be no passage from one matter to another, that there can be no transsubstantiation – which had, however, been established as a dogma by the Council of Trent, in 1551. Of course, no physical science could demonstrate the symbolic – and real – range of identification. At best it could only relegate it to subjectivity: you 'imagine' that you are identical to X . . . We had to wait for another Galileo, the Galileo of the Unconscious, in order to claim, in a new way, the real value of symbolic identification, including its somatic modifications.

A hardy explorer of the same psychic landscapes, the artist pours or spends the identificatory symptom into original discourse: into style. Neither subservient like the believer, nor subjected to of somatic conversion like the hysteric, but sometimes both of these, he constantly produces multiple identifications, but he *speaks* them. Hypothesis: because more than any other he is in the grip of the 'father in the individual prehistory'. Contrary to the widespread myth of the artist subject to the desire for his mother, or rather in order to defend himself against this desire, he takes himself . . . not for the phallus of the mother, but for this ghost, the third party to which the mother aspires, for the loving version of the third party, for a pre-

Oedipal father 'who loved you first' (say the Gospels), a conglomerate of both sexes (suggests Freud) . . . 'God is *Agape*'.

Joyce between Eros and Agape[5]

Joyce's Catholicism,[6] his profound experience of trinitary religion to the point of derision, confronted him with its centre, the eucharist, the rite *par excellence* of identification with the body of God, the fulcrum of all other identifications, including the artistic profusion of imagination favoured by Catholicism. This Catholic cultural context, intensely assimilated by Joyce, probably encountered a mechanism which is, moreover, the drive behind his fictional experiment, and allowed him to concentrate his efforts at representation and elucidation upon the identificatory substratum of psychic operation, placed so authoritatively at the centre of the last of the religions.

Quite emphatically, the many different ways in which Joyce – *the grace hoper* – insists on transsubstantiation or on the heresy of Arius, as well as on the consubstantiality of the father and the son in *Hamlet*, but also between Shakespeare, his father, his son Hamnet and the whole body of the playwright's work, as a real filiation, are the finest expression of the Joycian obsession, via the theme of the eucharist. We might recall the condensation between 'trinity' and 'transsubstantiation' in *contransmagnificandjewbangtantiality* . .

More indirectly, the orality of Bloom, avid consumer of livers, gizzards and other animal entrails; the vertiginous assimilation of knowledge by Mulligan or Stephen; the meal that constitutes the scene for the finally real encounter between Stephen and Bloom, leaving the way open for exchange, which extends to their sexual exchange of women; but also the assimilation by the narrator of the character of Molly, whose final monologue, more strikingly than any other use of the mask of a character by an author, indicates the displacement and realization, in the narrative themes as well as the very dynamic of the fiction, of the *topos* of identification.

In any case, it is probably in the two variants of amorous experience as they are illustrated by Stephen Dedalus and Leopold Bloom – in Stephen's *Agape* and Bloom's *Eros*[7] – that I would see the most pertinent and, analytically, the most *successful* attempt that Joyce undertook in order to explain the identificatory movement specific to artistic existence. We should say immediately that, if the exposure of intra-psychic identification in a literary text may be interpreted as a 'return of the repressed' (we repress the processes which have governed the constitution of our pyschic space, and it is only by means of a liberation of repression or a modification of the barrier of repression that this repressed can manifest itself) and if, in this respect, the massive presence of identificatory narrative themes or processes may be considered as a symptom, then it is surely a proliferating, unstable and problematic identification which is the symptom *par excellence* of the act of writing, as described by Mallarmé.

But Joyce knows this, with a knowledge that is perhaps unconscious, or at any rate with a knowledge illuminated by theological science, and consequently he turns the symptom around, pours it out and claims its profound logic as a necessary part of our everyday lives.

We need multiple, plastic, polymorphous and polyphonic identifications and, if the eucharist has lost the overarching power which gave us the opportunity to have them, then two possibilities at least remain open to us: let us read literature on the one hand, and attempt to reinvent love on the other. Amorous experience and artistic experience, as two interdependent aspects of the identificatory process, are our only means of preserving our psychic space as a 'living system', that is, open to the other, capable of adaptation and change. Such an integration of polymorphism or perversion is inseparable from a practice of language that is not restricted to calculation, however vertiginous, of pure signifiers, but which integrates pre- or trans-verbal representations, embracing a vast *semiotic* range which extends from gesture to colours and sounds, and turns the use of language not into a logical exercise but into a ritual theatre, a carnivalized liturgy.

Does this mean that this closeness to psychosis (in the manipulation of words as if they were things) broached by an identificatory polymorphous-ness of such extraordinary perversity, is due to one ultimate identification with an archaic mother, the supreme authority in which the identity of the constantly defiant narrator takes refuge, and, persistently, the law of paternal identity, the guarantee of all normative identity? C. G. Jung seems to believe so when he asserts that Joyce 'knows the female soul, as if he were the devil's grandmother'. But it is a strange grandmother who takes on the ways of a sensual Jew, and whose phallic *jouissance*, not unfamiliar with real decantings into female bodies (e.g. Bloom's masturbation while facing Gertie), is still finally inspired by the dominant power of the text and the sacred imposition of the proper name.

Or on the other hand is Joyce perhaps a 'holy man' who has turned the perverse symptom of identification with the woman inside out, like a glove, and brought out, in place of castration, the projection of style – as Lacan has it?

I would say instead that Joyce succeeds where Orpheus fails. Does his adventure not reveal the modern, post-Christian version of the Greek myth in which the hero-artist is forbidden to see something, to seek Eurydice in hell, to return to the mystery of femininity? For as we know, if he does so he loses his loved one, and this impossible love is paid for by a sacrifice (he is torn to pieces by the maenads), but also by an immortality (he lives on, scattered in his songs). On the contrary, Dedalus-Bloom does not divert his gaze from the infernal night that swallows Eurydice, but still does not disappear himself. Any more than Joyce, in spite of the difficulties of his existence, sacrificed his social being to the myth of *l'art maudit*, but rather ironically guided his boat between patrons and female guardians of litera-ture. Only, and tragically, the madness of Lucia perhaps testifies to the ludic metamorphoses of a father who will not stay fixed in one place.

But the Joycian odyssey towards the fatherland of the work does not, on the other hand, release him from the task of returning to the invisible secret of femininity which Freud described as the inaccessible part of the personality in both sexes. The narrator watches her, his Euridice–Molly, insolent, aggressive and obscene (we might consider, in counterpoint to this, the scatological letters beteen Joyce and Nora) and, without a hint of fear, he draws her from the inferno of passion . . . into his monologue-song.

People have mistakenly sought, in this ending of *Ulysses*, an acknowledgement or, on the other hand, a censure of female sexuality. It is more a matter of the male artist, gorged with an ultimate appropriation-identification giving us back a Bacchante . . . swallowed by Orpheus. And it is then that Dedalus–Bloom fulfils the plenitude of his body-text, that he can finally leave us his text as if it were his body, his transsubstantiation. 'This is my body', the narrator seems to say, the narrator whose identifications with HCE will be remembered from *Finnegans Wake*. And the reader, this time like the maenads, assimilates through the signs of the text the real presence of a complex masculine sexuality. Entirely without repression.

Something that is doubtless the condition of an enigmatic *sublimation*: the text bars but does not repress the libido, and has its cathartic effect upon the reader. But this spiriting away of repression doubtless explains the horror, the embarrassment, the bewitchment and, crucially, the surrender of the reader. Everything is visible, and all positions are there to be taken. *Nothing is missing*; there is nothing hidden that could be actually present. Thus it is that the inferno of passion, diabolical femininity, is reabsorbed into the themes of representation as well as language, to become comedy or derision. The personal secret may remain within such an economy, but not the reserve of feelings that feeds psychological life: it is reabsorbed by the ubiquity of a greedy and unstoppable identificatory process.

The father lives so that the son may live, the son dies so that the father may be incarnated in his work and become his own son. In this truly Dedalian labyrinth, *cherchez la femme*. The Christian *agape* of transsubstantiation was opposed to the Greek *Eros* which, before being sublimated in the mystical quest for the good and the beautiful in the words of Diotima in Plato's *Symposium*, or in the second part of the *Phaedrus*, was announced in the Greek philosopher as a violent, sado-masochistic and, *in extremis*, murderous psychodrama, between the lover and the loved one whom Plato had no hesitation in describing as a wolf and a lamb.

In fact, the amorous swallowing of the father which concludes the act of identification should not conceal the violence of *underlying aggressiveness*. An aggressiveness against him, or rather against his body, in as much as he *is* the body and bears the memory of the body of the mother, that is, of an outer body, which arises from the period of archaic symbiosis between the ego and its narcissistic attributes. By imagining the decay, or simply the sexuality – weakness, *jouissance*, sin – of the *paternal* body, I rid myself of my dependence on the *maternal* body. Moreover, this act of imagination-transposition turns my own neotenic weakness . . . into the fate of another: it is not I but he who is the passionate invalid, the sacrificial victim . . .

However, in the fantasm, and within the movement of identification-idealization with the father, it is the mother who receives the lightning bolts of rejection, at least for a while, from anyone, and finally from the perverse. In the end, identification, as a *heterogeneous transference* (body into meaning, mystical metaphor–metamorphosis) instead of the father, initially places me within the improbable and the uncertain: in *meaning*. But it is by separating myself from the *amor matris* (genitive subjective and objective) that I enter the legal fiction that constitutes my identity as a subject. In any case, this infinite erotic separation is the matrix of my eroticism – a constant double for my agapeian identifications.

Stephen's eroticism is cunningly mobilized around his mother, for whose death he is keen to believe himself responsible (who kills a mother: her son or cancer?). In any case, Stephen's malevolent passion is addressed to her: 'The corpsechewer! Raw head and bloody bones!'

Is Joyce sick? Or esoteric? Or postmodern? A host of questions present themselves, however non-normative we try and make our reading. I shall answer personally that his symptom and his obscurity, even in their most abstruse Dedalian puzzles, pose the crucial question of postmodernism: identification, representation. Without eliminating them as the vertiginous acceleration of *Finnegans Wake* will do, or the later poetic avant-garde, *Ulysses* confronts us with the very space in which an unstable image coagulates, for psychical linguistic and translinguistic experience, ready to turn into flesh *and* into meaninglessness. The themes of *Ulysses* are a perfect illustration of this incandescence of imaginary space which, because of its two-dimensionality – body and meaning – because of this transcorporeality, rivals the place of the sacred. Was this not Joyce's final ambition, which so much 'literature' makes us forget?

This practice of writing in Joyce – an extraordinary modern attempt to secularize transsubstantiation, with its joys and its deadly dangers – raises an important question for the analytic cure, which confronts problematic identifications (but is there any other kind?). In order to refer the subject to *one* identity, the analytic process perhaps assures him of a certain symbolic stability, but it must use the decisive and polymorphous qualities of the analyst's discourse, to avoid drying up the fluidity of the subject's imagination. And, finally, should the somewhat depressive disillusion that comes at the end of analysis not also take account of the real, however unattainable, as the ultimate motive for identification?

The lost father of the individual prehistory, a real body conditions my *jouissance* as a speaking being and, while making my analysis interminable, conditions my identificatory surges which simply ensure the act of living.

Notes

1 [Editor's note.] Jean Oury contributed to the colloquium on 'Identification' at which a version of this paper was read.
2 [Editor's note.] J. Schotte presided at the 'Identification' colloquium. For the texts of Oury's and Schotte's contributions, see: *Les Identifications: Confrontation de la clinique et de la théorie de Freud à Lacan*, avant-propos de Gérôme Taillandier (Paris: Denoël (L'Espace analytique), 1987).
3 [Editor's note.] The allusion is to Zaddeh's mathematics.
4 Cf. Richard Ellman, *The Consciousness of Joyce* (London: Faber and Faber, 1977).
5 This theme was developed at the *International Symposium on James Joyce*, Frankfurt, June 1974.
6 Cf. Robert Boyle, S.J., *James Joyce* (Pauline Vision: South Ill. University Press, 1978), and J. -L. Houdebine, 'James Joyce: obscénité et théologie' *Tel Quel*, 83.
7 On the subject of *Eros* and *Agape*, Anders Nygren, *Eros et Agapè* (Paris: Aubier, 1936), and my analytic interpretation of this distinction in *Histoires d'Amour* (Paris: Denoël, 1983).

Part IV

ELAINE SHOWALTER

Feminism and Literature

Although feminism as a political ideology can be traced back at least to the seventeenth century, feminist literary criticism is a very recent invention. We can look back on a rich ancestry of women's criticism informed by feminist concerns, including the work of Madame de Staël, Mary Wollstone-craft, George Eliot, Margaret Fuller, Charlotte Perkins Gilman, Olive Schreiner, Rebecca West, Virginia Woolf and Simone de Beauvoir; but only after the revolutionary year of 1968 did women begin to think of themselves as 'feminist critics', approaching literature with both a political perspective formed by the women's liberation movement, and a training in the contem-porary institutions of literary study. 'More than any other radical movement', Rosalind Coward has argued, 'feminism is aware of the material effects of images and words and the oppression or resistance which can be involved in them.'[1] Feminist criticism began when women who were stu-dents, teachers, writers, editors, or simply readers, began to note the limited and secondary roles allotted to fictional heroines, women writers and female critics, and to ask serious questions about their own relation to literary study. How were women represented in men's literary texts? What was the relationship between the textual harassment of women and the oppression of women in society? Why were women absent from literary history? If literature, as Roland Barthes had said, was 'what gets taught', was women's writing, rarely taught, not 'literature'? Was there a tradition of women's writing, or an autonomous female aesthetic? And if one could talk about women's writing, was 'men's writing' also marked by gender?

In attempting to answer these questions, feminist criticism has drawn on work in cultural anthropology, linguistics, psychoanalysis, Marxism, deconstruction, semiotics and discourse theory for important theoretical tools, revising each of these in terms of its own ideological position. The intellectual trajectory of feminist criticism in the past 20 years has taken us from a concentration on women's literary subordination, mistreatment and exclusion, to the study of women's writing, to an analysis of the construction and representation of gender within literary discourse. As it has evolved, then, feminist criticism has demanded not just the recognition of women's writing, but a radical rethinking of the conceptual grounds of literary study. Along with this process, the project of creating a criticism of our own has led a number of feminist critics in the United States to think about our relationship to other critical factions and revolutions on what Henry Louis Gates has called 'the cultural Left'. The challenge for the future of feminist criticism will be maintaining its internal cohesion while it builds intellectual and political coalitions with other minority and radical positions within literary study.

By now, there are several book-length metacritical studies of feminist criticism available which claim to give introductions or overviews of the field. While they signal an important phase in the evolution and institution-alization of feminism as a critical theory and practice, such studies are necessarily partial and biased. No one, including myself, speaks for feminist criticism; there is no mother-narrative from which it derives a charter, and no Sibyl upon whose lessons it stands or falls. While some would claim that feminist criticism is unified by its political commitments, feminist critics are far from consensus on what a political commitment means. For many, a politically responsible feminist criticism should struggle to use scholarship in the interests of improving the lives of women and should not make the impossibility of speaking for all women an excuse for inaction. For others, however, these are deluded humanist goals based on an essentialist view of 'women', and politics means a proper analysis of patriarchal metaphysics and aesthetics. Readers who want to understand the current state of feminist criticism will have to look at a variety of texts, especially at the anthologies now available which bring together a wide range of critics and positions.[2] This essay traces the history of feminist criticism from the position of someone who believes in the importance of social, historical and economic, as well as textual and psychic, factors in shaping gender ideology; and whose intellectual and political alliances have been shaped by participation in radical movements as well as by literary theory. I focus on a number of controversial themes within the field as of 1988, and I have tried to quote from a wide range of feminist critics in order to convey some sense of the multiplicity of voices and positions within the field.

Paradoxically, poststructuralist critics who scoff at the humanist 'notion of the unitary self' have tended to write about feminist criticism as the story of a few individual women, whom they either set up as heroines or attempt to discredit.[3] Similarly, critics who follow Jacques Derrida in deconstructing the hierarchal binary oppositions that dominate traditional Western thought, have represented feminist criticism as a battle between 'American' and 'French' feminist thought. In such a confrontational paradigm, 'American' (or sometimes 'Anglo-American') feminist criticism is taken to mean 'naive' empiricism and humanism, (as K. K. Ruthven observes, 'in francoph-ile circles, "Anglo-American" is a derogatory term')[4] while the French side is held to have a 'sophisticated' allegiance to poststructuralist theory and anti-humanist scepticism. These loaded terms echo classical European stereotypes of the 'enthusiastic' but gauche American girl and the elegant and aloof French woman of the world; they are constructed by suppressing the history of black and lesbian feminist theory; and they have to be sustained by celebrating (or scapegoating) a few women as 'representatives', since looking at issues across national boundaries and in a wide range of significant texts would present a far more complicated set of relations. Like other modes of contemporary literary theory, feminist criticism is international in its sources, and feminist critics criss-cross national boundaries. The effort to find a nationalist niche for such internationally mobile and theoretically complex figures as Gayatri Chakravorty Spivak, Mieke Bal, Hazel Carby, Cora Kaplan, Shoshana Felman, Nancy Huston, Dale Spender, Sylvia Bovenschen, Rosi Braidotti, Monique Wittig, Toril Moi, or Mary Jacobus seems almost comically futile. The future of feminist criticism, in the words of Naomi Schor, should lie in the 'interpenetration of different national traditions' and 'the multiplication of all differences – national, racial, sexual, and class', not in 'the perpetuation of myths of segregation and national superiority'.[5]

Rather than trying to label *theoretical* positions by real or metaphorical nationality, or to hitch them to specific individuals in mid-career, I think it makes more sense to look briefly at the different ways feminist criticism evolved in four countries which have produced important work – the United States, England, Germany and France – and then to look at the issues and themes of work in feminism and literature as they have been discussed from a variety of theoretical perspectives. One way of thinking about national differences in the evolution of feminist criticism is to ask how the women's movement in a particular country was related to the political and cultural left, and whether it went through a separatist phase. Although socialist or Marxist-feminist criticism cuts across national lines, countries with a feminist tradition of women-only groups were more likely to have developed theories of a female aesthetic than countries where the women's movement was closely tied to male-dominated socialist or leftist organizations. In structures of higher education where women's studies courses and programmes have been relatively strong such as the United States, Canada, West Germany, England, Australia and The Netherlands, more work has been done on women's literary history than in countries where university structures and disciplinary boundaries are more rigid. A major aspect of feminist criticism has been its relationship to contemporary women's writing, and its economic, critical, and professional support of women's access to publication. This support is connected to the emergence of women's presses and feminist publishing collectives, many of which appeared in the early 1970s, such as the Feminist Press in the US, des femmes and Editions Tierce in France, Virago and The Woman's Press in England, Frauenoffensive in Germany, Cooperativa Editorial des Mulhares in Portugal, Førlaget Hønsetryk in Denmark, Sara in The Netherlands, or Awakening in Taiwan. The ability to maintain these independent presses made it possible for feminist publishers in some countries to become effective disseminators of women's writing and feminist critics outside of academia. While feminist literary theory today is academically based, the real impact of the feminist literary revolution is best experienced through visiting women's bookstores in cities throughout North America and Europe, such as *Dulle Griet* in Leuven, *Libruella* in Bologna, *New Words* in Boston, or *Sisterwrite* in London.

United States

The American women's liberation movement began in the late 1960s, in the wake of the Civil Rights and antiwar movements; in addition to numerous small groups all over the country, it generated an autonomous national activist and lobbying group, NOW. There were many women academics and writers active in the movement in its earliest years. Among the most important books of both women's liberation and feminist criticism were Kate Millett's *Sexual Politics* (1970); the anthology *Woman in Sexist Society* (1971), edited by Vivian Gornick and Barbara Moran; and texts by such feminist poets and novelists as Tillie Olsen, Toni Morrison and Adrienne Rich. The early 1970s marked a strongly separatist phase of what is sometimes called 'cultural feminism' in the American movement, with Mary Daly, Rich, Susan Griffin, and others as its leading figures; and this was a healthy and invigorating period of self-definition and political solidarity. A large female reading audience for feminist books spread the message of women's liberation through such best-sellers as Erica Jong's *Fear of Flying*, Marilyn French's *The Women's Room*, Rita Mae Brown's *Ruby Fruit Jungle*, and Alice Walker's *The Color Purple*; in the United States, it has been said, 'feminist poets have powerfully influenced feminist politics'.[6] Feminist publishing also began early, with the formation of Daughters, Inc., the Feminist Press, Alicejames Books, and other women's publishing collectives.

Nevertheless American feminist criticism has always had its strongest institutional base in the university, both within departments of literature and in women's studies programmes. Thanks to a large number of women holding advanced degrees in literature, a relatively prosperous university press, and flexible curricular structures, American academic feminist criticism has been enormously productive, influential, and diverse. Feminist literary journals in the United States have mainly been financed by universities, including *Signs*, *Women's Studies*, *Feminist Studies*, *Tulsa Studies in Women's Literature*, *The Women's Review of Books*, and the more recent journals *Legacy*, *Genders* and *Differences*. In this setting, American feminist criticism has been repeatedly invigorated by interaction with the methods and assumptions of other critical fields and other disciplines, especially Afro-American criticism, poststructuralism and gender theory. In addition, American feminist criticism has been concerned with academic and professional issues, including challenges to the canon and the curriculum; the representation of women in professional journals, organizations, and institutes; and the gender subtexts of other critical schools. Black and lesbian feminist critics have both participated in the general field and developed their own journals and conferences. Hazel Carby points out that black feminist theory has followed the same trajectory as other modes of feminist inquiry, from the concentration on racism and misogyny in literary practice, to the analysis of a black female literary tradition and aesthetic, to a concern with theory and the conceptual grounds of literary study.[7]

England

Radical feminism in England first came from within the New Left, and was then influenced by the American women's movement and by European intellectual currents. As in Italy and Scandinavia (where, according to Toril Moi, 'the overwhelming majority' of feminists identify with socialism and 'feel at home somewhere on the political Left'[8]) British feminist theory was 'heavily influenced by socialist values and politics'.[9] By the early 1970s a number of feminist reading groups had formed around the country, looking not only at feminist theory but at the work of European Marxist theorists such as Louis Althusser, Pierre Macherey, Antonio Gramsci and Walter Benjamin. While there were women-only groups in Great Britain, the movement as a whole did not go through a strong separatist phase; according to the sociologist Olive Banks, 'there was never the deep rift between radical men and women that occurred, and indeed persisted, in the United States'.[10] Women's studies courses, which have been successful in England in the polytechnics and in adult education, made little headway in English universities, which were undergoing economic decline and were structurally more resistant to curricular innovation; indeed, Janet Todd argues that 'the hostility to the whole enterprise of feminist criticism is far greater in Britain than in the USA, both in universities and in the cultural establishment'.[11] The most powerful institutional base for British feminist criticism has been publishing. Many women editors in presses such as Routledge, Basil Blackwell, Harvester, Methuen and Tavistock, have supported the publication of feminist texts and series. Publishing houses, rather than universities, have also supported the English feminist journals, such as the *International Journal of Women's Studies*, the *Feminist Review*, and *m/f*. Women's writing has been an important aspect of English feminist criticism, less because prominent women writers spoke for feminism – indeed, contemporary English women writers have been among the most cautious in the world about endorsing feminism – than because publishing houses like Virago and The Women's Press made a rediscovered wealth of women's texts available in paperback editions. While Marxist-feminists like Rosalind Coward have questioned the identification of 'women's novels' with 'feminist novels', the public awareness of women's literature and feminist issues has increased through this mass-marketing. Both established novelists such as Doris Lessing, Maya Angelou, Margaret Drabble and Fay Weldon, and newcomers such as Jeanette Winterson have reached wide audiences.

Some of the most important work in English feminist criticism has come from the Marxist-Feminist Literature Collective, which met during 1976–9 in London, and whose membership included Cheris Kramer, Cora Kaplan, Helen Taylor, Jean Radford, Jennifer Joseph, Margaret Williamson, Maud Ellmann, Mary Jacobus, Michèle Barrett and Rebecca O'Rourke. As Cora Kaplan has recalled, the members of the group, students, teachers and writers of literature, wanted 'an analysis of literature that took account of both class and gender but saw them as separate and equal determinants'.[12] Using a synthesis of theory from Marxism and psychoanalysis, the women in the group also wrote a collective critical text, *Women's Writing*, which they presented at the 1977 Sociology of Literature Conference at Essex, challenging the unspoken assumptions about individuality, rivalry, and ownership of ideas in the male left.

In addition to its emphasis on the relation between gender and class, and its work on popular culture, English feminist criticism has made outstanding contributions to international feminist theory in film criticism, through the journal *Screen* and the work of such critics as Laura Mulvey, Annette Kuhn and Stephen Heath; in psychoanalytic theory through the work of Jacqueline Rose, Rosalind Coward and Juliet Mitchell; and in cultural studies through the work of Catherine Belsey, Rachel Bowlby, Michèle Barrett and Cora Kaplan, among many others. Work on race and gender is only beginning to appear in the late 1980s.

France

French feminist thought has long been split between the activist and materialist factions of the MLF (Mouvement de la Libération des Femmes), and the psychoanalytic discourse promoted by the powerful group known as psych et po, which always described itself as 'postfeminist',[13] and by influential poststructuralist theorists. For many French women university students, May 1968 'provided a first political *prise de conscience*'.[14] By the autumn of 1968, several radical women's groups had been formed in Paris, Lyons and Toulouse. The most influential of these was Psychanalyse et politique (psych et po), originally composed of women at the Sorbonne. Its charismatic leader and spokeswoman was the psychoanalyst Antoinette Fouque; its original star writer was Hélène Cixous, novelist and professor at Vincennes; and its financier was Sylvia Boissonas, a member of a wealthy industrialist family who funded the publishing house éditions des femmes, and the Paris bookstore *des femmes*. From the beginning, psych et po disdained feminism as 'a bourgeois avant-garde that maintains, in inverted form, the dominant values'. Instead, they argued, 'If capitalism is based on the sexual division of work, the women's struggle is based on sexual difference. The only discourse on sexuality that exists is the psychoanalytic discourse. Therefore the women's struggle must of necessity deal with the dialectical relationship between historical materialism and psychoanalysis'.[15]

French women's interest in psychoanalysis echoed the general trend of Parisian intellectual life after 1968. As Sherry Turkle explains in *Psychoanalytic Politics*, a psychoanalytic culture emerged in France after the collapse of the revolutionary left. Disillusioned with the utopian promise of radical politics, 'people . . . now turned to psychoanalytic ideas to explain what had happened' and entered analysis to understand what it had meant to them.[16] Most of the controversies revolved around the iconoclastic seminars of Jacques Lacan, gadfly of the Freudian establishment, and common property of gauchiste, literary and feminist Paris. In 1972–3, the subject of Lacan's Seminar XX was 'Femininity', and, according to Lacan's American disciple Stuart Schneiderman, it 'spoke to women in a way that few psychoanalytic texts have ever done'.[17]

Lacanian psychoanalysis played an important role in effecting the transition from the concrete and political orientation of the French feminist movement to the more abstract theorizing of 'the feminine' that has dominated the past decade. Women's oppression, women's history, women's texts, women's actual lives, *le vécu*, paled in significance beside the problems of language, fantasy and desire generated by Lacanian analysis and by Derridean deconstructive philosophy. The three French women theorists who have had most influence on crosscultural feminist thought, Cixous, Luce Irigaray and Julia Kristeva, are very different in their orientation, ideas and styles; but they see post-Saussurean linguistics, psychoanalysis, philosophy, semiotics and deconstruction as the most powerful means to understanding the production of sexual difference in language, reading and writing. 'Their common ground', according to Ann Rosalind Jones, 'is an analysis of Western culture as fundamentally oppressive, as phallogocentric. . . . Symbolic discourse (language in various contexts) is another means through which man objectifies the world, reduces it to his terms, speaks in place of everything and everyone else – including women'.[18] In French feminist thought, then 'Woman', or the category of the feminine, is 'the privileged site from which western phallocentric thinking can be deconstructed. The feminine . . . is seen as a negation of the phallic, and thus the privileged carrier of utopian visions'.[19] For deconstructionists, however, 'women', rather than 'Woman', are not important; 'for Derrida and his disciples', Alice Jardine notes, 'the question of how women might accede to subjecthood, write texts or acquire their own signatures, are *phallogocentric* questions'.[20]

Thus there has been very little work produced in France on women writers, and 'there is no new French feminist literary-critical practice to speak of to accompany the new French feminist theories'.[21] As Toril Moi notes, French theorists have contributed to feminist discourse by working on 'problems of textual, linguistic, semiotic or psychoanalytic theory', and by writing texts 'in which poetry and theory intermingle in a challenge to established demarcations of genre'.[22] While French theory has been widely translated and influential in the United States, England, Italy and Germany, virtually no foreign feminist literary criticism seems to have influenced the evolution of French theory, which continues its debates with classical philosophy and male modernism. While Sandra Gilbert, for example, has written the introduction to the English translation of *La Jeune Née, The Madwoman in the Attic* has yet to be translated in France. Furthermore, there is at present little support for feminist work either within French universities or within French university or commercial publishing. The feminist journals, such as *Nouvelles Questions Feministes*, that flourished in France in the 1970s, have all folded. With a few exceptions, for work on French women writers, the French literary canon, and gender, race and class, one has to look to feminist critics and scholars working in other countries, such as Alice Jardine, Jane Gallop, Naomi Schor, Nancy Miller, Toril Moi, Nicole Ward Jouve, Joan de Jean, Tilde Sankovich, Susan Suleiman, Nancy Huston and Rosi Braidotti.

West Germany

The women's movement in the German Federal Republic began in the autumn of 1968 as a split from the socialist students' movement; and it was intensely separatist. Compared to England or Scandinavia, West German feminists remain alienated from the left.[23] Politically, they have particular interest in the economics of housework and motherhood, and in ecology and peace. By the mid-1970s, a vigorous feminist counter-culture had developed, with such mass-circulation magazines as *Courage* and *Emma*, and a number of women's publishing collectives, such as the Munich-based Frauenoffensive. Verena Stefan's novel *Häutungen (Shedding)*, published in 1975, was a huge best-seller, selling 135,000 copies in its first two years; it was followed by many other popular novels on the theme of women's discontent and revolt. By 1976, French feminist theory was being discussed in Germany and translations of Irigaray and Cixous had begun to appear. German feminist criticism has been influenced by poststructuralist thought, but also by German hermeneutics, the Frankfurt School, and reader-response theory.[24] It is particularly concerned with the question of a feminist aesthetic in all the arts, from architecture to writing.

While West Germany is probably the most active centre for feminist criticism among the German-speaking countries, there has also been important work produced in East Germany, where officially there is no women's movement, since women are assumed to be emancipated under socialism. Novelists including Christa Wolf, Irmtraud Morgner and Helga Königsdorf have produced fiction that takes a strong position on issues of women's language and identity. Slower to reach women in other countries than French thought, German feminist criticism has begun to be widely translated in the 1980s.

The Female Aesthetic

The early interest in a female aesthetic, an *écriture feminine*, or a *'weibliche Ästhetik'*, developed out of the women-only groups of the early women's movement in the United States, France, Italy, The Netherlands and West Germany, as a radical response to a past in which the assumed goal for women's literature has been a smooth passage into a neuter, androgynous and allegedly 'universal' aesthetic realm. Instead the female aesthetic maintained that women's writing expressed a distinct female consciousness, and constituted a coherent literary tradition; and argued that feminist critics should reject the misogynistic formulas of patriarchal literary thought to forge a criticism of their own. The female aesthetic proposed the empowerment of the common woman reader, and the celebration of an intuitive female critical consciousness in the interpretation of women's texts, a consciousness often seen as literally or metaphorically lesbian.

In the United States, the female aesthetic was strongly influenced by the Black Arts movement of the 1960s, and its efforts to define a black aesthetic theory dealing both with indigenous principles of literary criticism, and with the relation of literature to political struggle. In striking parallels to the black aesthetic, the female aesthetic also spoke of a lost nation or motherland; of a female vernacular or Mother tongue; and of a powerful but neglected women's culture. In her introduction to an anthology of international women's poetry, for example, Adrienne Rich put forth the compelling hypothesis of a female diaspora:

> The idea of a common female culture – splintered and diasporized among the male cultures under and within which women have survived – has been a haunting though tentative theme of feminist thought over the past few years. Divided from each other through our dependencies on men – domestically, tribally, and in the world of patronage and institutions – our first need has been to recognize and reject these divisions, the second to begin exploring all that we share in common as women on this planet.[25]

Via the female aesthetic, women experimented with efforts to inscribe a female idiom in critical discourse and to define a feminist critical stylistics based on women's consciousness. In 'Toward a Feminist Aesthetic' (1978), Julia Penelope Stanley and Susan J. Wolfe (Robbins) proposed that 'the unique perceptions and interpretations of women require a literary style that reflects, captures, and embodies the quality of our thought', a 'discursive, conjunctive style instead of the complex, subordinating, linear style of classification and distinction'.[26]

In France, *écriture feminine* was represented by the work of Hélène Cixous, Luce Irigaray and Marguerite Duras, among others. Since there is no adjectival distinction between 'female' and 'feminine' in French, *écriture féminine* could mean both a 'female' writing that is related to woman's sexuality and body, and a 'feminine' avant-garde stylistics available to both sexes, and employing such techniques as gaps, breaks, questions, metaphors of excess, 'double or multiple voices, broken syntax, repetitive or cumulative rather than linear structure, and open endings'.[27] Irigaray described a woman's language or *parler femme* in which to inscribe female desire; Cixous urged women to write as resistance to phallogocentric power; and novelists like Monique Wittig experimented with techniques that emphasized the gender-structures of language.

In Germany, too, the women's movement generated an outpouring of autobiographical and confessional feminist literature, and 'asserting women's subjectivity as an epistemological model opposed to dominant male structures of thought . . . became a form of feminist resistance and struggle'.[28] In her introduction to *Shedding*, Verena Stefan described her efforts to create a women's language outside of patriarchal discourse: 'When I wanted to write about sensitivity, experiences, eroticism among women, I could not find the words . . . .Only now can I begin to concentrate systematically on sexism in language, on feminine language, on a feminine literature; only now can I begin reporting on life among women'.[29] In Italy, as well, theoretical work on a separate language of women attracted much attention, in attacks on grammatical gender, and in the fiction of such writers as Elsa Morante and Dacia Maraini. As Marina Yaguello wrote in 1978, 'The struggle for equality, for freedom, for cultural identity implies, for women as for all oppressed groups . . .the battle for the right to expression, to words, for the right to define themselves and determine themselves'.[30]

Despite its utopian vision and political force, however, the Female Aesthetic was a formulation with serious weaknesses. The hypothesis of a distinctive women's language could not be proven empirically, and the concepts of female style or *écriture féminine* described only one *avant-garde* mode of women's writing that privileged the non-linear, experimental, and surreal. Julia Kristeva declared that there was no stylistic distinctiveness inherent in women's writing: 'Nothing in women's past or present publications seems to allow us to affirm that there is a feminine writing'.[31] In so far as the female aesthetic suggested that only women were qualified to read women's texts, feminist criticism ran the risk of ghettoization. Moreover, the hypothesis of the female imagination was open to charges of essentialism and racism; the female imagination seemed also to be white. As women of colour protested against the inattention to racial and class differences between women, the idea of a common women's culture had to be re-examined.

Gynocriticism

None the less, feminist critics continued to ask whether there could be a disciplined way of defining the specificity of women's texts and constructing a female literary tradition, that did not depend on experience, that recognized differences between women, and that made use of contemporary methods of literary interpretation. Feminist criticism was not alone in its struggle with such problems in the 1970s. Afro-American, Canadian and postcolonialist critics were asking the same kinds of questions about literary history and critical difference: What is the relationship between a dominant and a muted culture? Does a muted culture have a history and a literature of its own, or must it always be measured by the chronology, standards and biases of the dominant? Can a minority criticism develop its own methods and theories inductively through extensive and careful reading of its own literary texts? How does culture change? These were the theoretical problems specific to a minority critical discourse, problems that were never raised within mainstream literary criticism and theory; for even when it is not overtly masculinist or anti-feminist, Western literary theory is both phallogocentric and ethnocentric, making universal claims on the basis of a literary history that is overwhelmingly white and male.

In many respects, the concepts necessary for answering such feminist questions came from disciplines very different than those that have been privileged by poststructuralism. Rather than looking to linguistics and philosophy for models, cultural critics needed to investigate symbolic anthropology, social history and ethnography. While this enterprise has been enormously fruitful, it has also been fraught with difficulties. On the one hand, black critics a decade ago were suspicious of white critics taking their work as a precedent. 'The idea of critics like Showalter *using* Black literature', wrote Barbara Smith in 1977, 'is chilling, a case of barely disguised cultural imperialism'.[32] On the other hand, while the relationship between black and white feminist criticism is at least open for discussion today, the term 'theory' has been so appropriated by 'poststructuralism' that any other kind of abstract thinking is rendered invisible and nonexistent. Either you have poststructuralism or you don't have any theory at all. And to claim an interest in culture, in the opinion of the Kristevan critic Toril Moi, is clearly to reject any interest in 'the text as a signifying process' in favour of a group of dubious 'empirical, extra-literary' influences that demonstrate a 'fear' of asking the really important theoretical questions: 'What is interpretation? What does it mean to read? What is a text?'[33] Very fundamental differences about the political, as well as the intellectual, goals of feminist criticism are reflected in such a taunting confrontation: my own view of the feminist theoretical project neither isolates the text in formalistic ways from its 'extra-literary' contexts, nor sees questions of interpretation, reading and textuality as apart from gender and culture.

All literary theory, most critics acknowledge, is text-specific; and in order for feminist criticism to develop, it had to identify women's writing as its distinctive text-milieu. In 1978, I proposed the word 'gynocriticism' to describe the feminist study of women's writing, including readings of women's texts and analyses of the intertextual relations both between women writers (a female literary tradition), and between women and men. My own work in this field had begun with a study of nineteenth- and twentieth-century English women novelists called *A Literature of Their Own* (1977). The title of the book came from a passage in John Stuart Mill's *The Subjection of Women* (not, as many reviewers claimed, from Virginia Woolf), and was intended to foreground my distance, as an American woman, from the English literary history I described. A pivotal text of gynocritical theory was Sandra Gilbert and Susan Gubar's monumental study, *The Madwoman in the Attic* (1979). Gilbert and Gubar offer a detailed revisionist reading of Harold Bloom's theory of the anxiety of influence, transforming his Freudian paradigm of Oedipal struggle between literary fathers and sons into a feminist theory of influence which describes the nineteenth-century woman writer's anxieties within a patriarchal literary culture.

As it has developed over the past 15 years, the fecundity of gynocriticism has been immense; Gilbert and Gubar alone have generated enough new ideas to keep feminist critics busy for the next 20 years. In a relatively short period of time, gynocriticism has generated a vast literature on individual women writers, persuasive studies of the female literary tradition from the Middle Ages to the present in virtually every national literature, and important books on what is called 'gender and genre': the significance of gender in shaping generic conventions in forms ranging from the hymn to the *Bildungsroman*.[34] It has been productive outside of the English and American context; one might point to the work of Esther Fuchs on Israeli women writers; Maaike Meijer and Ria Lemaire in The Netherlands; or Birgitta Holm, Jette Lundboe Levy, Irene Engelstad and Janneken Overland in Scandinavia. We now have a coherent, if still provisional, narrative of women's literary history. Women's writing has moved through several evolutionary phases of subordination, protest and autonomy in relation to the literary mainstream; but these stages are connected throughout history and across nationality by recurring images, metaphors, themes and plots that emerge from women's social, psychic and literary experience, and from reading both maternal and paternal precursors. Strongly influenced by the work of Gilbert and Gubar, the theoretical programme of gynocritics in the 1980s has been marked by increasing attention to 'the analysis of female talent grappling with a male tradition', both in literature and criticism, a project that defined both the female literary text and the feminist critical text as the sum of its 'acts of revision, appropriation, and subversion', and its differences of 'genre, structure, voice, and plot'.[35]

Gynocriticism assumes that all writing is marked by gender; as Alicia Ostriker notes, 'writers necessarily articulate gendered experience, just as they necessarily articulate the spirit of nationality, an age, a language'.[36] Although feminist critics recognize that the meaning of gender needs to be interpreted within a variety of historical, national, racial and sexual contexts, they maintain that women writers are not free to renounce or transcend their gender entirely. Women can differentiate their positions from any number of stereotypes of femininity, and define themselves also in terms of being black, lesbian, South African or working-class; but to deny that they are affected by being women at all is self-delusion or self-hatred, the legacy of centuries of denigration of women's art. As Sandra Gilbert asks,

If a writer is a woman who has been raised as a woman – and I daresay only a very few biologically anomalous human females have not been raised as women – how can her sexual identity be split off from her literary energy? Even a denial of her femininity . . . would surely be significant to an understanding of the dynamics of her aesthetic creativity.[37]

Furthermore, feminist critics *were* women writers; writing criticism that challenged the conventions of academic style as well as content. Every insight and discovery that women who were feminist critics made about women's writing and its relationship to a dominant tradition had transformative personal implications in our own work, for, as Roland Barthes observed in an early essay on 'Criticism and Language', 'it is inconceivable that the creative laws governing the writer should not be valid for the critic'. To say, then, that gynocritical theories were proved on feminist critics' pulses is not to invoke an image of female *biological* experience (as Mary Jacobus charges); indeed, even as a metaphor the pulse can hardly be seen as a sign of sexual difference. Rather, it is to emphasize that the history of women's writing inevitably is recapitulated in feminist criticism.

A second assumption of gynocriticism is that women's writing is always 'bitextual', in dialogue with both masculine and feminine literary traditions.[38] In an essay called 'Feminist Criticism in the Wilderness' (1981), I argued against feminist fantasies of a wild zone of female consciousness or culture outside of patriarchy, declaring instead that 'there can be no writing or criticism outside of the dominant culture'. Thus both women's writing and feminist criticism were of necessity 'a double-voiced discourse', embodying both the muted and the dominant, speaking inside of both feminism and criticism.[39] In reading women's texts, gynocriticism has freely experimented with a wide variety of interpretative tools; it does not prescribe a particular mode of textual analysis, and has made extensive use of poststructuralist insights, especially those having to do with the signification of the feminine.

Despite its achievements, or perhaps because of them, gynocriticism has for some years been the target of attacks from every point on the critical spectrum. A frequent attack on gynocriticism is that studying women's writing is 'separatist', that is, that it practises a kind of inverse sexism. K. K. Ruthven, for example, claims that gynocriticism repeats the same mistake for which feminists take 'male critics to task, namely an exclusive preoccupation with the writings of one sex'.[40] The charge of separatism is probably the weakest and most cynical in the anti-gynocritical armament, since no one charges that it is 'separatist' to write about American literature, Romantic poetry, or the Russian novel, nor insists that the typical anthology of men's writing should be accurately titled 'Great Male Poets of the Eighteenth Century'. Only feminist critics, it would seem, are required to defend their choice of subject matter. Furthermore, what feminist critics deplore is not an exclusive *preoccupation* with male writers, but critical *blindness* to the fact that to write exclusively about men is not simply to write universally about 'literature'. Gynocriticism always emphasized the spurious nature of such one-sided male claims to universality and emphasized the impossibility of separating women's writing from its contexts in a masculine tradition, even when these were not the main subject. 'A feminist critic cannot simply refuse to read patriarchal texts', Patsy Schweickart comments, 'for they are everywhere, and they condition her participation in the literary and critical enterprise. In fact, by the time she becomes a feminist critic, a woman has already read numerous male texts – in particular, the most authoritative texts of the literary and critical canons. She has introjected not only androcentric texts, but also androcentric reading strategies and values'.[41]

Gynocriticism has also been attacked for its emphasis on realist or nineteenth-century texts. In order to be truly revolutionary, many poststructuralists insist, feminist criticism must reject 'patriarchal aesthetics', such as the belief in a unified human subject, an interest in a linear narrative, or an interpretation of literature as mimetic rather than purely verbal and linguistic. The appropriate subject-matter for feminist criticism, they argue, is the *avant-garde* text of modernism or postmodernism.

The textual field of gynocriticism cannot now be described as limited to any particular period or genre. Historically, there has been an expansion of work ranging from the Middle Ages through the present; generically, poetry, drama, diaries, autobiographies, films and postmodernist forms have received attention as well as novels. In fact, work on women's writing now extends to every century and mode, so the charge that gynocritics privileges realism is out of date. Yet this is a good example of the need to look historically at critical as well as literary discourse. Many of the first feminist readings were indeed of nineteenth-century women's poetry and fiction, primarily English, but also European. This was so in part because the nineteenth century was the only literary period in which women writers had been accepted as canonical, although their numbers even there were severely restricted to a handful of writers. Secondly, the appearance of the male pseudonym among British and European women writers in the nineteenth century, from 'Ernst Ahlgren' (Victoria Benedictson) in Sweden, to George Eliot in England, George Sand in France, and 'Fernan Caballero' (Cecelia Böhl) in Spain, was a clear historical marker of a literary consciousness based on gender, and a new awareness among women that choosing male pen names could invest them with male authority and freedom. It was for this reason, and not out of ignorance of the work of eighteenth-century women novelists, that I chose to begin *A Literature of Their Own* in the 1840s. Finally, for American critics in the late 1960s, Victorian studies was a field undergoing exciting change. It was interdisciplinary in orientation, and unusually hospitable to feminist interventions. Flavia Alaya has recalled the way that the two were connected: 'Feminist criticism (and feminist critics) came of age just behind the vogue in Victorian studies. . . . These new women inherited a field the gravitational center of which had just begun to shift from the major poets to the great social thinkers . . . and whose center (for now) has shifted again to the study of fiction'.[42]

While in the 1970s, partly because of the invigorating impact of feminist criticism, the Victorian period became the dominant field of literary studies in the United States. In the past decade, through the influence of French thought, it has undergone a devaluation; what is most privileged now in fiction is modernism and postmodernism. Yet, as George Levine so convincingly demonstrates in *The Realistic Imagination*, Victorian narrative realism is far from being a simplistic mimetic rendering of 'experience', or a complacent domestication of the unconscious. It is rather a highly developed set of literary conventions of representation, including the romantic, the monstrous, the tragic and the irrational. Similarly, there is nothing uniquely revolutionary or subversive about the *avant-garde*, or the *avant-garde* literary style, however difficult or transgressive it may originally appear. Postmodernist metafiction, for example, is constructed through a set of literary conventions, as readily appropriated and commodified as any other. There is no reason to see Gertrude Stein as a more intrinsically feminist writer, by means of her style, than George Eliot or Kate Chopin.

In terms of racial and ethnic diversity, however, there is still much work to be done. One of the most serious by-products of the early concentration on Victorian women's texts was the omission of black women writers. It is true, as Hortense Spillers points out, that on a theoretical level, 'the gynocritical themes of recent feminist inquiry' evolved apart from a 'black women's writing community'.[43] Attention to black women's writing has begun to address this issue, both revising some of the basic metaphors of women's writing and adding new ones coming out of the black women's literary experience.

Canon-formation

As gynocriticism developed, an alternative canon of women's texts has begun to take shape. Canon-formation, the emergence of certain writers and texts as central to the understanding of a particular literary history and tradition, is now understood as a historically grounded process, rather than an assertion of aesthetic value. First of all, as John Guillory points out, 'strong revaluations of devalued figures' are very much a part of 'critical revolutions'.[44] Secondly, the gynocritical project had uncovered intertextual relations between women writers that had previously gone unnoticed, and demonstrated traditions of influence and revision that did not come from an essential female consciousness, but from mutual engagements with genre. Parallel traditions were emerging in other minority literatures as well; as Henry Louis Gates explained,

Literary works configure into a tradition not because of some mystical collective unconscious determined by the biology or race or gender, but because writers read other writers and *ground* their representations of experience in models of language provided largely by other writers to whom they feel akin. It is through this process of literary revision, amply evident in the *texts* themselves – in formal echoes, recast metaphors, even in parody – that a 'tradition' emerges and defines itself.[45]

The debate over feminist canonization came to a head with the publication of Gilbert and Gubar's proposal of such a tradition in the *Norton Anthology of Literature by Women: The Tradition in English* (1985). The book provided a field day for conservative male critics, who ridiculed the whole idea of such a project, hooted at the notion of a tradition of women's writing, and invariably ended by trotting out the allegedly satiric demand for an anthology of literature by men, as if they were not surrounded by such volumes. But men were not the only critics of the *NALW*. In a review in the *New York Times*, the novelist Gail Godwin complained that it was insulting to be called a woman writer, and that her own work (not reprinted in the anthology) was primarily influenced by Conrad. The literary historian Janet Todd objected that it was too soon to construct a canon, since we haven't done enough research. Chicana feminists, angry that no Chicana writer was included in the book, threatened a boycott.

Some feminists have argued that gynocriticism must abstain from all canonical gestures. Toril Moi, for example, protests that work like mine aims 'to create a separate canon of women's writing, not to abolish all canons'.[46] Yet, as Moi herself declares when she is bashing another feminist critic in a different context, 'to be against power is not to abolish it in a fine, post-1968 libertarian gesture, but to hand it over to someone else'.[47] Canon-formation is an aspect of the power of critical discourses and institutions; simply to be against canons is to leave the power of canon-formation to someone else. We cannot expect that women's writing will make an impact on the canon on its own; as Richard Brodhead has observed, new canons 'will not surface except through the force of someone's or some group's interests. And whether they will stay above water on future maps of the literary continents is a question exactly *not* of their innate value (which never saved a past yet) but of whether those interests can successfully institutionalize themselves and win old ones to the cause of making theirs be the past worth remembering'.[48] Furthermore, the fantasy that canons can be abolished rather than transformed misunderstands the complex process by which the construction of a literary canon is not simply the result of individual authority, but involves a non-conspiratorial cultural network of 'publishers, reviewers, editors, literary critics, and teachers'.[49]

Although we will never abolish canons, gynocriticism demystifies their pretenses to be absolute and permanent monuments of greatness, and instead reveals their material contexts and circumstances, and the 'social and historical relativity of aesthetic standards'.[50] Feminist criticism also is committed to expanding the canon to include neglected genres of women's writing, such as diaries, letters, science fiction and the romance.

The female subject

The most persistent attack from the poststructuralist left is that talking about women's writing assumes belief in a single category of 'woman', and posits the existence of a unified or monolithic female subject. According to some poststructuralists, the subject is no longer a person but a position; in women's case, femininity means marginality. To others, the subject-position is simply a linguistic construct. Thus to speak of 'women' or to assume that gender is the common denominator that unites people of the female persuasion is to commit the most heinous theoretical offense.

It's ironic that the poststructuralist critique of the unified female subject appeared just at the time when women were making a claim to their own subjectivity. As materialist feminists and other minority critics insist, subjectivity and group identity are fundamental aspects of political action, of contestation against the dominant. In the words of Henry Louis Gates, 'the dimension of agency is of crucial importance to the marginal spokesperson'.[51] 'If we have deconstructed the *female* out of existence', Toril Moi concedes, 'it would seem that the very foundations of the feminist struggle have disappeared'.[52] Biddy Martin is one of several feminist critics who believe that it is possible and indeed necessary to retain the notion of a female subject; 'work that moves in the direction of historically specific analysis can reconceptualize "the subject," power and knowledge without forfeiting a belief (if only a strategic one), in a subjective agency, in the possibility of change, and in the importance of (admittedly partial) narratives and representations of women's lives'.[53] Teresa de Lauretis too sees emerging in feminist writings 'the concept of a multiple, shifting, and often self-contradictory identity . . . an identity made up of heterogeneous and heteronomous representations of gender, race, and class and often indeed across languages and cultures; an identity that one decides to reclaim from a history of multiple assimilations, and that one insists on as a strategy'. 'The female subject', according to de Lauretis, 'is a site of differences . . . that are not only sexual or only racial, economic, or (sub)cultural, but all of these together, and often enough at odds with one another'.[54]

The difference dilemma

Much feminist thinking today seems to be caught up in what can be called 'the difference dilemma', the paralysing contradictions that are endlessly rehashed in poststructuralist thought. If 'Woman' is an essentialist concept, are there still women? How can we speak about 'women' without ignoring the differences between them? And if there are no women to speak for, why do we need feminist criticism? Much of the dilemma, in my opinion, is the result of a logical fallacy or misconception in poststructuralist thought, and need not be incapacitating or represent a contradiction.

Let's look at the way the poststructuralist argument about feminist identity is articulated by Julia Kristeva. Toril Moi summarizes Kristeva's view of feminism as a three-stage process:

1 Women demand equal access to the symbolic order. Liberal feminism. Equality.

2 Women reject the male symbolic order in the name of difference. Radical feminism. Femininity extolled.

3 Women reject the dichotomy between masculine and feminine as metaphysical.[55]

The last position is Kristeva's own. In 'Women's Time', she writes that 'in the third attitude, which I strongly advocate – which I imagine? – the very dichotomy man/woman as an opposition between two rival entities may be understood as an opposition belonging to *metaphysics*. What can "identity," even "sexual identity," mean in a new theoretical and scientific space where the very notion of identity is challenged?'[56]

Kristeva follows a Derridean strategy of identifying a binary opposition, reversing it, and then deconstructing it. But why deconstruct the opposition of masculine and feminine, rather than the opposition of equality and difference? As the historian Joan W. Scott has cogently argued, the binary opposition of 'equality' and 'difference' has been created to limit the choices available to feminists, but 'in fact, the antithesis itself hides the interdependence of the two terms, for equality is not the elimination of difference, and difference does not preclude equality'.[57] In a political context, Scott explains, 'equality' means the deliberate setting-aside of differences in a specific context, such as the workplace. To talk about 'difference' is not to declare an essentialist belief; differences always have to be defined contextually. Thus to demand equality for women does not mean to say that women are identical to men, nor that all women are alike. Similarly, to investigate difference is not to insist that all women are different from men in the same way, or to celebrate motherhood or any other trait as the fundamental condition of femininity. Scott concludes that we must 'refuse to oppose equality to difference and insist continually on differences,' but not to abandon crucial terms of identity that enable us to act.

Gender theory

The latest and most rapidly growing mode of American feminist criticism is gender theory, corresponding to the Third World critic's focus on 'race'. Within feminist scholarship, the term 'gender' is used to mean the social,

cultural and psychological constructs imposed upon biological sexual difference. Unlike the emphasis on women's writing that informs gynocritics, or
on the signification of 'the feminine' in poststructuralism, gender theory
explores the ideological inscription and the literary effects of the sex/gender
system. Joan W. Scott has identified three goals of gender theory: to
substitute the analysis of social constructs for biological determinism in the
discussion of sexual difference; to introduce comparative studies of women
and men into the specific disciplinary field; and to transform disciplinary
paradigms by adding gender as an analytic category.[58] Gender theory
promises to introduce the subject of masculinity into feminist criticism, and
to bring men into the field as students, scholars, theorists and critics.

But the politics of gender studies within feminist criticism are extremely
controversial. 'There is a danger', writes Janet Todd, 'that the study of men,
masculinity or homophobia in literature will aim to supersede feminist
criticism with its political aim and dimension, will cause not a swerve from
and return to feminist issues and women's writings, but a straightforward
march out of them'.[59] While gynocriticism, as I have shown, long maintained
that all writing was gendered, in practice feminist critics applied this insight
only to women's writing. At the beginning of this decade, few feminist critics
were analysing *men*'s writing as a gendered literary discourse; instead they
looked for the representation of women in male texts. Furthermore, while
a number of prominent male theorists took up the question of feminist
criticism in the early 1980s, few perceived masculinity as a subject; unlike
femininity, it seemed 'natural, transparent, and unproblematic'.[60] Thus for
this first wave of 'male feminists', the call to develop an awareness of gender
was initially heard as a challenge to master feminist criticism and to correct
what they saw as its shortcomings and flaws. Such mastery of the feminine
has long been a stance of masculine authority; and from Fanny Hill to
Benny Hill, some men have achieved enormous skill and success in female
impersonation. Until men questioned their own reading practices, however,
male feminism was just a form of critical cross-dressing that made female
masquerade a way to take over women's newly-acquired power. In order
to make a genuine contribution to feminist theory, male theorists had to
confront 'what might be implied by reading as a man, and questioning or
surrender of paternal privileges'.[61] Many feminist critics worried that male
critics would appropriate, penetrate, or exploit feminist discourse for professional advantage, without accepting the risks and challenges of investigating masculinity, or analysing their own critical practice. Some of these
controversies were vividly demonstrated in the often bitter exchanges of the
1980s that took place between 'male feminists' and feminist critics at
conferences, in journals, and in the book *Men in Feminism* (1987).

Nevertheless, by the mid-1980s, serious inquiries into masculine modes
of creativity, interpretation and representation began to develop in a number
of contexts: in the writing of a generation of male critics influenced by
feminist critical theory; in the work of the New Historicists; and most of
all, in the emergent fields of men's studies and gay studies. A significant

step in the development of gender criticism was Eve Kosofsky Sedgwick's
Between Men: English Literature and Male Homosocial Desire (1985). Sedgwick
analysed the inscriptions of male homosexuality in relation to class, race,
and the gender system as a whole. Following on work by Freud, Lévi-
Strauss, René Girard, Gayle Rubin, and others, she focused on the exchange
of women to mediate male bonding, and on the repressed bonds between
male rivals in erotic triangles. By placing relationships between men along
a continuum from the homosocial to the homoerotic, and by studying the
ways in which society exercised 'secular power over male bonds', Sedgwick
made it possible to look at 'the shape of the entire male homosocial spectrum
and its effects on women'.[62] As several gay critics have noted, Sedgwick's
woman-centred and feminist work brought both homophobia and male
homosexuality 'to center stage in the discussion of the construction of
gender'.[63] While men's studies, gay studies, and feminist criticism have
different politics and priorities, together they are moving beyond 'male
feminism' to raise challenging questions about masculinity in literary texts,
questions that enable gender criticism to develop.

As of the late 1980s, this revisionary process has had important effects
on work within several periods of English and American literature, especially
the Renaissance, the eighteenth century, the Romantic period, the *fin de
siècle*, and modernism. An analysis of the construction and representation
of gender within all literary discourse also provides a way of discussing
the gender subtexts of criticism and theory. The addition of gender as a
fundamental analytic category within literature, rather than its perpetuation
as a feminine supplement to the mainstream, obviously has revolutionary
transformative potential for the ways that we read, think and write.

Such a transformation, however, depends on the degree to which gender
theory does not mean a depoliticization of feminist criticism. One danger is
that 'gender' will continue to be read as a synonym for 'femininity', so
that men who come into the field will continue to pontificate about the
representation of women without accepting the risks and opportunities of
investigating masculinity, or analysing their own critical practice. Another
danger, seemingly paradoxical but actually related, is that gender will
become a postfeminist term that declares the study of women, and women's
writing, obsolete, or what Ruthven denounces as 'separatist'. The most
troubling risk is that critics will adopt the academic terminology of gender
while refusing to call themselves feminists, and ignoring the relationships
between gender, racial and class hierarchies. I think that the fundamental
conditions have been met that enable us to form a genuine critical coalition
around the issue of gender; but in order for gender to be a useful expansion,
rather than a displacement, of our work, it needs to be defined within a
feminist framework that insists on continued work on women, and on a
commitment to the continuing struggle against sexism, racism and homophobia.

Postfeminism and literature

The relationship between the women's movement and feminist criticism in the late 1980s is at the least problematic. In France today, the women's movement seems dead as last year's Lacroix, even under a socialist government. In Italy *dopofemminismo*, or postfeminism is the new by-word of a women's movement that survives in subdued fragments. In the United States, the *New York Times* announces that literary feminism has come of age, while the Reagan and Bush governments campaign successfully against every advance of the women's movement from abortion to affirmative action. In England, Cora Kaplan notes, 'feminist criticism has become legitimate within the academy . . . at a moment when education is contracting'. Kaplan warns that without an 'ongoing social movement to criticize and encourage it', feminist criticism, 'like all cultural movements that outlive their immediate political moment', can 'become smug, institutionalized, reflexive, and stale'.[64]

Radical movements inevitably go through phases of activity and decline, but those of us who remain to speak for their ideas and visions within universities have a responsibility to keep those ideas alive and fresh for the future. I believe that the next step for feminist criticism must involve the development of a comparative literature and theory, a poetics of the Other, that comes out of a theoretical coalition of minority critics. As literary work has progressed within feminist, black, postcolonialist, Chicano and gay criticism, to name several of the most active fields, we begin to see the emergent shape of a critical shadow cabinet. Within each specific field, critics have located in their own texts and cultures the particular images, metaphors, genres and structures that define literary difference. They have each confronted the problems of subjectivity, essentialism, integrity and intertextuality that mark late twentieth-century literary discourse. But when we look at them together, we see similar patterns of shared tropological systems, and a shared history of opposition, resistance, self-representation and accommodation to the dominant culture. Respecting our differences, yet investigating our mutual interests and correspondences, we could begin to work together for an understanding of literature that is truly universal, and for a criticism that accepts contradictions and limitations, but that does not make them an excuse to avoid working for social change.

Notes

1 Rosalind Coward, 'Are Women's Novels Feminist Novels?' in Elaine Showalter (ed.), *The New Feminist Criticism* (London: Virago, 1986), p. 238.
2 See, for example, Nancy K. Miller (ed.), *The Poetics of Gender* (New York: Columbia University Press, 1986); Edith Hoshino Altbach et al. (eds), *German Feminism: Readings in Politics and Literature* (Albany: SUNY Press, 1984); Judith Newton and Deborah Rosenfelt (eds), *Feminist Criticism and Social Change* (New York: Methuen, 1985); Gayle Green and Coppelia Kahn (eds), *Making a*

Difference (London: Methuen, 1985); Hortense Spillers and Marjorie Pryse, *Conjuring* (Bloomington: Indiana University Press, 1985); Gisela Ecker (ed.), *Feminist Aesthetics* (London: The Women's Press, 1985); Teresa de Lauretis (ed.), *Feminist Studies, Critical Studies* (Bloomington: Indiana University Press, 1986); and Robert Young (ed.), *Sexual Difference*, special issue of the *Oxford Literary Review*, 8 (1986).

3   Toril Moi, *Sexual/Textual Politics* (London: Methuen, 1985), p. 7.

4   K. K. Ruthven, *Feminist Literary Studies: An Introduction* (Cambridge: Cambridge University Press, 1984), p. 22.

5   Naomi Schor, 'Introducing Feminism', *Paragraph* 8 (October 1986), p. 101.

6   Newton and Rosenfelt, 'Introduction', *Feminist Criticism and Social Change*, p. xvii.

7   Hazel Carby, *Reconstructing Womanhood* (New York: Oxford University Press, 1987), p. 16.

8   Moi, *Sexual/Textual Politics*, p. 93.

9   Stephen Lehmann and Eva Sarton, *Women's Studies in Western Europe* (Chicago: American Library Association, 1986), p. 97.

10   Olive Banks, *Faces of Feminism: A Study of Feminism as a Social Movement*, (New York: St Martin's Press, 1981), p. 238.

11   Janet Todd, *Feminist Literary History* (London: Polity Press, 1988), p. 12.

12   Cora Kaplan, *Sea Changes: Culture and Feminism* (London: Verso, 1986), p. 62.

13   'Antoinette', in Claire Duchen (ed.), *French Connections* (Amherst: University of Massachusetts Press, 1987), p. 52.

14   Carolyn G. Burke, 'Report from Paris: Women's Writing and the Women's Movement', *Signs*, 3 (Summer 1978), p. 844.

15   *New French Feminisms*, ed. Elaine Marks and Isabelle de Courtivron (Amherst: University of Massachusetts Press, 1980), pp. 117–18.

16   Sherry Turkle, *Psychoanalytic Politics: Jacques Lacan and Freud's French Revolution* (London: Burnettt Book, 1979), p. 9.

17   Stuart Schneiderman, *Jacques Lacan: The Death of an Intellectual Hero* (Cambridge: Cambridge University Press, 1983), p. 30.

18   Ann Rosalind Jones, 'Writing the Body: L'écriture féminine', in *The New Feminist Criticism*, p. 362.

19   Ecker, *Feminist Aesthetics*, p. 18.

20   Jardine, 'Pre-Texts for the Transatlantic Feminist', *Yale French Studies* 62 (1981) p. 225; and *Gynesis: Configurations of Women and Modernity* (Ithaca: Cornell University Press, 1985), pp. 61–3.

21   Schor, 'Introducing feminism', p. 100.

22   Moi, *Sexual/Textual Politics*, p. 97.

23   Edith Altbach, 'The New German Women's Movement', in *German Feminism*, p. 10.

24   Ecker, *Feminist Aesthetics*, p. 11.

25   Rich, *The Other Voice* (New York: Morrow, 1975), p. xvii.

26   'Toward a Feminist Aesthetic', *Chrysalis*, 6 (1978), pp. 59, 67.

27   Ann Rosalind Jones, 'Inscribing femininity: French theories of the feminine', in *Making a Difference*, p. 88.

28   Sara Lennox, 'Trends in Literary Theory: The Female Aesthetic and German Women's Writing', *German Quarterly*, 54 (January 1981), p. 63.

29   'Foreword to *Shedding*', in *German Feminism*, p. 54.

30 Susan Bassnett, *Feminist Experiences: The Women's Movement in Four Cultures* (London: Allen and Unwin, 1986), p. 123.

31 Julia Kristeva, 'A partir de *Polylogue*', 1977; quoted in Moi, *Sexual/Textual Politics*, p. 163.

32 Barbara Smith, 'Toward a Black Feminist Criticism', in Showalter, *The New Feminist Criticism* p. 172.

33 *Sexual/Textual Politics*, pp. 76–7.

34 Alicia Ostriker, *Stealing the Language* (Boston: Beacon Press, 1986), p. 6.

35 Elizabeth Abel, 'Introduction', *Writing and Sexual Difference* (Chicago: University of Chicago Press, 1982), p. 2.

36 Ostriker, *Stealing the Language*, p. 9.

37 Sandra Gilbert, 'Feminist Criticism in the University: An Interview', in Gerald Graff, *Criticism in the University* (Evanston: Northwestern University Press, 1986), p. 117.

38 The term 'bitextual' comes from Naomi Schor, 'Dreaming Dissymetry: Barthes, Foucault, and Sexual Differences', in *Men in Feminism*, ed. Alice Jardine and Paul Smith (London: Methuen, 1987), p. 110.

39 Showalter, 'Feminist Criticism in the Wilderness', in *The New Feminist Criticism*, p. 263.

40 Ruthven, *Feminist Literary Studies*, p. 125.

41 *Gender and Reading*, ed. Elizabeth Flynn and Patrocinio Schweikart (Baltimore: Johns Hopkins University Press, 1986), p. 50.

42 Flavia Alaya, 'Feminists on Victorians', *Dickens Studies Annual*, 15 (1986), pp. 346–7.

43 Spillers and Pryse, *Conjuring*, p. 261.

44 John Guillory, 'The Ideology of Canon-Formation: T. S. Eliot and Cleanth Brooks', *Critical Inquiry*, 10 (September 1983), p. 198, n.30.

45 Henry Louis Gates, 'Introduction' to *Schomburg Library of Nineteenth-Century Black Women Writers* (New York: Oxford University Press, 1988), p. xviii.

46 *Sexual/Textual Politics*, p. 78.

47 Ibid., p. 148.

48 Richard Brodhead, *The School of Hawthorne* (New York: Oxford University Press, 1986), p. 7.

49 Sharon O'Brien, 'Becoming Noncanonical: The Case Against Willa Cather', *American Quarterly* 40 (March 1988), p. 111.

50 Judith Newton and Deborah Rosenfelt, 'Introduction', *Feminist Criticism and Social Change*, p. xxiv.

51 Henry Louis Gates, 'The Subject Position', unpublished manuscript, June 1988, p. 1. Thanks to Skip Gates for sharing his enormously useful and inspiring work.

52 Moi, *Sexual/Textual Politics*, p. 18.

53 Biddy Martin, 'A Study in Contrasts', *Women's Review of Books*, 4 (October 1986), p. 22.

54 Teresa de Lauretis, 'Issues, Terms, and Contexts', in *Feminist Studies/Critical Studies*, p. 15.

55 Moi, *Sexual/Textual Politics*, p. 12.

56 'Women's Time', in *The Kristeva Reader*, ed. Toril Moi (London: Basil Blackwell, 1986), p 209.

57 Joan W. Scott, 'Deconstructing Equality-versus-Difference: Or, the Uses of

Poststructuralist Theory for Feminism', *Feminist Studies*, 14 (Spring 1988), p. 38.

58 'Gender: A Useful Category of Historical Analysis', *American Historical Review*, 91 (December 1986), pp. 1053–75.

59 Todd, *Feminist Literary History*, p. 134.

60 Catherine MacKinnon, 'Feminism, Marxism, Method, and the State', *Signs*, 7 (Spring 1982), p. 537.

61 Elaine Showalter, 'Critical Cross-Dressing', (1983) reprinted in *Men in Feminism*.

62 Eve Kosofsky. Sedgwick, *Between Men: English Literature and Male Homosocial Desire* (New York: Columbia University Press, 1985), p. 88.

63 See Richard Dellamora, 'Masculine Desire and the Question of the Subject', paper presented at the MLA December 1987, and Craig Owens, 'Outlaws: Gay Men in Feminism', *Men in Feminism*, p. 231. Thanks to Richard Dellamora for sharing his ground-breaking work on gay subjectivity and criticism.

64 Kaplan, *Sea Changes*, p. 65.

HOMI K. BHABHA

Articulating the Archaic: Notes on Colonial Nonsense

How can the mind take hold of such a country? Generations of invaders
have tried, but they remain in exile. The important towns they build
are only retreats, their quarrels the malaise of men who cannot find
their way home. India knows of their trouble. . . . She calls 'Come'
through her hundred mouths, through objects ridiculous and august. But
come to what? She has never defined. She is not a promise, only an
appeal.

E. M. Forster, *A Passage to India*[1]

The Fact that I have said that the effect of interpretation is to isolate in
the subject a kernel, a *kern*, to use Freud's own term, of *non-sense*, does
not mean that interpretation is in itself nonsense.

Jacques Lacan, 'The Field of the Other'[2]

I

There is a conspiracy of silence around the colonial truth, whatever that
might be. Around the turn of the century there emerges a mythic, masterful
silence in the narratives of Empire, what Sir Alfred Lyall called 'doing our
Imperialism quietly', Carlyle celebrated as the 'wisdom of the Do-able –
Behold ineloquent Brindley . . . he has chained the seas together',[3] and
Kipling embodied, most eloquently, in the figure of Cecil Rhodes – 'Nations
not words he linked to prove / His faith before the crowd.'[4] Around the
same time, from those dark corners of the earth, there comes another, more
ominous silence that utters an archaic colonial 'otherness', that speaks in
riddles, obliterating proper names and proper places. It is a silence that
turns imperial triumphalism into the testimony of colonial confusion and

This chapter is based on an address made at a conference on Cultural Value at
Birkbeck College, the University of London, on 16 July 1988.

those who hear its echo lose their historic memories. This is the Voice of early modernist 'colonial' literature, the complex cultural memory of which is made in a fine tension between the melancholic homelessness of the modern novelist, and the wisdom of the sage-like storyteller whose craft takes him no further afield than his own people.[5] In Conrad's *Heart of Darkness*, Marlow seeks Kurtz's Voice, his words, 'a stream of light or the deceitful flow from the heart of an impenetrable darkness' and in that search he loses 'what is in the *work* – the chance to find yourself'.[6] He is left with those two unworkable words, 'the Horror, the Horror!' Nostromo embarks on the most desperate mission of his life with the silver tied for safety around his neck 'so that it shall be talked about when the little children are grown up and the grown men are old', only to be betrayed and berated in the silence of the Great Isabel, mocked in the owl's death call 'Ya-acabo! Ya-acabo! it is finished, it is finished.'[7] And Aziz, in *A Passage to India*, who embarks jauntily, though no less desperately, on his Anglo-Indian picnic to the Marabar caves is cruelly undone by the echo of the Kawa Dol: 'Boum, ouboum is the sound as far as the human alphabet can express it . . . if one spoke silences in that place or quoted lofty poetry, the comment would have been the same ou-boum.'[8]

As one silence uncannily repeats the other, the sign of identity and reality found in the work of Empire, is slowly undone. Eric Stokes, in *The Political Ideas of British Imperialism*[9] describes the mission of work – that medium of recognition for the colonial subject – as a distinctive feature of the imperialist mind which, from the early nineteenth century, effected 'the transference of religious emotion to secular purposes'. But this transference of affect and object is never achieved without a disturbance, a displacement in the representation of Empire's work itself. Marlow's compulsive search for those famous rivets, to get on with the work, to stop the hold, gives way to the compulsive quest for the Voice, the words that are half-lost, lied about, repeated. Kurtz is just a word, not the man with the name; Marlow is just a name, lost in the narrative game, in the 'terrific suggestiveness of words heard in dreams, of phrases spoken in nightmares'.

What emerges from the dispersal of work is the language of a colonial nonsense that displaces those dualities in which the colonial space is traditionally divided: nature/culture chaos/civility. Ouboum or the owl's deathcall – the horror of these words! – are not naturalized or primitivistic descriptions of colonial 'otherness', they are the inscriptions of an uncertain colonial silence that mocks the social performance of language with their non-sense; that baffles the communicable verities of culture with their refusal to translate. These hybrid signifiers are the intimations of a colonial Otherness that Forster describes so well in the beckoning of India to the conquerors: 'She calls "Come" . . . But come to what? She has never defined. She is not a promise, only an appeal.' It is from such an uncertain invitation to interpret, from such a question of desire, that the echo of another significant question can be dimly heard, Lacan's question of the alienation of the subject in the Other: 'He is saying this to me, but what does he

want?[10] 'Yacabo! Yacabo! It is finished . . . finished': these words stand not
for the plenitudinous place of cultural diversity, but at the point of culture's
'fading'. They display the alienation between the transformational myth of
culture as a language of universality and social generalization, and its tropic
function as a repeated 'translation' of incommensurable levels of living and
meaning. The articulation of nonsense is the recognition of an anxious
contradictory place between the human and the not-human, between sense
and non-sense, which no dialectic can deliver. In that sense, these 'senseless'
signifiers pose the question of cultural choice in terms similar to the Lacanian 'vel', between being and meaning, between the subject and the other,
'neither the one nor the other'. Neither, in our terms, 'work' nor 'word' but
precisely the work of the colonial word that leaves, for instance, the surface
of Nostromo strewn with the detritus of silver – a fetish, Emilia calls it; an
evil omen, in Nostromo's words; and Gould is forever silent. Bits and pieces
of silver recount the tale that never quite adds up either to the narcissistic,
dynastic dream of Imperial democracy, nor to Captain Mitchell's banal
demand for a narrative of 'historical events'.

The work of the word impedes the question of the transparent assimilation
of cross-cultural meanings in a unitary sign of 'human' culture. In-between
culture, at the point of its articulation of identity or distinctiveness, comes
the question of signification. This is not simply a matter of language; it is
the question of culture's representation of difference – manners, words,
rituals, customs, time – inscribed without a transcendent subject that knows,
outside of a mimetic social memory, and across the – Ouboum – kernel of
non-sense. What becomes of cultural identity – the ability to put the right
word in the right place at the right time – when it crosses the colonial non-
sense – neither the one – meaningful – nor the other – meaningless? Such
a question impedes the language of relativism in which cultural difference
is usually disposed of as a kind of ethical naturalism, a matter of cultural
diversity. 'A fully individual culture is at best a rare thing' Bernard Williams
writes in his interesting new essay *Ethics and the Limits of Philosophy*.[11] Yet,
he argues, the very structure of ethical thought seeks to apply its principles
to the whole world. His concept of a 'relativism of distance', which is
underwritten by an epistemological view of society as a given whole, seeks
to inscribe the totality of other cultures in a realist and concrete narrative
that must beware, he warns, the fantasy of projection. Surely, however, the
very project of ethical naturalism or cultural relativism is spurred precisely
by the repeated threat of the *loss* of a 'teleologically significant world', and
the compensation of that loss in projection or introjection which then
becomes the *basis* of its ethical judgement. From the margins of his text,
Williams asks, in parenthesis, a question not dissimilar from Forster's India
question or Lacan's question of the subject; 'What is this talk of projection
[in the midst of naturalism] really saying? What is the screen?' He makes
no answer.

The problematic enunciation of cultural difference becomes, in the discourse of relativism, the perspectival problem of temporal and spatial dis-

tance. The threatened 'loss' of meaningfulness in cross-cultural interpretation, which is as much a problem of the structure of the signifier as it is
a question of cultural codes (the *experience* of other cultures), then becomes
a hermeneutic project for the restoration of cultural 'essence' or authenticity.
The issue of interpretation in colonial cultural discourse is not, however, an
epistemological problem that emerges because cultural objects appear *before*
(in both senses) the eye of the subject in a bewildering diversity. Nor is it
simply a quarrel between pre-constituted holistic cultures, that contain
within themselves the codes by which they can legitimately be read. The
question of cultural difference as I want to cast it, is not what Adela Quested
quaintly identified as an 'Anglo-Indian difficulty', a problem caused by
cultural plurality. And to which, in her view, the only response could be
the sublation of cultural differentiation in an ethical universalism: 'That's
why I want Akbar's "universal religion" or the equivalent to keep me decent
and sensible.'[12] Cultural difference, as Adela experienced it, in the nonsense
of the Marabar caves, is not the acquisition or accumulation of additional
cultural knowledge; it is the momentous, if momentary, extinction of the
recognizable object of culture in the disturbed artifice of its signification, at
the edge of experience.

What happened in the caves? *There*, the loss of the narrative of cultural
plurality; *there* the implausibility of conversation and commensurability; *there*
the enactment of an undecidable, uncanny colonial present, an Anglo-Indian
difficulty, which repeats but is never itself fully represented: 'Come . . . But
come to what?'; remember India's invocation. Aziz is incurably inaccurate
about the events, because he is sensitive, because Adela's question about
polygamy has to be put from his mind. Adela, obsessively trying to think
the incident out, somatizes the experience in repeated, hysterical narratives.
Her body, Sebastian-like, is covered in colonies of cactus spines, and her
mind which attempts to disavow the body – hers, his – returns to it
obsessively: 'Now, everything transferred to the surface of my body . . . He
never actually touched me once . . . It all seems such nonsense . . . a sort of
shadow.' It is the echochamber of memory: '"What a handsome little
oriental . . . beauty, thick hair, a fine skin . . . there was nothing of the
vagrant in her blood . . . he might attract women of his own race and rank:
Have you one wife or many? . . . . Damn the English even at their best," he
says . . . "I remember, remember scratching the wall with my finger-nail to
start the echo . . ." she says . . . And then the echo . . . "Ouboum".'[13]

In this performance of the text, I have attempted to articulate the enunciatory disorder of the colonial present, the writing of cultural difference. It
lies in the staging of the colonial signifier in the narrative uncertainty of
culture's in-between: between sign and signifier, neither one nor the other,
neither sexuality nor nationality, neither, simply, memory nor desire. The
articulated opening in-between that I am attempting to describe, is well
brought out in Derrida's placing or spacing of the hymen. In the context
of the strange play of cultural memory and colonial desire in the Marabar
caves, Derrida's words are uncannily resonant. 'It is neither desire nor

pleasure but between the two. Neither future nor present, but between the two. It is the hymen that desire dreams of piercing, of bursting in an act of violence that is (at the same time or somewhere between) love and murder. If either one *did* take place, there would be no hymen. . . . It is an operation that both sows confusion between opposites and stands *between* the opposites 'at once'.[14] It is an undecidability that arises from a certain culturalist substitution that Derrida describes as 'anti-ethnocentrism think-ing itself as ethnocentrism . . . silently imposing its standard concepts of speech and writing'. For neither can the epistemological object of cultural identity nor the dialectical, structuralist sign of arbitrary difference contain the effect of such colonial nonsense.

In the language of epistemological cultural description, the object of culture comes to be inscribed in a process that Richard Rorty describes as that confusion between justification and explanation, the priority of know-ledge 'of' over knowledge 'that': the priority of the visual relation between persons and objects above the justificatory, textual relationship between propositions. It is precisely such a priority of eye over inscription, or Voice over writing, that insists on the 'image' of knowledge as confrontation between the self and the object of belief seen through the mirror of Nature. In such a visibility of truth the metonymy of the colonial moment comes to be disavowed because its narrative ruse lies in proferring a visibility or totality of the event of cultural authority, or the object of race, only to alienate it from itself, to replicate identity as iteration. The signifiers of ambivalent, hybrid, cultural knowledges – neither 'one' nor 'other' – are ethnocentrically elided in the search for cultural commensurability, as Rorty describes it: 'to be rational is to find the proper set of terms into which all contributions should be translated if agreement is to become possible'.[15] And such agreement leads inevitably to a transparency of culture that must be thought outside of the signification of difference; what Ernest Gellner has simplistically resolved in his recent work on relativism, as the diversity of man in a unitary world. A world which, if read, as 'word' in the following passage illustrates the impossibility of signifying, within its evaluative langu-age, the values of anteriority and alterity that haunt the colonial non-sense.

Gellner writes: 'Assume the regularity of nature, the systematic nature of the world, not because it is demonstrable, but because anything which eludes such a principle also eludes real knowledge; if cumulative and communicable knowledge is to be possible at all, then the principle of orderliness must apply to it . . . Unsymmetrical, idiosyncratic explanations are worthless – they are not explanations.'[16]

It is the horizon of holism, towards which cultural authority aspires that is made ambivalent in the colonial signifier. To put it succinctly, it turns the dialectical 'between' of culture's disciplinary structure – *between* uncon-scious and conscious motives, *between* indigenous categories and conscious rationalizations, *between* little acts and grand traditions, in James Boon's[17] words – into something closer to Derrida's 'entre', that sows confusion between opposites and stands between the oppositions at once. The colonial signifier – neither one nor other – is, however, an act of ambivalent signification, literally splitting the difference between the binary oppositions or polarities through which we think cultural difference. It is in the enunciatory act of splitting that the colonial signifier creates its strategies of differentiation that produce an undecidability between contraries or oppositions.

Marshall Sahlins' 'symbolic synapses'[18] produce homologous differentiations in the conjunction of oppositions from different cultural planes. James Boon's cultural operators produce the *Traviata* effect – when Amato del Passato turns into the sublime duet Grandio – as a moment that recalls, in his words, the genesis of signification. It is a moment that matches the right phones to the language system, producing from different orders or oppositions a burst of cross-referencing significance in the 'on-going' cultural performance. In both these influential theories of the culture-concept, cultural generalizability is effective to the extent to which differentiation is homologous, the genesis of signification recalled in the performance of cross-referencing.

What I have suggested above, for the colonial cultural signifier, is precisely the radical loss of such a homologous or dialectical assemblage of part and whole, metaphor and metonymy. Instead of cross-referencing there is an effective, productive cross-cutting across sites of social significance, that erases the dialectical, disciplinary sense of 'Cultural' reference and relevance. It is in this sense that the culturally unassimilable words and scenes of nonsense, with which I started – the Horror, the Horror, the owl's death call, the Marabar caves – suture the colonial text in a hybrid time and truth that survives and subverts the generalizations of literature and history. It is to the ambivalence of the on-going colonial present, and its contradictory articulations of power and cultural knowledge, that I now want to turn.

II

The enunciatory ambivalence of colonial culture cannot, of course, be derived directly from the 'temporal pulsation' of the signifier; the rule of Empire must not be allegorized in the misrule of writing. There is, however, a mode of enunciation that echoes through the annals of nineteenth-century Indian colonial history where a strange discursive figure of undecidability arises within cultural authority, between the knowledge of culture and the custom of power. It represents the moment when the authority of the master word is as much installed as *Entseelt*. It is a negation of the Traviata moment; it is a moment when the impossibility of naming the difference of colonial culture, alienates, in its very form of articulation, the colonialist cultural ideals of progress, piety, rationality and order.

It is heard in the central paradox of missionary education and conversion, in Alexander Duff's monumental *India and India Missions* (1839): 'Do not send men of compassion here for you will soon break their hearts; do send men of compassion here, where millions perish for lack of knowledge'.[19] It can be heard in the aporetic moment of Sir Henry Maines's Rede Lecture (1875) and is repeated again in his contribution to Humphry Ward's definitive commemorative volume on The Reign of Queen Victoria:

> As has been truly said, the British rulers of India are like men bound to keep true time in two longitudes at once. Nevertheless, the paradoxical position must be accepted in the most extraordinary experiment, the British Government of India, the virtually despotic government of a dependency by a free people.[20]

The paradox is finally fully exposed in Fitzjames Stephen's important essay on 'The Foundations of the Government of India', in his opposition to the Ibert Bill – an opportunity which he uses to attack the utilitarian and liberal governance of India.

> A barrel of gunpowder may be harmless or may explode, but you cannot educate it into household fuel by exploding little bits of it. How can you possibly teach great masses of people that they ought to be rather dissatisfied with a foreign ruler, but not much; that they should express their discontent in words and in votes, but not in acts; that they should ask from him this and that reform (which they neither understand nor care for), but should on no account rise in insurrection against him.[21]

These statements must not be dismissed as imperialism's double-think; it is, in fact, their desperate acknowledgement of an aporia in the inscription of empire that makes them notable. It is their performance of a certain uncertain writing in the anomalous discourse of the 'present' of colonial governmentality that is of interest to me. And not to me alone. For these enunciations represent what I take to be that split-second, that ambivalent temporality that demonstrates the turn from evolutionism to diffusionism in the culturalist discourse of colonial governmentality; an ambiguity that articulated the otherwise opposed policies of the utilitarians and comparativists in the mid-nineteenth century debate on colonial cultural 'progress' and policy.

According to John Burrows such an ambivalence was signally representative of cultural governance, as he writes in *Evolution and Society*: 'when [they] want to emphasise the fact of continuity, the similarity between barbaric institutions and those of the European past, or even present, they speak in an evolutionary manner. But almost equally often they speak in terms of a straight dichotomy: status and contract, progressive and non-progressive, barbarous and civilized'.[22]

These statements reveal a particular ideological space that Benedict Anderson has described, so well, as the inner incompatibility of empire and nation, they alienate the idea of the commensurability of culture or the dialectical sign of its meaning and, in that sense, they echo a colonial nonsense 'neither one nor the other' but somewhere in between. In these

gnomic, yet crucial, historical utterances, are displayed the margins of the
disciplinary idea of culture enacted in the colonial scene: British/India,
Nostromo, Ouboum – each cultural naming represents the impossibility of
cross-cultural identity or, symbolic synapses; each time there repeats the
incompletion of translation. It is such a figure of doubt that haunts Henry
Maine's naming of India: in his essay on the 'Observation of India', India is
a figure of profound intellectual uncertainty and governmental ambivalence.

If India is a reproduction of the common Aryan origin, in Maine's
discourse it is also a perpetual repetition of that origin as a remnant of the
past; if that remnant of India is the symbol of an archaic past, it is also
the signifier of the production of a discursive past-in-the-present; if India
is the imminent object of classical, theoretical knowledge, India is also the
sign of its dispersal in the exercise of power; if India is the metaphoric
equivalence, authorizing the appropriation and naturalization of other cultures, then India is also the repetitive process of metonymy recognized only
in its remnants' that are, at once, the signs of disturbance and the supports
of colonial authority. If India is the originary symbol of colonial authority,
it is the sign of a dispersal in the articulation of authoritative knowledge;
if India is a runic reality, India is also the ruin of time; if India is the seed
of life, India is a monument to death. India is the perpetual generation of
a past–present which is the disturbing, uncertain time of the colonial
intervention and the ambivalent truth of its enunciation.

These aporia must not be seen merely as contradictions in the idea of
ideology of empire. They do not effect a symptomatic repression of domination or desire that will eventually either be sublated or will endlessly
circulate in the dereliction of an identificatory narrative. Such enunciations
of culture's colonial difference are closer in spirit to what Foucault has
sketchily, but suggestively, described as the material repeatability of the
statement. As I understand the concept – and this is my tendentious
reconstruction – it is an insistence on the *surface of emergence* as it structures
the present of its enunciation: the historical caught outside the hermeneutic
of historicism; meaning grasped not in relation to some un-said or polysemy,
but in its production of an authority to differentiate. The meaning of the
statement is neither symptomatic nor allegorical. It is a status of the subject's
authority, a performative present in which the statement becomes both
appropriate and an object of appropriation; repeatable, reasonable, an
instrument of desire, the elements of a strategy. Such a strategic repetition
at the enunciative level requires neither simply formal analysis nor semantic
investigation nor verification but, and I quote, 'the analysis of the relations
between the statement and the spaces of differentiation, in which the statement itself reveals the differences'.[23] Repeatability, in my terms, is always
the repetition in the very act of enunciation, something other, a difference
that is a little bit uncanny, as Foucault comes to define the representability
of the statement: 'Perhaps it is like the over-familiar that constantly eludes
one', he writes, like 'those famous transparencies which, although they

conceal nothing in their density, are nevertheless not entirely clear. The enunciative level emerges in its very proximity'.[24]

If at first sight these statements by Duff and Maine and Fitzjames Stephen are the uncommon commonplaces of colonial history, then doubly inscribed their difference emerges quite clearly between-the-lines; the temporal in-between of Maine's past–present that will only name India as a mode of discursive uncertainty. From the impossibility of keeping true time in two longitudes and the inner incompatibility of empire and nation in the anomalous discourse of cultural progressivism, emerges an ambivalence that is neither the contestation of contradictories nor the antagonism of dialectical opposition. In these instances of social and discursive alienation there is no recognition of master and slave, there is only the matter of the enslaved master, the unmastered slave.

What is articulated in the enunciation of the colonial present – in between the lines – is a splitting of the discourse of cultural governmentality at the moment of its enunciation of authority. It is, according to Frantz Fanon, a 'Manichean' moment that divides the colonial space: a Manichean division, two zones that are opposed but not in the service of a 'higher unity'.[25] Fanon's Manichean metaphors resonate with something of the discursive and affective ambivalence that I have attributed to the archaic nonsense of colonial cultural articulation, as it emerges with its significatory edge, to disturb the disciplinary languages and logics of the culture concept itself – not simply the one or the other. For Fanon, the native lives on the knife-edge, in a state of muscular and psychic tension, split between his carceral space and his dreams of possession, muscular prowess, aggression. 'The symbols of the social – the police, the bugle calls in the barracks, military parades and the waving flags – are at one and the same time inhibitory and stimulating: Don't dare to budge . . . Get ready to attack'.[26] And if Fanon sets the scene of splitting around these uncanny and traumatic fetishes of colonial power, then Freud in describing the social circumstances of splitting in his essay on 'Fetishism', echoes the political conditions of my enunciatory aporia. 'A grown man', Freud writes, 'may experience a similar panic when the cry goes up that throne and Altar are in danger, and similar illogical consequences will ensue'.[27]

Splitting constitutes an intricate, non-repressive strategy of defence and differentiation in the colonial discourse, if it is read outside the canon of 'castration' as principally a problem of the enunciation of 'ambivalence'. The splitting of two contradictory and independent attitudes that inhabit the same place, one taking account of reality, the other under the influence of instincts which detach the ego from reality, results in the production of multiple and contradictory belief. If this mode of articulation is read – heretically without the cause of castration, that visible invisibility – then the enunciatory moment of multiple belief is less of a defence against the anxiety of difference, but is itself productive of differentiations – between knowledges. Splitting is then a form of enunciatory, even intellectual uncertainty that stems from the fact that what is articulated in-between each belief, what articulates contradictoriness is not so much a meaningful principle of negation, not so much a denial of what was seen, but a loss of the significatory function itself between the contradictory yet coeval and coterminous statements of belief. If you can imagine it, a *language-less-meaning*, in the articulation of cultural authority, with the cut appearing in-between the time of signification, just as I have written it. And this refusal to represent, where culture cuts up and power, momentarily, cuts out, is itself productive of a mode of ambivalence at the point of disavowal (*Verleugnung*) which Freud describes as the vicissitude of the idea, as distinct from the vicissitude of affect, repression (*Verdrängung*). It is crucial to understand – and not often noted – that the process of disavowal is the negation of a visual epistemology, that is productive of other fantasmatic knowledges, multiple belief, that make sense of the trauma, and substitute for the absence of visibility. It is precisely such a vicissitude of the idea of 'culture' in its colonial enunciation, culture articulated at the point of its erasure, that makes a non-sense of the disciplinary meanings of culture itself. A colonial non-sense, however, that is productive of powerful, if ambivalent, strategies of cultural authority and resistance.

There occurs then, what we may describe as the 'normalizing' strategy of discursive splitting, a certain anomalous containment of cultural ambivalence. It is visible in Fitzjames Stephen's attack on the 'undecidability' of liberal and utilitarian colonial governance. What structures his statement is the threatening production of 'uncertainty' that haunts the discursive subject and taunts the enlightened liberal 'subject' of culture itself. But the threat of 'meaninglessness', the reversion to chaos, is required to maintain the vigilance towards Throne and Altar; to reinforce the 'belligerence' of British civilization, which if it is to be authoritative, Fitzjames Stephens writes, must not shirk from the open, uncompromising, straightforward assertion of the anomaly of the British government of India. An insoluble anomaly that preoccupied enlightened opinion throughout the nineteenth century, in Mill's words: 'the government of a people by itself has a meaning and a reality; but such a thing as government of one people by another does not and cannot exist'. The open assertion of the 'anomalous' produces an impossible cultural choice: civilization or the threat of chaos – either one or the other – whereas the discursive 'choice' continually requires both and the practice of power is imaged, anomalously yet again, 'as the virtually despotic government of a dependency by a free people' – once more neither one nor the other.

If this mistranslation of democratic power repeats the 'anomaly' of colonial authority – the colonial space without a proper name – then Evangelical pedagogy in the 1830s turns the 'intellectual uncertainty', between the Bible and Hinduism, into an anomalous strategy of interpellation. With the institution of what was termed 'the intellectual system' in 1829, in the mission schools of Bengal, there developed a mode of instruction which continually set up – on our model of the splitting of colonial discourse –

contradictory and independent textualities of Christian piety and heathen idolatry in order to elicit, between them, in an uncanny doubling, undecidability. It was an uncertainty between truth and falsehood whose avowed aim was conversion, but whose discursive and political strategy was the production of doubt; not simply a doubt in the content of beliefs, but a doubt, or an uncertainty in the native place of enunciation; at the point of the colonizer's demand for narrative, at the moment of the master's interrogation. This is Duff writing in 1835:

> When asked whether it is not an imperative ordinance of his faith that, during the great festival of Ramadan, everyone of the faithful should fast from sunrise to sunset – [the Mohammedan] unhesitatingly, and without qualification, admits that this is a command which dare not be broken – an act of contempt against Mohammed . . . You then appeal to the indisputable geographical fact that in the Arctic and Antarctic regions, the period from sunrise to sunset annually extends to several months . . . either his religion was not designed to be universal, therefore not Divine, or he who framed the Koran was unacquainted with the geographical fact . . . and therefore an ignorant imposter. So galled does the Mohammedan feel . . . that he usually cuts the Gordian Knot by boldly denying the geographical fact . . . and many, many are the glosses and ingenious subterfuges to which he feels himself impelled to resort.[28]

The Brahmans treat with equal contempt, not only the demonstrations of modern science but 'the very testimony of their eyes'. The avowed aim of this systematic mistranslation, of 'this drawing from the metaphysics of the Koran its physical dogmata' is to institutionalise a narrative of 'verisimilitude of the whole statement' for in Duff's words, 'no sooner was the identity of the two sets of phenomena announced as a fact, than the truth of the given theory was conceded'. The normalizing strategy is however a form of subjection that requires precisely the anomalous enunciation – the archaic nonsense of the banal misreading of mythology as geographical fact – so that, as Duff writes, 'there was a sort of silent warfare incessantly maintained . . . self-exploding engines that lurked unseen and unsuspected . . . When the wound was once inflicted, honourable retreat for the native was impossible'.[29]

The aim is the separation of the heathen soul from the subterfuge of its 'subtile system'. The strategy of splitting is the production of a space of contradictory and multiple belief, even more sly and subtle, between Evangelical verisimilitude and the poetry of the Vedas or the Koran. A strategic space of enunciation is produced – neither the one nor the other – whose truth is to place the native in that moment of enunciation which both Benveniste and Lacan describe, where to say 'I am lying' is strangely to tell the truth or vice versa. Who, in truth, is addressed in the verisimilitude of such translation, which must be a mistranslation? In that subtle warfare of colonial discourse lurks the fear that in speaking in two tongues, language itself becomes doubly inscribed and the intellectual system uncertain. The colonizer's interrogation becomes anomalous, 'for every term which the

Christian missionary can employ to communicate divine truth is already
appropriated as the chosen symbol of some counterpart deadly error'.[30] If
the word of the master is already appropriated and the word of the slave
is undecidable, where does the truth of colonial nonsense lie?

Underlying the intellectual uncertainty generated by the anomaly of
cultural difference is a question of the displacement of truth that is at
once between and beyond the hybridity of images of governance, or the
undecidability between codes and texts, or indeed the impossibility of Sir
Henry Maine's colonial problematic: the attempt to keep true time in two
longitudes, at once. It is a displacement of truth in the very identification
of culture, or an uncertainty in the structure of 'culture' as the identification
of a certain discursive human truth. A truth of the human which is culture's
home; a truth which 'differentiates' cultures affirms its human significance,
the authority of its address. When the Mohammedan is forced to deny the
logical demonstration of geographical fact and the Hindu turns away from
the evidence of his eyes, we witness a form of ambivalence, a mode of
enunciation, a coercion of the native subject in which no truth can exist.
It is not simply a question of the absence of rationality or morality: it leads
through such historical and philosophical distinctions of cultural differences,
to rest in that precariously empty discursive space where the question of
the human capacity of culture lies. To put it a little grandly, the problem
now is of the question of culture itself as it comes to be represented and
contested in the colonial imitation – not identity – of man. As before, the
question occurs in culture's archaic undecidability.

On the eve of Durgapuja in the mid 1820s, the Reverend Duff walks
through the quarter of Calcutta where the image-makers are at work. A
million images of the goddess Durga affront his eyes; a million hammers
beating brass and tin assault his ears; a million dismembered Durgas, eyes,
arms, heads, some unpainted, others unformed, assail him as he turns to
reverie:

> The recollections of the past strangely blend with the visible exhibitions of
> the present. The old settled convictions of home experience are suddenly
> counterpoised by the previously unimagined scene. To incline [your quivering
> judgement] in one way or other, to determine the 'dubious propendency' you
> again and again watch the movements of those before you. You contemplate
> their form and you cannot doubt that they are men . . . Your wonder is vastly
> increased; but the grounds of your decision have multiplied too.[31]

My final argument interrogates, from the colonial perspective, this cultural compulsion to 'be, become, or be seen to be human'. It is a problem
caught in the vacillatory syntax of the entire passage; heard finally in the
'cannot' in 'You cannot doubt that they are men'. I will suggest that the
coercive image of the colonized subject produces a loss or lack of truth that
articulates an uncanny truth about colonialist cultural authority and its
figurative space of the human. The infinite variety of man fades into
insignificance when, in the moment of the discursive splitting, it oversigni-

fies; it says something beside the point, something beside the truth of culture, something *Abseits*. A meaning that is culturally alien not because it is spoken in many tongues but because the colonial compulsion to truth is always an effect of what Derrida has called the Babelian performance, in the act of translation, as a figurative transference of meaning across language systems. I quote from Derrida:

> When God imposes and opposes his name, he ruptures the rational transparency but interrupts also the . . . linguistic imperialism. He destines them to the law of translation both necessary and impossible . . . forbidden transparency, impossible univocity. Translation becomes law, duty and debt, but the debt one can no longer discharge.[32]

It is a performance of truth or the lack of it that, in translation, impedes the dialectical process of cultural generality and communicability. In its stead, where there is the threat of overinterpretation, there can be no ethical or epistemological commensurate subject of culture. There is, in fact, the survival across culture and cultures of a certain interesting, even insurgent, madness that subverts the authority of culture in its 'human' form. It will hardly surprise you then, at this juncture, if having glimpsed the problem in those dismembered images of the goddess Durga, I now turn to that other living doll, Olympia, from Hoffmann's *The Sandman* on which Freud bases his essay on *The Uncanny*, to explicate this strategy of cultural splitting: human/non-human; society/Ouboum.

In keeping with our taste for contraries, I suggest that we read the fable of the Double uncannily, in-between Freud's analytic distinctions between 'intellectual uncertainty' and 'castration', between 'surmounting' and 'repression'. Such doubts bedevil the essay to the point at which Freud half-suggests an analytic distinction between 'repression proper' as appropriate to psychical reality, and 'surmounting' – which extends the term repression beyond its legitimate meaning – as more appropriate to the repressive workings of the cultural unconscious.[33] It is through Freud's own 'intellectual uncertainty', at the point of his exposition of psychic ambivalence that, I believe, the cultural argument of the uncanny double emerges.

The figure of Olympia stands between the human and the automaton, between manners and mechanical reproduction, embodying an aporia: a living doll. Through Durga and Olympia, the ghostly magical spirit of the double embraces, at one time or another, my entire colonial concert party: Marlow, Kurtz, Adela, Aziz, Nostromo, Duff, Maine, the owl, the Marabar caves, Derrida, Foucault, Freud, master and slave alike. All these comedians of culture's non-sense have stood, for a brief moment, in that undecidable enunciatory space where culture's authority is undone in colonial power – they have taught culture's double lesson. For the uncanny lesson of the double, as a problem of intellectual uncertainty, lies precisely in its double-inscription. The authority of culture, in the modern episteme, requires at once imitation and identification, the archaic survival of the Ego-istical in the superego, the culture is *heimlich*, with its disciplinary generalizations, its mimetic narratives, its homologous empty time, its seriality, its progress, its customs and coherence. But cultural authority is also un*heimlich*, for to be distinctive, significatory, influential and identifiable, it has to be translated, disseminated, differentiated, inter-disciplinary, intertextual, international, inter-racial. In between these two plays the time of a colonial paradox in those contradictory statements of subordinate power. For the repetition of the 'same' can in fact be its own displacement, can turn the authority of culture into its own non-sense precisely in its moment of enunciation. For to imitate is to cling to the denial of the ego's limitations; to identify is to assimilate conflictually. It is from between them where the letter of the law will not be assigned as a sign, that culture's double returns uncannily – neither the one nor the other, but the imposter – to mock and mimic, to lose the sense of the masterful self and its social sovereignty. It is at this moment of intellectual and psychic 'uncertainty' that representation can no longer guarantee the authority of culture; and culture can no longer guarantee to author its 'human' subjects as the signs of humanness. Freud neglected the cultural uncanny but Hoffmann was far more canny. If I started with colonial nonsense, I want to end with metropolitan bourgeois burlesque. I quote from Hoffmann's *The Sandman* a passage Freud failed to note.

> The history of the automaton had sunk deeply into their souls, and an absurd mistrust of human figures began to prevail. Several lovers, in order to be fully convinced that they were not paying court to a wooden puppet required that their mistress should sing and dance a little out of time, should embroider or knit or play with her little pug etc. when being read to, but above all things else that she should frequently speak in such a way as to really show that her words presupposed as a condition some thinking and feeling . . . Spalanzani was obliged, as has been said, to leave the place in order to escape a criminal charge of having fraudulently imposed an automaton upon human society.[34]

We are now almost face to face with culture's double bind – a certain slippage or splitting between human artifice and culture's discursive agency. To be true to a self one must learn to be a little untrue, out-of-joint with the signification of cultural generalizability. As Hoffmann suggests, sing a little out of tune; just fail to hit that top E in James Boon's *Aida* concept; speak in such a way to show that words presuppose feeling, which is to assume, that a certain nonsense always haunts and hinders them. But how untrue must you be to fail to be happily, if haphazardly human? That is the colonial question; that, I believe, is where the truth lies – as always a little beside the point.

Native 'folly' emerged as a quasi-legal, cultural category soon after the establishment of the Supreme Court in Calcutta in the 1830s, almost as the uncanny double of the demand for verisimilitude and testimony – the establishment of the Law. Folly is a form of perjury for which Halhed assures us, in his preface to the *Code of Gentoo Laws*, no European form of words exists. To our delight and horror, however, we find that its structure repeats that enunciatory splitting that I have been attempting to describe. It consists, Halhed writes, 'in falsehoods totally incompatible with each other and utterly contrary to their own opinion, knowledge and conviction . . . It is like the madness so inimitably delineated in Cervantes, sensible enough upon some occasions and at the same time completely wild and unconscious of itself'.[35] Despite adequate contemporary juridical and sociological explanations for perjury, the myth of the lie persists in the pages of power, even down to District Officers' reports in the 1920s. What is the truth of the lie?

When the Muslim is coerced into speaking a Christian truth he denies the logic of his senses; the Hindu denies the evidence of his eyes; the Bengalee denies his very name as he perjures himself. Or so we are told. Each time what comes to be textualized as the truth of the native culture is a part that becomes ambivalently incorporated in the archives of colonial knowledge. A part like the geographical detail that is specious and beside the point. A part like 'folly' that is untranslatable, inexplicable, unknowable yet endlessly repeated in the name of the native. What emerges in these lies that never speak the 'whole' truth, come to be circulated from mouth to mouth, book to book, is the institutionalization of a very specific discursive form of paranoia, that must be authorized at the point of its dismemberment. It is a form of persecutory paranoia that emerges from culture's own structured demand for imitation and identification. It is the archaic survival of the 'text' of culture, that is at once the demand and desire of its translations, never the authority of its originality. Its strategy, as Karl Abrahams has described it, is a partial incorporation; a form of incorporation that deprives the object of a part of its body in that its integrity may be attacked without destroying its existence. 'We are put in mind of a child', the psychoanalyst Karl Abrahams writes, 'who catches a fly and having pulled off a leg, lets it go again'.[36] The existence of the disabled native is required for the next lie and the next and the next – 'The horror! the horror!' Marlow, you will remember, had to lie as he moved from the heart of darkness to the West's whited sepulchre. As he replaces the words of horror for the name of the Intended we read in that palimpsest, neither one nor the other, something of the awkward, ambivalent, unwelcome truth of empire's lie.

Notes

1 E. M. Forster, *A Passage to India*, (Harmondsworth: Penguin) 1979, p. 135.
2 J. Lacan, *The Four Fundamental Concepts of Psycho-Analysis*, (Harmondsworth: Penguin) 1979, p. 250.
3 Carlyle, *Essays*.
4 Rudyard Kipling, 'The Burial' quoted in Eric Stokes, *The Political Ideas of English Imperialism* (London: Oxford University Press, 1960) p. 28. I am indebted to Stokes' suggestive remarks on the value of 'inarticulateness' attributed to the mission of colonial enterprise.

5   W. Benjamin, *Illuminations*, trans. Harry Zohn (London: Jonathan Cape, 1970), pp. 98–101.

6   J. Conrad, *Heart of Darkness* (Harmondsworth: Penguin, 1979).

7   J. Conrad, *Nostromo* (Harmondsworth: Penguin, 1979) p. 345.

8   E. M. Forster, *A Passage to India* (Harmondsworth: Penguin 1975), p. 145.

9   E. Stokes, *Political Ideas*, p. 29.

10 J. Lacan, *The Four Fundamental Concepts of Psychoanalysis* (Harmondsworth: Penguin, 1979), p. 214.

11 B. Williams, *Ethics and the Limits of Philosophy* (London: Fontana, 1985).

12 E. M. Forster, *Passage to India*, p. 144.

13 This is a collage of words, phrases, statements made in/around the entry to the Marabar caves. They represent a fictional re-enactment of that crucial moment as an act of memory.

14 J. Derrida, *Dissemination*, trans. Barbara Johnson (Chicago: Chicago University Press, 1981), pp. 212–3.

15 R. Rorty, *Philosophy and the Mirror of Nature* (Princeton: Princeton University Press, 1979), p. 318.

16 E. Gellner, *Relativism and the Social Sciences* (Cambridge: Cambridge University Press, 1985), p. 90.

17 J. Boon, 'Further operations of "culture" in anthropology: a synthesis of and for debate', *Social Science Quarterly*, vol. 52, pp. 221–52.

18 M. Sahlins, *Culture and Practical Reason* (Chicago: Chicago University Press, 1976).

19 Rev. A. Duff, *India and India Missions: Including Sketches of the Gigantic System of Hinduism etc.* (Edinburgh: John Johnstone, 1839) 3, p. 211.

20 Sir Henry Maine, *The Effects of Observation of India on Modern European Thought*, (Cambridge: The Rede Lecture, 1875).

21 James Fitzjames Stephen, 'The Foundations of the Government of India' *Nineteenth Century*, 14, pp. 551 ff. (October, 1883).

22 J. W. Burrow, *Evolution and Society, A Study in Victorian Social Theory* (Cambridge: Cambridge University Press, 1966), p. 159.

23 M. Foucault, *The Archaeology of Knowledge* (London: Tavistock, 1972), p. 92.

24 Ibid., p. 111.

25 F. Fanon, *The Wretched of the Earth* (Harmondsworth: Penguin, 1969), p. 29.

26 Ibid., p. 41.

27 S. Freud, 'Fetishism' in *On Sexuality* (Harmondsworth: Pelican Freud Library, 1977, vol. 7), p. 352.

28 Duff, *India and Indian Missions*, p. 564.

29 Ibid. p. 563.

30 Ibid. p. 323.

31 Ibid. p. 225.

32 J. Derrida, 'Des Tours de Babel', *Difference in Translation*, ed. Joseph F. Graham (Ithaca: Cornell University Press, 1985), p. 174.

33 S. Freud, 'The "Uncanny"', in *Art and Literature* (Harmondsworth: Pelican Freud Library, vol. 14).

34 E. T. A. Hoffmann, *The Sandman*,

35 N.B. Halhed, trans. and ed., *A Code of Gentoo Laws, or Ordinations of the Pundits* (London, 1776), pp. li–lii.

36 K. Abrahams, *Selected Papers On Psychoanalysis* (London: Karnac, 1988), p. 487.

GAYATRI CHAKRAVORTY SPIVAK

Poststructuralism, Marginality, Postcoloniality and Value

This essay is not about the difference between Africa and Asia, between the United States and Britain. It is about the difference and the relationship between academic and 'revolutionary' practices in the interest of social change. The radical academic, *when she is in the academy*, might reckon that names like 'Asian' or 'African' (or indeed 'American' or 'British') have histories that are not anchored in identities but rather secure them. We cannot exchange as 'truth', in the currency of the university, what might be immediate needs for identitarian collectivities. This seems particularly necessary in literary criticism today, with its vigorous investments in cultural critique. If academic and 'revolutionary' practices do not bring each other to productive crisis, the power of the script has clearly passed elsewhere. There can be no universalist claims in the human sciences. This is most strikingly obvious in the case of establishing 'marginality' as a subject-position in literary and cultural critique. The reader must accustom herself to starting from a particular situation and then to the ground shifting under her feet.

I am speaking at a conference on Cultural Value at Birkbeck College, the University of London, on 16 July 1988. The speaker is obliged to think of her cultural identity in such a case. From what space is she speaking, in what space is the representative member of the audience placing her? What does the audience expect to hear today, here?

Presumed cultural identity often depends on a name. In Britain in July of 1988 a section of underclass 'Asians' was vigorously demanding to be recognized as different from underclass 'Blacks', basically because they felt that on account of their cultural attributes of mildness, thrift, domesticity and industriousness, they were, unlike the lazy and violent peoples of African origin, responsible and potentially upwardly mobile material.

Distinguishing between Africa and Asia in terms of kinship to Europe is

This chapter is based on an address made at a conference on Cultural Value at Birkbeck College, the University of London, on 16 July 1988.

an old story. As a politically correct Asian, I find this story deplorable. Yet it can be said that a well-placed Asian academic can afford to find it deplorable. To a London audience, academics and cultural workers, eager to hear a speech on cultural value, it is important that the speaker's identity that afternoon was 'Asian', with underclass differentiations out of sight. Unless we continue to nurse the platitudinous conviction that the masses are necessarily identical with 'the revolutionary vanguard', or conversely that, stepping into the university, 'The truth has made us free', we must attend to the possibility of such dissension, and their imbrication with the history and burden of names. Identitarianism can be as dangerous as it is powerful, and the radical teacher in the university can hope to work, however indirectly, toward controlling the dangers by making them visible.[1]

In the United States, where the speaker lives and teaches, her cultural identity is not 'Asian', although it would be recognized as a geographically correct description by most people. In the United States, 'Asians' are of Chinese, Japanese and, of late, Vietnamese extraction. The complex and class-differentiated scenario of the absence or presence of their solidarity with African-Americans is yet another story. In the United States, she is 'Indian'. Subterfuges of nomenclature that are by now standard have almost (though not completely) obliterated the fact that that name lost some specificity in the first American genocide.

The feeling of cultural identity almost always presupposes a language. In that sense, I suppose I feel a Bengali. Yet in the London of July 1988, that name was negotiable as well. The places of 'Bengali' concentration are populated by disenfranchized immigrant Bangladeshis. This seems to me to have a real political logic, not unrelated to national languages, which probably escapes most metropolitan British users of the name. Yet, considering the two-hundred-year-old history of the British representation (in both senses) of Bengal and vice versa, my loss of that name in that place is not without a certain appropriate irony.[2]

To whom did they want to listen, then, this representative audience in London? Since, if they had been attending to the coding of proper names, the references were up for grabs.

The name 'Third World' is useful because, for any metropolitan audience, it can cover over much unease. For these listeners, the speaker's identity might well have been 'Third World'. (In the United States this would undoubtedly have been the case. It nicely marks the difference between Britain as the central ex-colonial, and the United States as a central neo-colonial power.)[3] Sociologists have been warning us against using this expression, contaminated at birth by the new economic programs of neo-colonialism.[4] And, indeed, in the discipline of sociology, in the decade spanning *The New International Division of Labour* and *The End of the Third World*, the genealogy of a culturalist use of that term seems rather shabby.[5] What need does it satisfy? It gives a proper name to a generalized margin.

A word to name the margin. Perhaps that is what the audience wanted to hear: a voice from the margin. If there is a buzzword in cultural critique now, it is 'marginality'. Every academic knows that one cannot do without labels. To this particular label, however, Foucault's caution must be applied, and we must attend to its *Herkunft* or descent. When a cultural identity is thrust upon one because the centre wants an indentifiable margin, claims for marginality assure validation from the centre. It should then be pointed out that what is being negotiated here is not even a 'race or a social type' (as in the passage below) but an economic principle of identification through separation.

> The analysis of *Herkunft* often involves a consideration of race or social type. But the traits it attempts to identify are not the exclusive generic characteristics of an individual, a sentiment, or an idea, which permit us to qualify them as 'Greek' or 'English' [or 'Third World']; rather, it seeks the subtle, singular, and subindividual marks that might possibly intersect in them to form a network that is difficult to unravel.[6]

The Academy

In order to bypass that comparison, the speaker can now provisionally choose a name that will not keep her in (the representation of) a margin so thick with context. With all the perils attendant upon a declared choice, she 'chooses' the institutional appellation 'teacher'. It is, most often for such speakers and audiences, writers and readers, a university, and I am a university teacher. That context is in its own way no thinner, but at least speaker and audience share it most obviously.

When we begin to teach 'marginality', we start with the source books of the contemporary study of the cultural politics of colonialism and its aftermath: the great texts of the 'Arab World', most often Frantz Fanon, a Christian psychoanalyst from Martinique.[7] (I mention these details in anticipation of the fifth section below).

It is also from this general context that we find the source book in our discipline: Edward Said's *Orientalism*.[8] (A word on *our* discipline: since the conference was held under the auspices of a Department of English with a small inter-disciplinary component in Culture Studies, I took it to be the collective professional identity of the majority, with all genealogy suspended; and this text is *Literary Theory Today*.)

Said's book was not a study of marginality, not even of marginalization. It was the study of the construction of an object, for investigation and control. The study of colonial discourse, directly released by work such as Said's, has, however, blossomed into a garden where the marginal can speak and be spoken, even spoken for. It is an important (and beleaguered) part of the discipline now.[9]

As this material begins to be absorbed into the discipline, the long-established but supple, heterogeneous and hierarchical power-lines of the institutional 'dissemination of knowledge' continue to determine and overde-

termine their condition of representability. It is at the moment of infiltration
or insertion, sufficiently under threat by the custodians of a fantasmatic
high Western culture, that the greatest caution must be exercised.[10] The
price of success must not compromise the enterprise irreparably. In that
spirit of caution, it might not be inappropriate to notice that, as teachers,
we are now involved in the construction of a new object of investigation –
'the third world', 'the marginal' – for institutional validation and certifi-
cation. One has only to analyse carefully the proliferating but exclusivist
'Third World-ist' job descriptions to see the packaging at work. It is as if,
in a certain way, we are becoming complicitous in the perpetration of a
'new orientalism'.

> No 'local centers', 'no pattern of transformation' could function if, through a
> series of successive linkages [*enchâinements successifs*], it were not eventually
> written into [*s'inscrivait*] an over-all strategy . . . The [disciplinary] apparatus
> [*dispositif*], precisely to the extent that it [is] insular and heteromorphous with
> respect to the other great 'manoeuvres'. . .'[11]

writes Foucault.

Let us attempt to read the possibility of our unwilling or unwitting
perpetration of a 'new orientalism' as the inscription of an 'overall strategy':

It is not only that lines separate ethnic, gender and class prejudice in the
metropolitan countries from *indigenous* co-operation with neo-colonialism
outside, in the Third World proper. It is also that arguments from culturalism, multi-culturalism and ethnicity, however insular and heteromorphous
they might seem from the great narratives of the techniques of global
financial control, can work to obscure such separations in the interests of
the production of a neo-colonial discourse. Today the old ways, of imperial
adjudication and open systemic intervention cannot sustain unquestioned
legitimacy. Neo-colonialism is fabricating its allies by proposing a share of
the centre in a seemingly new way (not a rupture but a displacement):
disciplinary support for the conviction of authentic marginality by the
(aspiring) elite.

If we keep the possibility of such inscriptions in mind, we might read
differently the specific examples of the working of 'local forces', close to
home. Here are three: The first two are more directly inscribed into the
economic text as it rewards the construction of objects of investigation:
funded proposals. What sells today? 'A pattern of transformation'. The third
works through what one might call the text of metropolitan representation
and self-representation. Here are examples:

(1) Quotation from a grant proposal written by a brilliant young Marxist
academic:

> Taking the 'magical realism' of Garcia Marquez as a paradigmatic case of Third World literary production, I will argue that science fiction . . . may be considered, so to speak, the Third World fiction of the industrial nations . . .

How is the claim to marginality being negotiated here? The radicals of the industrial nations want to *be* the Third World. Why is 'magical realism' paradigmatic of Third World literary production? In a bit, and in the hands of the less gifted teacher, only that literary style will begin to count as ethnically authentic. There is, after all, a reason why Latin America qualifies as the norm of 'the Third World' for the United States, even as India used to be the authentic margin for the British. It is interesting that 'magical realism', a style of Latin American provenance, has been used to great effect by some expatriate or diasporic subcontinentals writing in English.[12] Yet as the Ariel–Caliban debates dramatize, Latin America has *not* participated in decolonization. Certainly this formal conduct of magical realism can be said to allegorize, in the strictest possible sense, a socius and a political configuration where 'decolonization' cannot be narrativized. What are the implications of pedagogic gestures that monumentalize *this* style as the right Third World style? In the greater part of the Third World, the problem is that the declared rupture of 'decolonization' boringly repeats the rhythms of colonization with the consolidation of recognizable styles.

(2) A feminist who has done inspiring and meticulous work on the European discursive text of mothering, a friend and ally. (Again, the interest of this essay lies in a general auto-critique of our moment in criticism, not in the exposure of an imagined enemy. That indeed is why the speaker put aside the name 'Asian/Indian/Bengali/Third World' and took the microphone as 'literary/culturalist/academic'.)

My friend was looking for speakers to comment on postmodern styles in the context of the third world. She did not want her funded institute on the *avant-garde* to be 'Eurocentric'. I told her that I could only comment on a handful of writers in my native language. Her question: but do these writers show their awareness of being in a minority, being marginals? No, I said, and asked a counter-question: Isn't it 'Eurocentric' to choose only such writers who write in the consciousness of marginality and christen them 'Third World'? Answer: One must begin somewhere.

'One must begin somewhere' is a different sentiment when expressed by the unorganized oppressed and when expressed by the beneficiary of the consolidated disciplinary structure of a central neo-colonialist power. If we were studying this move in the perspective of nineteenth-century colonial discursive production, what would we say about the margin being constituted to suit the institutional convenience of the colonizer? If the 'somewhere' that one begins from is the most privileged site of a neo-colonial educational system, in an institute for the training of teachers, funded by the state, does that gesture of convenience not become the normative point of departure?

Does not participation in such a privileged and authoritative apparatus require the greatest vigilance?

'If a genealogical analysis of a scholar were made . . . his *Herkunft* would quickly divulge the official papers of the scribe and the pleading of the lawyer – their father – in their apparently disinterested attention. . . .' (*LCP*, p. 147). Should we imagine ourselves free of this analysis? Should we not attempt also to 'write the history of the present?' Why, as we clear ourselves of the alibi of occupying the centre or seeking validation by/as the centre, should we think that we do not resemble 'the confused and anonymous European' of the nineteenth century, 'who no longer knows himself or what name he should adopt', to whom 'the historian offers . . . the possibility of alternate identities, more individualized and substantial than his own?' (*LCP*, p. 160).

As a result of a decade of colonial discourse studies percolating into disciplinary pedagogy and its powerful adjuncts, and of the imbrication of techniques of knowledge with strategies of power, who claims marginality in the larger post-colonial field? What might this have to do with the old scenario of empowering a privileged group or a group susceptible to upward mobility as the authentic inhabitants of the margin? Should we not cast a genealogical eye over what we have spawned in literary criticism and the study of culture, since a study of the strategies of the margin must not be stopped?

> One must not suppose that there exists a certain sphere of 'marginality' that would be the legitimate concern of a free and distinterested scientific inquiry were it not the object of mechanisms of exclusion brought to bear by the economic or ideological requirements of power. If 'marginality' is being consti-tuted as an area of investigation, this is only because relations of power have established it as a possible object; and conversely, if power is able to take it as a target, this is because techniques of knowledge [disciplinary regulations] were capable of switching it on [*investir*].[13] Between techniques of knowledge and strategies of power, there is no exteriority, even if they have specific roles *and are linked together on the basis of their difference* . . . Not to look for who has the power in the order of marginality . . . and who *is* deprived of it . . . But to look rather for the pattern of the modifications which the relationships of force imply by the very nature of their process. (*HS*, p. 98–9, emphasis and contextual modification added.)

(3) My third example comes from Benita Parry. Ms Parry is, once again, an ally, and she was kind enough to draw my attention to the fact that in a recent issue of the *Oxford Literary Review* on colonialism, she had charged Homi Bhabha, Abdul JanMohammed and Gayatri Spivak basically with not being able to listen to the voice of the native.[14]

Postcoloniality

It is in my response to her that the name 'postcolonial' comes fully into play, which, incidentally, makes the Latin-American as paradigmatic (stylistic) example, tremble.

In a piece on J. M. Coetzee's novel *Foe*, I have approached Benita Parry's question by contrasting Defoe's Robinson Crusoe, the mercantile capitalist who trains Friday, represented as the willing proto-colonial subject, with Coetzee's Susan Barton, the anachronistic eighteenth-century English-woman who longs to give the muted racial other a voice.[15] Rather than repeat my argument, I will take the liberty of quoting myself, with contextual modifications:

> When Benita Parry takes us to task for not being able to listen to the natives, or to let the natives speak, she forgets that the three of us, post-colonials, are 'natives' too. We talk like Defoe's Friday, only much better. Three hundred years have passed, and territorial imperialism has changed to neo-colonialism. The resistant post-colonial has become a scandal.
>
> Why is the name 'post-colonial' specifically useful in our moment?
>
> Those of us present in that room in Birkbeck College, or indeed the writers and readers of this collection, who are from formerly colonized countries, are able to communicate to each other, to exchange, to establish sociality, because we have had access to the culture of imperialism. Shall we then assign to that culture, to borrow Bernard Williams's phrase, a measure of 'moral luck?'[16] I think there can be no doubt that the answer is 'no'. Ths impossible 'no' to a structure, which one critiques, yet inhabits intimately, is the deconstructive philosophical position, and the everyday here and now named 'post-coloniality' is a case of it.[17]

Further, whatever the identitarian ethnicist claims of native or fundamental origin (implicit for example, in Benita Parry's exhortation to hear the voice of the native), the political claims that are most urgent in decolonized space are tacitly recognized as coded within the legacy of imperialism: nationhood, constitutionality, citizenship, democracy, even culturalism. Within the historical frame of exploration, colonization, decolonization – what is being effectively reclaimed is a series of regulative political concepts, the *supposedly* authoritative narrative of whose production was written else-where, in the social formations of Western Europe. They're being reclaimed, indeed claimed, as concept-metaphors for which no historically adequate referent may be advanced from postcolonial space, yet that does not make the claims less important. A concept-metaphor without an adequate referent is a catachresis. These claims for founding catachreses also make postcoloniality a deconstructive case.

> The centre, on the other hand, still longs for the object of conscientious traditional ethnography: 'where women inscribed themselves as healers, ascetics, singers of sacred songs, artisans and artists,' writes Benita Parry.

I have no objection to conscientious ethnography, although I am a bit frightened by its relationship to the history of the discipline of anthropology. My especial word to Parry, however, is that her efforts as well as mine are judged by the exclusions practised through the intricate workings of the techniques of knowledge and the strategies of power, which have a history rather longer and broader than our individual benevolence and avowals.[18]

Value

The persistent critique of what one must inhabit, the persistent consolidation of claims to founding catachreses, involve an incessant re-coding of diversified fields of value. Let us attempt to imagine 'identity', so cherished a foothold, as flash-points in this re-coding of the circuitry.

Let us, then, for the moment at least, arrest the understandable need to fix and diagnose the identity of the most deserving marginal. Let us also suspend the mood of self-congratulation as saviours of marginality. Let us peer, however blindly, into the constantly shifting and tangling network of the techniques of knowledge and the strategies of power through the question of value. This is not an invitation to step into the sunlit arena where values are so broad that philosophers can wrangle about it with reference to imaginary societies: ethical universals and cultural particularity.[19]

In fact, Marx's use of the word 'value' may be seen as catachrestical to the philosophical usage. Which amounts to saying that the appropriate definitions of value might be versions of the re-coding of what Marx names 'value'.[20]

'Value' is the name of that 'contentless and simple [*inhaltslos und einfach*]' thing by way of which Marx rewrote not mediation, but the possibility of the mediation that makes possible in its turn all exchange, all communication, sociality itself.[21] Marx's especial concern is the appropriation of the human capacity to produce, not objects, nor anything tangible, but that simple contentless thing which is *not* pure form; the possibility of mediation (through coding) so that exchange and sociality can exist. Marx's point of entry is the economic coding of value, but the notion itself has a much more supple range. As Marx wrote, to Engels, 'the issue of the matter of value is too decisive for the whole book' (what subsequently became the three volumes of *Capital* and the *Theories of Surplus Value*).[22]

In the early 1970s, *Anti-Oedipus* attempted to extend the range of the Marxian argument from value by applying it to the production and appropriation of value in affective and social rather than merely economic coding. This was their appeal against Althusser, to read again the first chapter of *Capital*, where the talk is of value – the contentless orginary thing of human production – *before* it gets fully coded into an economic system of equivalences and entailed social relations. Their suggestion was that, since capital decoded and deterritorialized the socius by releasing the abstract as such, capitalism must manage this crisis via many reterritorializations, among which the generalized, *psychoanalytic* mode of production of affective value operates by way of a generalized systemic institution of equivalence, however spectacular in its complexity and discontinuity.

The codings of value in the politico-cognitive sphere, through the discursive system of marginality, whether by way of psychoanalysis, culturalism, or economism, is still part of this crisis-management. In the discipline, to take the most familiar everyday examples: 'What is worth [the German word for 'value'] studying, teaching, and talking about' appears as 'What can best be parcelled out into a fourteen- or ten-week format'; 'What are the best available textbooks' (where 'best' and the 'production of the best' are altogether coded); 'What are the most manageable paper topics' (produced by the techniques of knowledge in the United States primary and *secondary* education system); 'How best can it be proved that this can be integrated into the English curriculum without disturbing the distribution requirements'; 'What projects funded'; 'What books marketed'. Paradoxically, as these necessary practicalities – 'one must begin somewhere' – become tacitly accepted working rules for the planners, the recipients (students, audiences) often think in terms of pedagogy as only consciousness-transformation, conference speech as only agenda. I am not suggesting that there is a positive space of 'marginality' to be recovered on the other side of the incessant coding. 'Marginality', as it is becoming part of the disciplinary–cultural parlance, is in fact the name of a certain constantly changing set of representations that is the condition and effect of it. It is coded in the currency of the equivalencies of knowledge. That currency measures the magnitude of value in the sphere of knowledge.

We cannot grasp values as such; it is a possibility for grasping, without content. But if we position ourselves *as identities* in terms of links in the chain of a value-coding as if they were persons and things, and go on to ground our practice on that positioning, we become part of the problem in the ways I am describing.[23]

Work in gendering in principle sees the socius as an affectively coded site of exchange and surplus. The simple contentless moment of value as it is gender-coded has historically led to the appropriation of the sexual differential, subtracted from, but represented as, the theoretical fiction of sexual identity. (Economically codable value is the differential subtracted from the theoretical fiction of use-value in the identity of production and consumption.)[24] Gayle Rubin's 'The Traffic in Women: Notes on the "Political Economy" of Sex' was a pathbreaking essay in the analysis of gender-coding.[25] Kalpana Bardhan's writings on the status of Indian women is the only scholarly work in the frame of post-coloniality in the subaltern context that I have seen which shares the presupposition that gender determinacy is the coding of the value-differential allowing for the possibility of the exchange of affective value, negotiating 'sexuality' rather than sexual identity.[26]

The operation of value makes every commitment negotiable, however urgent it might seem or be. For the *long* haul emancipatory social intervention is not *primarily* a question of redressing victimage by the assertion of (class- or gender- or ethno-cultural) identity. It is a question of developing a vigilance for systemic appropriations of the social capacity to produce a *differential* that is one basis of exchange into the networks of cultural of class- or gender-identity.

In the field of ethno-cultural politics, the post-colonial teacher can help to develop this vigilance rather than continue pathetically to dramatize victimage or assert a spurious identity. She says 'no' to the 'moral luck' of the culture of imperialism while recognizing that she must inhabit it, indeed invest it, to criticize it.

(Indeed, the specificity of 'post-coloniality' understood in this way can help us to grasp that no historically (or philosophically) adequate claims can be produced in any space for the guiding words of political, military, economic, ideological emancipation and oppression. You take positions in terms not of the discovery of historical or philosophical grounds, but in terms of reversing, displacing, and seizing the apparatus of value-coding. This is what it means to say 'the agenda of onto-cultural commitments is negotiable'. In that sense 'postcoloniality', far from being marginal, can show the irreducible margin in the centre: We are always *after* the empire of reason, our claims to it always short of adequate. In the hands of identitarians, alas, this can lead to further claims of marginality. 'We are all post-colonials . . .')

Claiming catachreses from a space that one cannot not want to inhabit and yet must criticize is, then, the deconstructive predicament of the postcolonial. It is my hope that this sense will put a particular constraint upon the metropolitan marginal or indigenous elite, in whose ranks I can belong, not to produce a merely 'antiquarian history' which seeks the continuities of soil, language and urban life in which our present is rooted and, 'by cultivating in a delicate manner that which existed for all time, . . . tr[y] to conserve for posterity the conditions under which we were born' (*LCP*, p. 162).

It is in this spirit that I will view *Genesis*, a film by Mrinal Sen.

Let me spell it out here. Postcoloniality in general is not subsumable under the model of the revolutionary or resistant marginal in metropolitan space. If 'black Britain' or the 'rainbow coalition' in the United States are taken as paradigmatic of, say, India or the new African nations, the emphasis falls on Britain or the States as nation-states. It is in this sense that the aggressive use made by an earlier nationalism of the difference between culture and political power has now been reversed only in political *intent*. The main agenda there is still to explode the fantasmatic 'whiteness' of the metropolitan nation. In a powerful recent essay, Tim Mitchell has suggested that the typical Orientalist attitude was 'the world as exhibition'.[27] The 'new orientalism' views 'the world as immigrant'. It is meretricious to suggest that this reminder undervalues the struggle of the marginal in metropolitan space. It is to remember that that struggle cannot be made the unexamined referent for all postcoloniality without serious problems. No 'two-way dialogue' in 'the great currents of international cultural exchange' forgets this.[28]

Thus an art film out of India (*Genesis*), or out of Mali (Cisse Souleymane's *Yeelen*) cannot resemble *Thé au harem d'Archimède* (Mehdi Charef, French/ Algerian). The last sequence of Alain Tanner's new film *Une flamme dans le coeur*, placing Mercedes (the Arab woman in Paris) in Cairo, attempts to point at this problematic.

Genesis: a film by Mrinal Sen (1986)

Current postcolonial claims to the names that are the legacy of the European enlightenment (sovereignty, constitutionality, self-determination, nation-hood, citizenship, even culturalism) are catachrestical claims, their strategy a displacing and seizing of a coding of value.[29] It can show us the negotiable agenda of a cultural commitment to marginality, whereas ethnicist academic agendas make a fetish of identity. The project, as always, is the recoding of value as the differential possibility of exchange and the channelling of surplus. Postcoloniality as agency can make visible that the basis of *all* serious ontological commitment is catachrestical, because negotiable through the information that identity is, *in the larger sense*, a text.[30] It can show that the alternative to Europe's long story – generally translated as 'great narratives' – is not only short tales (*petits récits*) but tampering with the authority of storylines.[31] In *all* beginning, repetition, signature:

> In order for the tethering to the source to occur, what must be retained is the absolute singularity of a signature-event and a signature-form ... But ... a signature must have a repeatable, iterable, imitable form; it must be able to be detached rom the present and singular intention of its production.[32]

The first sequence of the film, repeating the formula, 'as always, yet once again', ends in a shot of recognizably north Indian men and women, peasantry or the urban poor dressed in their best, lining up to be perfunc-torily interrogated and put their thumbprints on a long scroll. As the voice-over intones: 'As always, yet once again, they lost everything they had and became slaves again.' In the manner of didactic allegories, some signals are clear to some groups tied together by the various value-codings (systems of representation) the elements of which are being manipulated by Sen with a certain panache. Indigenous radicals sense the pervasiveness and ubiquity of bonded labor as a mode of production.[33] India fanciers perceive the famous Indian cyclical time. Slightly more knowledgeable Indians perhaps catch an ironic reference to Krishna's famous promise in the *Gita*: 'I take on existence from eon to eon, for the rescue of the good and the destruction of the evil, in order to reestablish the Law.'[34]

Some would notice an *in medias res* reference to the sequential narrative of the modes of production, a reminder of the young Marx's impatience with the question of origins, an impatience that was never given up: 'If you ask about the creation of nature and of man, then you are abstracting from nature and man. . . . Do not think and do not ask me questions, for as soon as you think and ask questions, your *abstraction* from the existence of nature and man has no meaning.'[35]

In this articulation of history in terms of the mode of production of (economic) value, the 'worker' is represented as collectively caught in the primitive signature (at its most proximate the thumbprint, the body's mark), the originary contract – the first codification/identification. Both of these things take on importance in the film's subsequent emphasis on the name of the father and its use of the radical counterfactual.

Banality and the desert

At any rate, it is only after this pre-originary scene of repetition that the title flashes on the screen: GENESIS. It looks a bit self-consciously solemn, in large letters by itself on the screen. The ethnographically savvy viewer would find it banal, the savvy diasporic would find it embarrassingly pre-postmodern, the metropolitan third worldist would perhaps suppress the embarrassment because it's a third-world allegory of the birth of a nation – 'genesis' does mean birth – which unfortunately misses the appropriate style of magical realism. The 'non-theoretical' metropolitan third-worldist would prefer something more de Sica style, like the recent *Salaam Bombay*, or Adoor Gopalakrishnan's *Face to Face* with its heavy contemporary cultural content, spelling out the fate of a Western theory in the context of the encroachment of industrial capitalism in rural India, or even Sen's earlier films, where the super-realistic technique achieved its obsessive brilliance by laying bare, for the most part, the workings of the urban lower middle class of West Bengal. The appropriate, indeed felicitous, viewer of the film, the participant in the active high-cultural life of New Delhi, would recognize that it taps a rather banal tourist genre, the recent spate of Indian films celebrating the local ethnic color of Rajasthan. This is a crude taxonomy, but it is still slightly more complex than first world/third world, Eurocentric/marginal.

If we look at the coding of these positions, it is possible to speculate that what leaves the viewer baffled is that Sen assumes *agency* of re-inscription rather than marginality of the postcolonial position. As the opening credits unroll, we notice that it is Sen's first collaborative film, with French and Belgian support. *Gandhi* had to pretend that its British and US casting and production were not 'part of the film'. Sen uses this to put together a film as a postcolonial, not as a Bengali for Bengalis.

The post colonial text is often the site of the re-negotiation of the banal for its telescoping of 'an infinity of traces, without . . . inventory'.[36] When a so-called Third-World text speaks a post-colonial (rather than nationalist) allegory, what lexicon is, after all, most readily to hand? It's the difference between, let us say, the hermeneutic reinterpretation of Freud and a look at the operation of 'pop-psych' in society to see how it has become an operative and allegorical lexicon: between fixing your glance at the thickness of signifiers and at the impoverishment of the referential.[37] In such a text the allegory works in bits and pieces, with something like a relationship with the postmodern habit of citing without authority. With a pedagogy that sees this as the mark of the fragmented postcolonial mode, the allegory can offer a persistent parabasis to the development of any continuous ethno-cultural narrative *or* of a continuous re-inscription.[38]

Genesis is the 'original', not the translated, title of the film. Why should a mainland Indian film not appropriate English as one of its moments, without the usual coyness of magical or teratological realism? Generally, in diasporic English fiction written by people who have no active contact with the native languages, the only way in which these native languages are denoted is through the monstrous mockery of a transformed standard English which reflects more the writer's lack of creative access to the languages of the country. Here the English word is, and is not, a *sub*-title when it flashes on the screen. That at least is the postcolonial Indian's relationship to English – a (sub)titular relationship that does not derive from an authentic title to the language. At the origin is something like a sub-title, something like a footnote, something like a postscript, and postcoloniality can be its scrupulous paradigm.

Among other things, the film records the origin myth of the Bible. Why should the centre of Hinduisim not appropriate Judaeo-Christianity with the haphazard points of contact and non-coherent re-inscription, appropriate to the post-colonial mode, *without* the heavy trappings of transcendentalism, unitarianism, and the nineteenth-century legitimizing projects, such as the Brahmo Samaj or the semitized Hinduism that masquerades as 'the real thing?' Postcolonial pedagogy must teach the over-determined play of cultural value in the inscription of the socius. Such unacknowledged appropriative overdeterminations are the substance of contemporary globality. Think for instance of the appropriative weaving of the great 'European' narratives of socialism and 'Christianity', (in this context 'Christianity' is not quite European, in its origins, either) with the 'Asian' narratives of 'Ethnicity' and 'Islam' in the fact that the trans-Caucasian autonomous region of Nagorno-Karabakh, representing five per cent of the territory of the Republic of Azebaijan was, in that very July, attempting to secede, under *glasnost*, from its Muslim-majority base to form the seventy-five per cent Christian-majority Artsakh Autonomous Republic of Armenia.[39] This story has proceeded much further at the time of revising. I have written elsewhere, at greater length, of the problems of cultural representation of Central and Eastern Europe and Central and Western Asia.[40]

A postcolonialist pedagogy, looking at the title *Genesis* on the screen, can help us acknowledge the overdeterminations, see *glasnost* and its attendant outbursts of sub-nationalisms in the Soviet periphery within the curious logic of postcoloniality. The fact that socialism can never fully (adequately) succeed is what it has in common with everything. It is *after* that fact that one starts to make the choices. And, in its perpetually postponed yet persistent establishment, there 'should be no room' for the persistent moment of totalitarianism. The apparent contemporary success of capitalism ('democracy') depends on a seemingly benevolent identitarian ignoring of the shifting mechanics of value-coding in the interest of the socially and nationally 'representative concrete individual'. A postcolonial pedagogy in the literary case can help undermine the prejudices attendant upon such benevolence (which would also fix a systemic 'marginal') by suggesting that the word 'catachresis' is at least no harder than expressions like 'freedom of choice'.

Genesis is not a continuist rewriting of the Judaeo-Christian story as one episode in an eternal return by way of the celebrated Hindu cycles of time. By the time we come to the end of the film, we do not conclude that capitalism is just another turn of the wheel. On the other hand, the Hindu story (available from high myth to 'folklore') of the ten consecutive incarnations, appearing accompanied by various natural catclysms, allows Sen to offer parallel descendants for the two men and the one woman who are the central characters of the story, the two men's from a drought, the woman's from a murderous flood. The woman is not produced by man or men. They share the same story with a difference: natural (their drought/ her flood) and social (their occupation weaving and farming; hers has been wifing, mothering, sharing work). This is not a story of 'primitive communism', for Marx arguably a 'presupposition', a theoretical fiction.[41] The snake appears at least twice, as a sort of reminder of one revised patriarchal story-line.

I have pointed out earlier that the film uses a banal tourist genre, recognizable by the felicitous viewer. It is not my intention to suggest that teaching within the postcolonial field of value should ignore the culturally 'felicitous' and the scholarly. We must rather learn to recognize it as another moment in the differential negotiation of ontological commitment to the object of investigation. We must, as teachers, make every effort to know what the appropriate diagnosis is (historically and in the present) and then speak of it as one case, rather than as the self-identical authority.[42] This permits one not to be trapped by authority, to look at other codings, other constellations. Let us try out this coding on the space named 'Rajasthan'.

In *Kiss of the Spider Woman*, the use of early Hollywood technicolour at the end is carefully framed in diverse filmic idioms, so that we can adjust our look. In *Genesis*, the unframed yet noticeably regressive use of lyric space and the wide screen, unproblematic light, primary colours, can be seen as denoting 'Desert'. Yes, this *is* the desert area of North-West India, but we are, rather aggressively, not in veridical space. The stones of the ruins move, to denote insubstantiality, and the sound of an anachronistic aeroplane is the response of a god created out of a skull before the dawn of serious technology. North West India pushes toward the desert of West Asia as the felicitous theatre of *Genesis*. No garden in the beginnning, but a desert in the middle of history. (West Asia, the Middle East, itself reveals the catachrestical nature of absolute directional naming of parts of the globe. It can only exist as an absolute descriptive if Europe is presupposed as the centre.) This is no particular place, negotiable as the desert area of North-West India, pushing toward West Asia, but not quite West Asia; perhaps the very looseness of this reference questions the heavy, scholarly, period films, the benevolent anti-racist films (sometimes the benevolent racist films, one can hardly tell the difference) that have been made about the Bible story in its appropriate geographical context.

There is something of this loose-knit denotation of space in the language of the film as well. The film is made by an Indian whose native language is not Hindi, the national language. Do you see it now? To be in a new 'nation' (itself catachrestical to the appropriate development of nations), speak *for* it, in a national language that is not one's mother-tongue. But what is a mother-tongue?

A mother-tongue is a language with a history – in that sense it is 'instituted' – before our birth and after our death, where patterns that can be filled with anyone's motivation have laid themselves down. In this sense it is '"unmotivated" but not capricious'.[43] We learn it in a 'natural' way and fill it once and for all with our own 'intentions' and thus make it 'our own' for the span of our life and then leave it without intent – as unmotivated and uncapricious as we found it (without intent) when it found us – for its other users: 'The "unmotivatedness" of the sign requires a synthesis in which the completely other is announced as such – without any simplicity, any identity, and resemblance or continuity – within what is not it.[44]

Thus the seemingly absurd self-differential of a non-native speaker of a national language can be used to show that this *is* the name of the game, that this is only an instantiated representation of how one is 'at home' in a language. There is no effort in *Genesis* to produce the rich texture of 'authentic' Hindi, nor its Beckettized skeleton. This is just the spare Hindi of a man slightly exiled from his national language. And as such, one notices its careful focusing.

The extreme edge of Hindi as the 'national language' is a peculiar concoction with a heavily Sanskritized artificial idiom whose most notable confection is the speech of the flight attendants on Indian airplane flights. By contrast, Hindi as it is spoken and written is enriched by many Arabic and Persian loan-words ('loan-words' is itself – you guessed it, a catachrestical concept-metaphor. 'Those French words which we are so proud of pronouncing accurately are themselves only blunders made by the Gallic lips which mispronounced Latin or Saxon, our language being merely a defective pronunciation of several others' said Proust's Marcel).[45] And, in Sen's predictable stock Hindi, those are some of the words emphasized in an eerie light, adding, as it were, to that non-specific desert aura, the cradle of genesis, Arabia and Persia, somewhere off the Gulf, real enough today as the stage of imperialist inhumanity. These 'loan words' move history out of the methodological necessity of a pre-supposed origin. You will see what I mean if I list the three most important: *zarurat* (necessity), *huq* (right), and the most interesting to me, *khud muqtar*.

The sub-title translates this last expression as 'self-reliant' or 'independent'. The trader keeps repeating this phrase with contempt to the weaver and the farmer, whom he exploits, as a kind of scornful reprimand: 'You went to the market yourself, to check up on the price of what you're producing for me. You want to represent yourself. You want to be *khud muqtar.*' 'Independent' gives the exchange too nationalist an aura. The actual phrase would be something more like pleading your own case, and would underscore an everyday fact: in spite of efforts at Sanskritization, much of the language of legal procedure in India comes, understandably, from court Persian.

The aura of a place which is the Semi-Japhetic desert, a semi-Japhetic language arranged by a non-native speaker; the perfect staging for *Genesis.* In the beginning is an impossible language marked with a star. Progress is made by way of the imagined identity of an original caught between two translations.[46] This is neither Africa nor East Asia, nor yet the Americas. It is an old score being actively reshuffled, not the rather youthful debate about a third world identity.

The postcolonial teacher can renegotiate some of the deceptive 'banality' of the film to insert the 'Third World' into the text of value.

Woman and Engels

The film loosens the tight logic of progression of the mode of production narrative most movingly by taking a distance from the tough, outdated, comprehensive, ambitious reasonableness of the Engelsian account of the origin of the family.[47] Rumour has it that the intellectuals of the majority left party in Calcutta have said about this part of the film that Sen hadn't really understood his Engels. Again, the authority of the authoritative account, the appropriate reading, are invoked. We are caught in a much more overdetermined web than you think – inappropriate use of Hindi, inappropriate use of Engels, India Tourist Board use of Rajasthan: and you think you're just watching an *Indian* film, even that you want just to listen to the voice of the native.

Woman in *Genesis* marks the place of the radical counterfactual: the road not taken of an alternative history which will not allow the verification of a possible world *by the actual one.*[48] The two moments that I would like to discuss are in that sense not 'true to history' but full of the possibility of pedagogic exactitude.

A work of art (I use this expression because I feel wary about our present tendency to avoid such old-fashioned phrases for no reason but to show that we are politically correct, although our presuppositions are in many ways unaltered) is a part of history and society, but its function is not to behave like 'history' and 'sociology' as disciplinary formations. My general argument, here as elsewhere, has been that, *in terms of this characteristic*, and as long as it does not itself become a totalizing masterword, art or the pedagogy of art can point at the ultimately catachrestical limits of being-human in the will to truth, life, or power. But with the resistance to the menace of catachresis (use or mention, mention as use) comes a tendency to dismiss such arguments as 'nothing but' the aestheticization of the political (the assumption being, of course, that the veridical is *eo ipso* political).[49] I leave the suggestion aside, then, and look at the representation of the woman as the radical counterfactual in history.

Engels finds the origin of class exploitation in the sexual division of labour in the structure of support around the reproduction of society. Woman's labour-power, the power to produce children, was according to Engels, fetishized into a relationship of dependence and subordination. It is quite possible that this Engelsian script has written the woman as she suddenly appears on the screen in the *Genesis*, for she is shown *after* the monogamian family. The flood has killed her former husband and children. But, in *this* historical moment, in *this* text, in *this* 'self-mediated birth', she negotiates reproduction as agent of production, able to articulate a position *against* the perversion of her agency.

In this counterfactual account, it is the woman who points out the problem of the fetish-character of the commodity. It is in answer to her question ('does the weaver have the right [*huq*] to satisfy the need [*zarurat*] of the farmer for a new cloth?') that the distinction between productive consumption and individual consumption and the meaning of bondage as non-ownership of the means of production emerge in the false haven. The trader lets the weaver weave a new cloth for his friend the farmer. This is not producing a use-value, but merely including the cloth as part of their real subsistence wage. But Sen represents another change in this moment inaugurated by the questioning of the curious woman (remember 'Genesis?'). The trader gives the weaver money. The desert is being inserted into generalized commodity exchange.

Is this how it happened? Probably not. And certainly not according to most great narratives, anthropological or politico-economic. Yet why not? Women's story is not the substance of great narratives. But women are curious, they have a knack of asking the outsider's uncanny questions, even though they are not encouraged to *take* credit for what follows. Thus, here too, the two men will tell her 'you won't understand' when they go to a distant market with their money, although her curiosity produced the money.

The point is not to contradict Engels but rather to see the counterfactual presentation of the woman as the motor of 'effective' history. It is no disrespect to Engels to suggest, *in this way*, that his text too is held by a certain value-coding where women's victimage rather than agency is foregrounded. And is this sequence in the film also a fragmentary transvaluation of Eve's much maligned responsibility for the inauguration of knowledge?

It is perhaps not surprising that it is within the most touristic footage in the film that Sen fabricates the emergence of the autonomous aesthetic moment. No knowledge of Indic aesthetics or ethnics is required to flesh out the bold strokes, which I list below:

1   The possibility of autonomous representation as one of the gifts of generalized commodity exchange: in order to dream, all you need is money.

2   The framing of the aesthetic as such so that its production can be hidden. The two men willingly hide themselves until the woman, decorated with silver anklets, appears as an aesthetic object.

3   True to the autonomy of the aesthetic in this allegorical context, the aesthetic object is endowed with a hermetically represented subjectship. The woman sings, without sub-titles. GENESIS in the beginning, in English(?) in the 'original', marks postcolonial accessibility. Here, framed in the film, is a parody of culturalist art, inaccessible except to the authentic native; the audience of postcoloniality has no access to the authentic text. The song is in a Rajasthani dialect, ironically the only verbal marker that this is 'Rajasthan'. It is, however, the most stunningly double-edged moment in the film. For it is also a negotiation of a banality belonging to the internationally accessible idiom of a general 'Indian' mass culture of long standing – the Bombay film industry: the woman breaking into a folk song. Unlike the rest of the film which creates interesting collages of musical idioms, this lilting singing voice is autonomous and unaccompanied. There is also an interesting manipulation of gazes here.

4   As the sequence cuts to a scene at the well, the wordless tune infects the noise of the pulley. Labour is aestheticized.

Aesthetic objectification and commodity exchange bring out the supplement of sexual possessiveness that was implicit in the text. The two men are individualized by jealousy. If we must quote Engels, the here and now of the film, preceded by all those cycles of disaster, is clearly post-lapsarian:

> Monogamy does not by any means make its appearance in history as the reconciliation of man and woman, still less as the highest form of such reconciliation. On the contrary, it appears as the subjection of one sex by the other, as the proclamation of a conflict between the sexes entirely unknown hitherto in prehistoric times. . . . The first class-antagonism which appears in history coincides with the development of the antagonism between man and woman in monogamian marriage, and the first class-oppression with that of the female sex by the male.[50]

The film is not an origin story, but a story of once again, once again. What we are watching here is not the 'first class-oppression', but the discontinuity between developed class oppression and gender oppression. The woman had shared class oppression with the weaver and the farmer. The men join the merchant, their master, in the role of gender oppressor. Neither truth to Engels, nor truth to Rajasthani kinship patterns is needed here, although both help in creating the aura of fields of meaning. Again, postcoloniality is a mode of existence whose importance and fragility would be destroyed by techniques of specialist knowledge as they work with strategies of power. I get a grasp on how the agency of the postcolonial is being obliterated in order to inscribe him and her as marginals, culture studies must use, but actively frame and resist specialisms. It must, at all costs, retain its skill as a strategy that works on cases with shifting identities. 'The overthrow of mother right was the *world-historic defeat of the female sex*. . . . In order to guarantee the fidelity of the wife, that is, the paternity of the children, the woman is placed in the man's absolute power.'[51]

The woman in the film is finally pregnant. The men are obsessed by the question of paternity. In the spare dialogue, a point is made that does not apply only to the 'third world' or 'the marginals'; the point that the real issue in the overthrow of mother right is not merely ownership but control. The woman is the subject of knowledge; she *knows* the name of the father in the most literal way. This scandalous power is modified and shifted into 'a strange reversal': power is consolidated *in* the name of the father and the woman is reduced to the figure who cannot know. Again counterfactually, the woman is given the right to answer the question of the name of the father and of mother right:

SHE:	*I* am the one to tell you?
HE (THE FARMER):	Then who else can?
HE (THE WEAVER):	It's my child, isn't it?
SHE:	Why are you asking me?
HE:	Who else shall I ask?
SHE:	Ask yourself. Ask your friend.

When the question of right (*huq*) is posed, she answers in terms of the men's need (*zarurat*). In the simple language of affective exchange she speaks mother right. This, too, is counterfactual, for it has little in common with the heavily coded exchange-system of matriarchal societies.

SHE:	What difference will it make who the father is?
HE:	Who has the right over it?
SHE:	I don't know who has the right over it. I accepted you bóth. In three we were one. Now you talk of rights, you want to be master. The enemy is not outside, but in. This child is mine.

This moment does not belong in the accounting of history, and the men do not get her point. 'Our first sin was to call her a whore', they mutter. The admission has, strictly speaking, no counterfactual consequence. The eruption of jealousy, the enmity between comrades, the defeat of the female sex seem to mark a moment of rupture. The tempo speeds up. This disaster is neither drought nor flood, but a quick succession of colonial wars – on camels, with bombs; succeeded by neo-colonialism, 'development' – a bulldozer.

In a completely unexpected final freeze-frame, what comes up from below is a Caterpillar bulldozer. You see the word CATERPILLAR on its nose and, again, it's not a subtitle; like GENESIS, it's a word that the postcolonial understands. The innumerable links between capitalism and patriarchy are not spelled out. The film ends with the immediately recognizable banality of the phallus – the angle of the shot focuses attention on the erect pipe so that you don't even quite know that it's a bulldozer. The sub-title becomes part of the text again, and the catachresis is brutally shifted into the literality of the present struggle.

Let us imagine a contrast between this bulldozer and the bulldozer in *Sammy and Rosie Get Laid*, so textualized that it can work as a rich symbol. In Sen the lexicon is resolutely and precariously 'outside'. Pedagogy here must try to retrench from that outside the presence of a banal globality, which must not be retranslated into the autonomy of the art object or its status as ethnic evidence, the particular voice of the marginal. Our agency must not be re-inscribed through the benevolence of the discipline.

Postscript

Not all 'postcolonial' texts have to look like *Genesis*. In fact, I do not know what the paradigmatic postcolonial stylistic production would be. At any rate, this essay is as much about a postcolonial style of pedagogy as about the look of a postcolonial text.[52]

We must, however, attend to taxonomic talk of paradigms and such, for 'no "local centre," no "pattern of transformation" could function if, through a series of sequences, it did not eventually enter into an over-all strategy'. (*HS*, p. 99). But this attention cannot be our goal and norm. We must arrest the emergence of disciplinary currency by keeping our eye on the double (multiple and irregular) movement of the local *and* the over-all.

In chapter 1 of *Capital* Marx speaks of four forms of value: the simple; the total or expanded; the general; and money.

The 'simple' form of value (20 yards of linen = one coat) is heuristic or accidental. The 'general', where all value is economically expressed in terms of *one* commodity, is on its way to the money form. The second form – 'the total or expanded' – is where 'z commodity A = u commodity B or v commodity C or = w Commodity D or = x commodity E or = etc.'[53].

In the Western European mid-nineteenth century Marx felt that the most appropriate object of investigation for an emancipatory critique was capital. In the analysis of capital (traffic in economic value-coding), which releases the abstract as such, it is necessary for both capitalist and critical activist to use the most logical form of value (general and then money) as his tool. This is a lesson that we cannot ignore. But in the analysis of contemporary capital*ism* in the broadest sense, taking patriarchy (traffic in affective value-coding) and neo-colonialism (traffic in epistemic–cognitive–political–institutional value-coding) into account, it is 'the total or Expanded Form of Value', where 'the series of [the] representations [of value] never comes to an end', which 'is a motley mosaic of disparate and unconnected expressions', where the endless series of expressions are all different from each other, and where 'the totality has no single, unified form of appearance', that Foucault, or Deleuze, or indeed, implicitly, Gayle Rubin choose as their analytical field.[54] 'We must conceive discourse as a series of discontinuous segments whose tactical function is neither uniform nor stable' (*HS*, p. 100).

Rubin, Deleuze and Guattari seem to know their relationship to Marx. Kalpana Bardhan, like Sen, although necessarily in a different form, gives us the ingredients for an expanded analysis from within the generalist position (adhering to the importance of the general or money form). Rubin's work is in some ways most exciting, because she comes to the threshold of the total expanded form (which she calls, somewhat metaphorically, 'political economy') from a staunchly humanist–structuralist position.

As for Marx's and Foucault's apparently opposed claims for their methodological choices, the only *useful* way to read them is as being dependent upon their objects of investigation.[55] Thus, *in the economic sphere*, 'the total or expanded form' is 'defective' as a form of analysis (Marx). And *in the cognitive–political sphere* 'it is a question of orienting ourselves to a conception of power which *replaces* the privilege of the law with the viewpoint of the stake [*enjeu*]' (Foucault, *HS*, p 102; emphasis added).[56] I have tried to flesh out their relationship by reading the production of 'marginality' as a taxonomic diagnosis in our trade; and suggesting that, here and now, 'postcoloniality' may serve as the name of a strategy that repeatedly undoes the seeming opposition.

Notes

1   It is my conviction of the power of collectivities that will not allow me to ignore that the realization of the 'potential' is an incessantly betrayed struggle undermined by the longing for upward class mobility in those among the non-revolutionary underclass who feel they might have the possibility of a foothold in the ladder. In the rest of this first section I try to argue that radical teachers at universities – an important apparatus of upward class mobility – should attend to the nature of the institution that is their contractual space – and not ignore their obligation by claiming a spurious marginality, and declare the desire for the revolution as its accomplishment. I believe the teacher, *while operating within the institution*, can foster the emergence of a committed collectivity by not making her institutional commitment invisible.

2   See Ranajit Guha, *A Rule of Property for Bengal: An Essay on the Idea of Permanent Settlement* (New Delhi: Orient Longman, 1981); and Victor Kiernan, *Marxism and Imperialism* (London: Edward Arnold, 1974), pp. 206f. I hope the reader will not consider this mention of the name 'Bengali' a proof of 'high flying Bengali cultural revanchism'. There seems no way around the fact that the speaker's native language is Bengali.

3   In 'Representing the Colonized: Anthropology's Interlocutors', Edward Said is quite correct in reminding us that 'We should first take scrupulous note of how . . . the United States has replaced the great earlier empires as *the* dominant outside force' (*Critical Inquiry*, 15 (Winter 1989), p. 215). It seems to me that

the displacements entailed by this shift in conjuncture must also be kept in mind. 'The West' is not monolithic.

4   See Carl Pletsch, 'The Three Worlds, or the Division of Social Scientific Labor, circa 1950–1975', *Comparative Studies in Society and History*, 23 (4) (October, 1981).

5   Folker Froebel, Jurgen Heinrichs and Otto Kreve, *The New International Division of Labour: Structural Unemployment in Industrialized Countries and Industrialization in Developing Countries*, tr. Pete Burgess (Cambridge: Cambridge University Press, 1980); Nigel Harris, *The End of the Third World: Newly Industrializing Countries and the Decline of an Ideology* (London: Penguin, 1986).

6   Michel Foucault, *Language, Counter-Memory, Practice: Selected Essays and Interviews*, tr. Donald F. Bouchard and Sherry Simon (Ithaca: Cornell University Press, 1977), p. 145. Hereafter cited in text as *LCP*.

7   Experts in the mainstream are not charitable to this impulse: 'Many acts of revenge have been and are still taken against citizens of the former colonial powers, whose sole personal crime is that of belonging to the nation in question . . . That Europe should in her turn be colonized by the peoples of Africa, of Asia, or of Latin America (we are far from this, I know) would be a "sweet revenge," but cannot be considered my ideal . . . This extraordinary success [that the colonized peoples have adopted our customs and have put on clothes] is chiefly due to one specific features of Western civilization which for a long time was regarded as a feature of man himself, its development and prosperity among Europeans thereby becoming proof of their superiority: it is, paradoxically, Europeans' capacity to understand the other' (Tzvetan Todorov, *The Conquest of America: the Question of the Other*, trans. Richard Howard (New York: Harper and Row, 1984), pp. 256, 258). Or to give only two examples, this comment on 'Sartre's creative use of terrorism. The true precursor of Sartre was not so much Marx as Sorel, whose belief in the efficacy of violence as a purgative anticipated his own. Curiously Sartre's apologia for "terrorism-fraternity" found its real home not on French soil, but in the underdeveloped countries of the third world, where terror was recommended, as a cure-all for colonial-induced psychopathologies' (Steven B. Smith, *Reading Althusser: An Essay on Structural Marxism* (Ithaca: Cornell University Press, 1984), p. 67.)

8   Said, *Orientalism* (New York: Pantheon Books, 1978).

9   For a more detailed consideration of the attendant pedagogical situation, see Spivak, 'The Making of Americans, the Teaching of English, and the Future of Culture Studies," *New Literary History* (forthcoming). For a brief checklist of required reading, see Chinua Achebe, 'Colonialist Criticism', *Morning Yet On Creation Day: Essays* (Garden City, Anchor Press, 1975); Ngugi Wa Th'iongo, *Writers in Politics* (London: Heinemann, 1981); Ashis Nandy, *The Intimate Enemy: Loss and Recovery of Self Under Colonialism* (New York: Oxford University Press 1983); Ranajit Guha and Gayatri Spivak (eds), *Selected Subaltern Studies* (New York: Oxford University Press, 1988); Stuart Hall and James Donald, *Politics and Ideology* (London: Open University Press, 1985); Hazel Carby, *Reconstructing Womanhood: the Emergence of Afro-American Women Novelists* (New York: Oxford University Press, 1987); Sneja Gunew (with Uyen Loewald), 'The Mother Tongue and Migration', *Australian Feminist Studies*, 1 (Summer, 1985); Trinh-Ti-Minh-Ha and Jean-Paul Bourdier, *African Spaces: Designs for Living in Upper Volta* (Homes and Meier, 1985); Paulin J. Hountondji, *African Philosophy: Myth and Reality*, trans. Henri Evans (Bloomington: Indiana University Press, 1983);

Henry Louis Gates, Jr, *Figures in Black: Worlds, Signs and the "Racial" Self* (New York: Oxford University Press. 1986); Lata Mani, 'Contentious Traditions: The Debate on SATI in Colonial India' *Cultural Critique*, (Autumn, 1987); Mick Taussig, *Shamanism, Colonialism and the Wild Man: A Study in Terror and Healing*, (Chicago: University of Chicago Press, 1987); Mary Louise Pratt, 'Scratches on the Face of the Country; or What Mr Barrow Saw in the Land of the Bushmen', *Critical Inquiry*, 12 (1) (Autumn 1985). Of the numerous journals coming out in the field, one might name *Cultural Critique, New Formations, Criticism, Heresy, and Interpretation, Inscriptions, Third Text.*

10   For a superb analysis of this fantasm in the context of the United States, see Barbara Herrnstein Smith, 'Cult-Lit: Hirsch, Literacy, and "The National Culture"', *South Atlantic Quarterly* (Winter, 1990).

11   Michel Foucault, *The History of Sexuality: Vol. 1: An Introduction*. trans. Robert Hurley (New York: Vintage books, 1980), p. 99. Hereafter cited in text as *HS*.

12   Fredric Jameson, 'On Magic Realism in Film', *Critical Inquiry*, 12 (2) (Winter, 1986). Most noticeable texts are, of course, V. S. Naipaul *Guerrillas* (New York: Alfred A. Knopf, 1975) and Salman Rushdie, *Midnight's Children* (New York: Alfred A. Knopf, 1981).

13   The Freudian term *'Besetzung'*, translated as 'cathexis' in the standard edition, is translated *'investissement'* [lit. investment] in French. The Freudian term means, roughly, 'to occupy with desire', Since Foucault did not use Freudian terms in their strict sense, 'cathecting' or 'occupying with desire' might be inadvisable here. On the other hand 'invest' has *only* an economic meaning in English and the psychoanalytic usage is never far below the surface in poststructuralist French writers. I decided on the somewhat odd 'switch it on'.

14   Benita Parry, 'Problems in Current Theories of Colonial Discourse', *Oxford Literary Review*, 9, i–ii (1987).

15   Coetzee, *Foe* (New York: Viking Penguin, 1987).

16   For interesting speculations on 'moral luck', see Bernard Williams, *Moral Luck: Philosophical Papers 1973–1980* (Cambridge: Cambridge University Press, 1981), pp. 20–39. But moral luck is an after-the-fact assignment. 'The justification, if there is to be one, will be essentially retrospective' (p. 24). The impossible and intimate 'no' might thus involve our consideration of the historical production of our cultural exchangeability. Why does it involve the long haul toward a future? I attempt to answer this in the text. (I am also aware that the delicacy of Williams's concern with the individual moral agent is travestied when transferred to something like 'the culture of imperialism'. It would be interesting to 'apply' Williams's brilliantly inconclusive speculations to individual imperialist reformists.)

17   Spivak, 'Theory in the Margin: Coetzee's *Foe* reading Defoe's *Crusoe/Roxana*', forthcoming in Jonathan Arac (ed.), *Proceedings of the 1988 English Institute.*

18   Spivak, 'Theory in the Margin'.

19   Most thoughtfully for example, in Richard Rorty, 'Solidarity and Objectivity?' in John Rajchman and Cornel West, (eds), *Post-Analytic Philosophy* (New York: Columbia University Press, 1985).

20   Whenever someone attempts to put together a 'theory of practice' where the intending subject as absolute ground is put into question, catachrestical masterwords become necessary, because language can never fully bypass the presupposition of such a ground. The particular word is, in such a case, the best that will serve, but also, and necessarily, a misfit. (There can, of course, be no

doubt that the marxian theory of ideology put into question the intending
subject as absolute ground.) The choice of these master-words obliges the taking
on of the burden of the history of the meanings of the word in the language
(paleonymy). Thus 'value' (as 'writing' in Derrida or 'power' in Foucault) must
necessarily *also* mean its 'ordinary' language meanings: material worth as well
as idealist values, and create the productive confusion that can, alone, give rise
to practice. It must be said, however, that these master-words are misfits only
if the ordinary use of language is presupposed to have fully fitting cases. Thus
'to fit' is itself a catachresis and points to a general theory of language as
catachrestical that must be actively marginalized in all its uses. For a development of 'active marginalization'. See Spivak, 'Theory in the Margins'.

21   Karl Marx, *Capital: A Critique of Political Economy*, trans. Ben Fowkes (New
York: Vintage Books, 1977), vol. 1, p. 90.

22   Karl Marx, *Selected Correspondence* (Moscow: Progress Publishers, 1975), p. 228.

23   Williams uses 'currency' in this sense in *Moral Luck*, p. 35. Yet because he can
only see value-coding as singular and rational, rather than heterogeneous and
coherent, he dismisses it as impossible in the moral sphere, and indeed is
sceptical about the possibility of a moral *philosophy* on related grounds. I am
in basic sympathy with his position though I cannot accept his presuppositions
and conclusions about 'currency'. Here perhaps attending to the metaphoricity
of a concept would help. For the metaphoricity of the concept of currency, as
for concepts and metaphors in general, see Derrida, 'White Mythology: Metaphor in the Text of Philosophy', in *Margins of Philosophy*, trans. Alan Bass
(Chicago: University of Chicago Press, 1982), pp. 207–71.

24   I have discussed this in 'Scattered Speculations on the Question of Value', in
Spivak, *In Other Worlds: Essays in Cultural Politics* (New York: Methuen, 1987).

25   Gayle Rubin, 'The Traffic in Women: Notes on the "Political Economy" of
Sex', in Rayna R. Reiter (ed.), *Toward an Anthropology of Women* (New York
Monthly Review Press, 1975). p. 157–210.

26   See for example, Kalpana Bardham, 'Women: Work, Welfare and Status.
Forces of Tradition and Change in India', *South Asia Bulletin*, 6 (1) (Spring,
1986). Because of the heavy weight of positivist empiricism in her discipline
(development economics), she has to be read somewhat against the grain.

27   Tim Mitchell, 'The World of Exhibition', *Comparative Studies in Society and History*,
31 (2) (April, 1989).

28   The *intellectual* kinship between Africa and African-Americans is an example of
such international cultural exchange. This is rather different from the issue of
the heterogeneity of the metropolitan underclass. I should of course also mention
the cultural and political solidarity between Arab-Americans and the Palestine
Liberation struggle as an example of two-way exchange. My general point
about academic practice in defining marginality and postcoloniality remains
generally unaffected by this.

29   The *OED* defines 'catachresis' as 'abuse or perversion of a trope or metaphor'.
We appropriate this to indicate the originary 'abuse' constitutive of language-
production, where both concept and metaphor are 'wrested from their proper
meaning'. Thus, in the narrow sense, a word for which there is no *adequate*
referent to be found.

30   Some of us have been intoning this larger sense, with not too much effect
against what Geoff Bennington calls 'the beginner's error of conflating "text"
in Derrida's sense with "discourse"' ('L'arroseur arrosé(e)', *New Formations*, 7

(Spring 1989), p. 36. See also Spivak 'Speculation on Reading Marx: After Reading Derrida', in Derek Attridge et al. (eds), *Post-structuralism and the Question of History* (Cambridge: Cambridge University Press, 197), p. 30.

31 Jean-François Lyotard, *The Postmodern Condition: A Report on Knowledge*, trans. Geoff Bennington and Brian Massumi (Minneapolis: University of Minnesota Press, 1984).

32 Derrida, 'Signature Event Context', in *Glyph 1*, p. 194.

33 For an extraordinary staging of this pervasiveness and ubiquity, and indeed a re-inscription of 'India' from that perspective, see Mahasweta Devi, 'Douloti the Bountiful', in Spivak, trans. *Imaginary Maps* (New York: Routledge, forthcoming).

34 J. B. van Bruitenen (trans), *The Bhagavadgita in the Mahabharata* (Chicago, 1981), p. 87.

35 Karl Marx, 'Economic and Philosophical Manuscripts', in Rodney Livingstone and Gregor Benton (trans.), *Early Writings* (Harmondsworth: Penguin, 1975), p. 20.

36 Antonio Gramsci, 'The Study of Philosophy', in *Selections from the Prison Notebooks*, trans. Quintin Hoare and Geoffrey Nowell Smith (New York: International Publishers, 1971), p. 324.

37 I take this distinction from Foucault, *The Archaeology of Knowledge*, trans. A. M. Sheridan Smith (New York: Pantheon Books, 1972), p. 88–105.

38 The *OED* defines 'parabasis' as 'going aside', 'address to the audience in the poet's name, unconnected with the action of the drama'. We appropriate this as a transaction between postcolonial subjct positions, persistently going aside from typical allegorical continuity.

39 For a treatment of the Armenian case from the point of view of catachrestical claims to nationhood, see Anahid Kassabian and David Kazanjian, 'Theorizing Armenian Genocide', *New Formations* (forthcoming); Boris Kagarlitsky, *The Thinking Reed: Intellectuals and the Soviet State: 1917 to the Present*, trans. Brian Pearce (London: Verso, 1988), fast becoming the text on the new USSR, does not yet take into account the breaking open of the available value-coding of ethnicity and nationalism.

40 'Cultural and Political Power of Cinematic Language', paper delivered at conference on 'Problems of Cultural Representation in Global Cinema', (Boston Film/Video Institute, 26–30 April 1989; forthcoming).

41 Umberto Melotti unwittingly exposes this in *Marx and the Third World*, trans. Pat Ransford (London: Macmillan, 1977), p. 28–9.

42 For 'truth' as one case of a general iterability, see Derrida, *Limited Inc. abc . . .*, trans. Samuel Weber (Baltimore: Johns Hopkins Press, 1977).

43 Derrida, *Of Grammatology*, trans. Spivak (Baltimore: Johns Hopkins University Press, 1976), p. 46.

44 Ibid., p. 47. I am naturalizing Derrida's general description. Derrida's next sentence makes clear that his concern is more sub-individual than language-acquisition.

45 Marcel Proust, *Cities of the Plains*, trans. C.K. Scott Moncrieff (New York: Vintage Books, 1970), p. 99. Professor Jessie Hornsby's extraordinary knowledge of Proust helped me locate a merely remembered passage.

46 Star: 'This *Ursprache* as German scholars termed it . . . which we might term Proto-Indo-European . . . could be reconstructed . . . The asterisk being used by convention to indicate reconstructed parent words which were not directly

attested by any language known . . . ' (Colin Renfrew, *Archaeology and Language: The Puzzle of Indo-European Origins* (New York: Cambridge University Press, 1987), p. 14). Caught between two translations: 'Indeed it was not until 1947 that a good bilingual inscription was found at the site of Karatepe, written in Phoenician (a well-known Semitic language) as well as in hieroglyphic Hittite, so that real progress could be made with it' (ibid., p. 51). Japhetic: 'the story in the book of Genesis of the three sons of Noah, Ham, Shem and Japheth was taken as a perfectly acceptable explanation of the divergence of early languages. The languages of Africa were thus termed Hamitic, those of the Levant Semitic, and those to the land of the north Japhetic' (ibid., p. 13). Since 'Semitic' is still in use, I am using 'Japhetic' within the allegorical frame of the authority still given to the Biblical myth in certain situations of global politics. See Volosinov's underscoring of a differentiated origin for 'Japhetic' languages' in his discussion of N. Ja Marr in *Marxism and the Philosophy of Language*, trans. Ladislav Mateika and I. R. Titunik (New York: Seminar Press, 1973), pp. 72, 76, 101.

47   Frederick Engels, *The Origin of the Family, Private Property, and the State* (New York: Pathfinder Press 1972). Gayle Rubin's sympathetic critique of Engels in 'Traffic' is exemplary.

48   This is in striking contrast to the story's 'source', Samaresh Basu's 'Uratiya', a poignant semi-fantastic staging of patriarchal conflict. Another case of the narrativization of an alternative history that will not allow the verification of a possible world by the actual world is brilliantly telescoped in the tribal half-caste woman's utterance in Mahasweta Devi's 'The Hunt': 'If my mother had killed her white daughter at birth . . . I would not have been' ('The Hunt', forthcoming in *Women in Performance*).

49   For my statement of the argument, see Spivak, *In Other Worlds*, pp. 241–7; for a dismissal where concept and rhetoric are resolutely identified with the disciplines of 'philosophy' and 'literary criticism (aesthetics), see Jürgen Habermas, *The Philosophical Discourse of Modernity*, trans. Fredrick Lawrence (Cambridge: MIT Press, 1987), pp. 161–210.

50   Engels, *Origin*, pp. 74–5.

51   Ibid., pp. 68–9.

52   For a taxonomy of possible diversity here, see for example the articles in *Cultural Critique*, 6 and 7 (Spring and Autumn, 1987).

53   Marx, *Capital I*, p. 156.

54   Marx, *Capital I*, pp. 156, 157.

55   For a detailed study of Marx and Foucault, see Barry Smart, *Foucault, Marxism and Critique* (London: Routledge, 1983).

56   Marx, *Capital I*, p. 156.

Index